D1274271

MOUNTAIN JUBILEE

MOUNTAIN JUBILEE

By

ARNOLD LUNN

Stulti autem malorum memoria torquentur; sapientes bona praeterita grata recordatione renovata delectant. Est autem situm in nobis ut et adversa quasi perpetua oblivione obruamus et secunda jucunde ac suaviter meminerimus.

Fools are tortured by the memory of evils, but memory is a joy to the wise, for by memory they taste again the pleasures that are past. We have the power, if we wish, not only to annihilate our misfortunes by a kind of permanent oblivion, but also to summon up pleasant and delightful memories of good fortune.

CICERO. *De Finibus*, i. 17.

London: 1943
EYRE & SPOTTISWOODE

THIS BOOK IS PRODUCED IN COMPLETE CONFORMITY
WITH THE AUTHORIZED ECONOMY STANDARDS

First published 1943
Reprinted January 1944
Reprinted July, 1945
Reprinted April, 1946

MADE AND PRINTED IN GREAT BRITAIN FOR EYRE AND SPOTTISWOODE (PUBLISHERS) LTD.
15, BEDFORD STREET, STRAND, LONDON, W.C.2

DEDICATORY LETTER

To Greta Raeburn and Doreen Elliott

North Atlantic,
Christmas Eve, 1942.

My Dear Greta and Doreen,

It is Christmas Eve, and I know that you will be thinking of the many Christmases which we spent together at Mürren, and you will remember not only the cheerful riot in the Palace ballroom, but also the gleam of moonlit snows and the evening star in the window of the Wetterlücke, and you will sigh for powder snow in the Blumental, and also for the noblest mountain-scape in the world, the north wall of the Oberland as seen from the terrace of Mürren. And it is, because you love not only ski-ing but mountains, that I dedicate to you this book of mountain and ski-ing memories.

I am crossing the Atlantic in a Norwegian freighter, and my heart leaped when I saw the Norwegian flag, which has a supra-national symbolism for all skiers. I remembered this flag flying from the grandstand on Holmenkollen Day, 1930, *and the swift dynamic succession of Norse jumpers, and stubborn duels between Norwegians, Swedes and Finns in the fifty-kilometre race, and I thought of that infinitely grimmer struggle which is being waged to-day, the unending battle between our indomitable friends in Norway and the Nazi invaders.*

The officers and crew who were not on duty joined us in the diminutive lounge, and sang Christmas hymns in Norwegian and the Norwegian national anthem which I last heard in Poland just before the opening of the World Championship of 1939. *Half of those who were present had been torpedoed, at least once. All of them had relations under the Nazi heel. The radio-telegraphist, a Canadian lady who had crossed the Atlantic some thirty times in this ship, could not join us, for she was on duty. Do you remember the old Norwegian taunt in the days when I was trying to win international recognition for slalom racing? "Such races are only suitable for untrained Englishmen and ladies." You can guess the chilly welcome which awaited the Canadian lady when she first took up her duties on this ship. It was a slight to Norway to appoint a woman for so responsible a position. The taciturn captain did not conceal his displeasure. That was a year ago. To-day the radio-telegraphist is the captain's wife.*

After the Norwegians had left us, the passengers carried on. We were lucky, for our small company included a very talented performer at the piano, Mr. Archie Turnbull, and of the rest of us some could sing, and all sang. We passed without any sense of incongruity from Christmas hymns to popular songs, and then suddenly Mr. Turnbull struck up Clementine *and* that, *as you will guess, rang a bell, for it was to the tune of* Clementine *that we sang the song which Alan d'Egville wrote to celebrate that first and most glorious of " Inferno " races.*

I hope that even my friend, Frank Smythe, who feels about iconoclastic racers much as Ruskin felt about mountaineers, will forgive the few pages devoted to a not inglorious chapter in the history of British sport, a chapter in which you both played a distinguished role. At least he will find in those pages abundant justification for the belief that sport reflects the social conditions of an age, and that the creeping leprosy of the Nazi infection was as disastrous in the realm of ski-racing as in the mountaineering world.

But it is the love of the mountains from which we are exiled, and not the ambition to chronicle sporting events which has provoked this book. You and I have two countries, our own and Switzerland. When France fell and when we watched the fires of burning dockland on the night of September 7th, 1940, *and wondered whether England could continue to take it, second only to the supreme horror of Hitler's evil face gloating over conquered London from the balcony of Buckingham Palace was the possibility that the swastika might fly from the roofs of Berne. And in those dark and difficult days many of us were sustained by the mountains of vision faintly showing against a background patterned by tracer bullets and searchlights and the dull glare of exploding shells. I have just been reading through the series of poignant letters which reached me after the publication of the* British Ski Year Book *in* 1940, *letters which prove how strong was the mountain tie even in the most anxious moments of the war.*

" *Two days ago,*" *wrote Mrs. E. Partington during the peak of the London blitz,* " *with every bone in my more than fifty years old body creaking like fury, I let myself into our maidless house, wondering, and not for the first time either, how much longer we'd got to stick it. Usually I can ' take it,' and even glory in being able to hit back a bit. But on Monday I thought that a fire, a cosy meal and the merry presence of my absent family would be the Kingdom of Heaven. Said absent family being far away cooking for and generally messing about attending to the needs of about* 30 *or more of other people's children, I had to look around for comforts and get a meal myself.*

" *There on the mat was the latest* British Ski Year Book, *and there I found my comfort. The day's canteen worries, more route marches and tired men than usual, cigarette supplies run out, gas geyser burst and a couple of sirens to make weight—all this just faded out and for the rest of the evening I let comfort pour over me in waves. We, too, have the deep and abiding joy of the mountains. Sixteen years of holidays, winter and summer, in the*

Alps and mostly at our beloved Grindelwald have been our lucky portions. Part of our hearts are there."

Pietas *is a tradition of the mountain brotherhood, and manv of us have read and re-read the old classics of our craft when the war was going badly, or the barrage made it difficult to sleep. I have little craving for, and no hope of, a posthumous public excepting for this book and its predecessor,* The Mountains of Youth, *but I should be sorry if I could not believe that those books will be read by mountain lovers as yet unborn. It may well be that these years when the Alps as such are inaccessible, will seem more remote from their experience than the years when individual peaks, such as the Matterhorn were still believed to be unclimbable. And if that be so, this book may find a niche on their shelves, as a period piece, the period of our Babylonish exile. By the waters of Lima and Lisbon, Yosemite and Potomac, I sat down and wept. Yea I wept when I remembered thee, oh Lütschine! And because the mere effort to find words to express grief has an anæsthetic effect, I have found consolation in the writing of this book. It has been written in a great variety of conditions, and of setting. Some chapters were written to the accompaniment of the London barrage, others at sea, others in hospital. But however varied the setting, the theme remains unchanged, the theme of mountain love in exile.*

There were months when we faced the peril of losing something even more precious than the mountains, our island fortress and with that fortress the last hope of enslaved Europe. The anxieties of those days are reflected in these pages, as is also the return of unquestioning faith in final victory. And, because the book is a period piece, I have published the chapters in the form in which they were written, sometimes adding date and place. Two unedited chapters, Between the Aare and the Reuss *and* Thanks to Bimbo *appear as published in that golden past before Europe was troubled even by the shadow of the swastika. The contrast between the mood of this earlier writing and of the chapters written during this war suggests a comparison between the respective merits of the Muse of Possession and the Muse of Privation.*

The greater part of this book has not yet appeared in print. The pages describing Switzerland while France was falling appeared in a book of war-time reminiscences, And the Floods Came, *and a few chapters were first published in* The British Ski Year Book.

Authors automatically retain the right to reproduce in book form such of their articles as appear in the Press or in periodicals, unless they explicitly sell, not only the serial rights but also the copyright. Though I have written many articles for newspapers and periodicals, I have never yet been asked to sign away my copyright, but in these days of disintegration I am all in favour of complying with quaint old customs, and as it is usual for authors to thank editors for granting a favour which they have no power to withhold, I beg to express my grateful thanks to my old and trusted friend, the Editor of The British Ski Year Book, *for the right to reproduce a few chapters which first saw the light of day in that admirable periodical. This gracious gesture on my part will, at least, serve to advertise the fact that one editor was sufficiently impressed by my work to take the responsibility of publishing it.*

Let me supplement this gratuitous acknowledgment of a favour which could not have been withheld with a very sincere expression of thanks to Phyllis Holt-Needham and to Colonel B. W. Bowdler, C.M.G., D.S.O., who have read the proofs of the book. Colonel Bowdler who, as you know, has been proof-reading the British Ski Year Book *for many years, can never be induced to remonstrate when he dislikes what I have written. He suffers in silence. Phyllis Holt-Needham on the other hand never conceals what the Psalmist calls " the roar of the heart's disquiet " when my views clash with hers or when my English offends her nice sense of words. I am grateful to her for criticisms which are always astringent and usually just, for I have never met her equal as the critic of a manuscript. It is only fair to her to record the fact that such passages in this book as displease you probably displeased her, and remain uncensored as evidence of my manly independence.*

Apologies follow acknowledgments in alphabetical order, and it might, perhaps, have been more courteous to my American readers had I concealed the nostalgic note which, I fear, is only too obvious in the chapters devoted to the mountains of the American continent. Before the war my happiness among the mountains of other ranges was never impaired by the fact that they were not the Alps. I remember a perfect autumn morning in the Yosemite in 1937. *No thought of the distant Alps disturbed my enjoyment of one of the loveliest and most impressive of mountain-scapes. So long as one was secure in the knowledge that one could return, when one wished, to the Alps, one's experiences in other ranges supplemented but did not compete with Alpine experiences. But the war altered all that. I remember a lovely walk in Vermont with a lover of Mürren, Stephanie Wade Martin. We climbed a little hill above the river. The Midas touch of autumn had turned the maples to gold, and the silver thread of the river wound through woods in all the glory of deciduous foliage. I remembered October days among the Alpine foothills, but there was a sad emptiness in the sky where the Oberland should have been, and instead of giving thanks for the beauty of Vermont, I was sad because these hills were not the Jura. Which was, perhaps, unreasonable. St. Augustine describes an analogous experience. He had lost a beloved friend and his own home had become a prison to him. And those for whom the Wetterhorn or Jungfrau are friends can echo his cry of sorrow.* Expetebant eum oculi mei, et non dabatur : et oderam omnia quod non haberent eum. "*My eyes sought for him everywhere, and I found him not, and I hated all places because they held him not.*"

Perhaps, if I loved our own mountains less, I should be happier among the mountains of other continents, but even so the pain of loss is a small price to pay for the ecstasy of possession, and I do not envy those whose gamut of emotions ranges only between tepid happiness and discrete distress. There are, of course, moments of unavailing protest against the inevitable, moods when one feels with Dante that the remembrance of past happiness is the greatest of griefs

Nessun magior dolore
Che ricordarsi del tempo felice
Nella miseria,

but these moods pass, and gratitude remains. Even if you and I were condemned to spend the rest of our days in the most unrelenting of plains, unrelieved even by the distant hope of the hills, we should be guiltless of the crime of regretting the glorious past, and of envying those who, because they had never lived on the heights, have no reason to rebel against the intolerable flatness of the plains.

To-morrow "the Father of all may hide from us the heavens with dark cloud or the sun may shine undimmed" but however uncertain the future we can still say with Horace

Vixi, cras vel atra
Nube polum pater occupat
Vel sole puro

Come what may, we have lived.

Christmas Greetings to you both, and may the New Year bring the Alps a little nearer.

ARNOLD LUNN.

CONTENTS

LIST OF ILLUSTRATIONS

Other Works by ARNOLD LUNN

COME WHAT MAY. An Autobiography
AND THE FLOODS CAME. A Chapter of War-time Autobiography
THE HARROVIANS
LOOSE ENDS
FAMILY NAME
WITHIN THE PRECINCTS OF THE PRISON

SPANISH REHEARSAL
COMMUNISM AND SOCIALISM
WHITHER EUROPE ?

THE FLIGHT FROM REASON
ROMAN CONVERTS
THINGS THAT HAVE PUZZLED ME
JOHN WESLEY
PUBLIC SCHOOL RELIGION. A Symposium
NOW I SEE
A SAINT IN THE SLAVE TRADE
WITHIN THAT CITY
THE GOOD GORILLA
THE THIRD DAY

DIFFICULTIES. (With Mgr. R. A. Knox)
IS CHRISTIANITY TRUE ? (With Professor C. E. M. Joad)
SCIENCE AND THE SUPERNATURAL. (With Professor J. B. S. Haldane, F.R.S.)
IS THE CATHOLIC CHURCH ANTI-SOCIAL ? (With G. G. Coulton, D.Lit.)

OXFORD MOUNTAINEERING ESSAYS
THE MOUNTAINS OF YOUTH
SWITZERLAND AND THE ENGLISH
THE COMPLETE SKI-RUNNER
A HISTORY OF SKI-ING
ALPINE SKI-ING
SKI-ING FOR BEGINNERS
THE ALPS
THE ENGLISHMAN IN THE ALPS. An Anthology
GUIDE TO MONTANA
THE ALPINE SKI GUIDE TO THE BERNESE OBERLAND
SWITZERLAND : Its Literary, Historical and Topographical Landmarks
THE ITALIAN LAKES AND LAKELAND CITIES
VENICE : Its Story, Architecture and Art

AUCTION PIQUET

In Preparation : Switzerland in English Prose and Poetry (an anthology).

CHAPTER I

Golden Jubilee

GRINDELWALD was celebrating its golden jubilee as a Winter Sports centre, and I had been asked to say a few words to the assembled guests at the Bear Hotel. My friend Grob, Kurdirector of Grindelwald, listened with exemplary patience to my speech and then piloted me towards the bar. " Do you realise," I asked, " that in 1942 I shall celebrate my own Golden Jubilee as a visitor to Grindelwald? I was born on April 18th, 1888, and my first vivid memory is of the great fire which destroyed the old Bear and half the village."

" We must give you a banquet in the Bear," said Grob.

Miracles sometimes happen, and I may yet celebrate my Golden Jubilee in the valley which I love, but not in the Bear, for the Bear was burnt in January, 1941, within two years of its fiftieth birthday.

The old Bear was associated with the golden age of mountaineering, the new Bear with the golden age of ski-ing; and the new Bear, like the old, has refused to survive the age of which it was a symbol.

The old Bear was the temple of the Alpine Club. It welcomed the elect, but its atmosphere was a little chilling to the profane, that is, to all who could be comprehensively damned as " trippers." The Alpine Club of those days was recruited from bishops, judges, parsons, barristers, dons and schoolmasters, as class-conscious as the most fanatic of Marxists.

The new Bear was built in the opening phase of winter sports. The English pioneers divided their days between the Byzantine orthodoxies of the English school of skating and tobogganing parties to the " Happy Valley." It was from the Bear that Fox set out to experiment on the unwieldly planks. That was as early as 1891, shortly before E. C. Richardson laid the foundations of British ski-ing at Davos.

Davos was the birthplace of British ski-ing, Mürren of modern ski-racing, for it was at Mürren that the Kandahar was founded and the slalom evolved. But though the oldest international downhill racing meeting, the Anglo-Swiss Universities Meeting, was organised at Mürren (where the Slalom was held), it was down the Tschuggen Glade that British and Swiss University skiers first raced against each other, and it was in the bar of the new Bear that we celebrated the gallant performance of the British team, beaten but far from disgraced.

Meanwhile, the skiers were beginning to return to Grindelwald, instead of merely exploiting the Grindelwald slopes of the Scheidegg from their bases at Wengen and Mürren. The Kandahar Ski Club opened a branch at Grindelwald in 1936, and in the last winter before the war, Robert Readhead, who had learned to ski at Grindelwald, won the Duke of Kent's Cup, an unofficial World Championship for skiers domiciled in the plains, and a fitting finale to the golden age of British ski-ing with a glorious victory.

During the first winter of the war, I revisited the Alps on my way back from the Balkans, and I last saw the Bear, shuttered and forlorn, in February, 1940.

I was in Florence when the Germans invaded Holland, and left Paris just after the Germans had turned the Maginot line at Sedan, and I did not set foot again on the mainland of Europe until I landed at Lisbon on October 11th, 1941.

I was very sorry to leave England, but when the Clipper took off for Lisbon my regrets were tempered by the thrill of returning to the Latin South, and I was awake long before the dawn searching the horizon for the first hint of land. Long after darkness had ebbed from the eastern sky night still reigned on the Atlantic. Thousands of feet below us the dark ocean showed through windows in the curtain of mist, on the surface of which a light sparkled intermittently, as if it were a fallen star checked on its downward flight by a net of clouds. And then the star revealed itself as the flashing beam of a lighthouse, the summit of which just pierced through the low mists above the sea. And what were those dark shapes to the east? Clouds? My heart leaped when the cloud-like shapes resolved themselves into mountains, real mountains. I had said good-bye to the Alps from the terrace of Berne, while the Panzers were breaking through at Sedan, and the next mountains which I saw were the Rockies from Denver. Beautiful in their way, but I missed the dead, the Roman, the Burgundian, and the Habsburg. For there are moments when the tramp of dead legions can still be heard on the roads which the Romans built, and the echoes of Roland's horn still linger in the gorge of Roncevalles. It was good to return to mountains which had their roots in the great centuries, mountains which had watched the Romans come and the Saracens retreat, mountains whose approaches are guarded by castles, and whose valleys are sanctified by shrines and watered by Virgilian rivers, *fluminaque subterlabentia muros*, the mirror of ancient walls.

The Clipper floated over toy castles, and made a perfect landing on the unruffled waters of the bay. Before the outbreak of the war I had been living in the enchanted garden of San Remigio, above Pallanza, and as I stood outside the Customs shed, and watched the Tagus awakening to the glory of the southern day, Maggiore seemed a little nearer. There was the same backwash of shadow as the sun climbed, the same golden shimmer of hills surrendering to the insistent heat, the same phantom breeze, ruffling the windless corridors of the dawn, and fretting the placid water by miniature ripples, the same gleaming expanses of burnished silver varied by pools of translucent blue.

I left that afternoon for Madrid, which I had last seen from the Campo Santo during the Civil War. The Madrid to which I returned was a sorrowful city, darkened by the shadow of an unpredictable future, and I was grateful to Miss Aileen O'Brien, who provided a car in which we escaped for a few hours into the hills. We drove through the ruins of the University City, past villages scarred by the war, towards the long line of the Sierra in which stands the Escorial. The serene beauty of the October hills, crested with premature snow, recalled the glory of the autumn Alps. I remembered the Oberland, the parched greens of the deserted cow alps showing through the dust of autumn snows, the noble curtain of forests which sweeps down to the lakes, the flame of larches set against the sombre background of evergreens, the purple of deciduous foliage, mirrored and reversed in the ultramarine of Brienz, and the mellow golden light, at once tender and discriminating, magical in its union of atmosphere and clarity.

The car stopped near the Escorial and suddenly I heard a sound which evoked a surge of memories, the jangle of a cowbell. A bullock was passing slowly in the street. I shut my eyes and tried to convince myself that I was listening to the unconducted orchestras of Buss or Wengernalp. But the mountains which overlook the Escorial evoke memories very different from those which are associated with the Alps, for I had last seen them during the Civil War. The son of a friend of mine was in command of a company, defending an outpost near the crest of the range. He came down to see his father, and I remember the whine of a spent bullet, as they wandered off together, and the contrast between the desolation of war on the mountain tops and the spring flowers in the valley below.

"You can see the Escorial," said my friend, "from the top of the mountain where my son is fighting."

The Escorial is autochthonous, for it is built of granite from the neighbouring Sierra. It is as austere as the mountain matrix from which it was hewed, as sombre as the Spain in which it was born, and as stern as the King who built it for his tomb. Magnificent, and yet I found myself sighing for the towers of Thun or Chillon. I remembered Byron's prisoner, the "little lake which in my very face did smile," and the blue distances of Lake Leman flecked by lateen sails ; and I recalled a remark of my wife's on our return to Switzerland shortly before Mr. Chamberlain flew to Munich. We had been living at San Remigio, and though the Italians were uninfected by the inspired Anglophobia of the Fascist Press, the shadow of cruel things to come obscured the Italian sunlight, and for the first time in my life I was glad to leave Italy. As the train swept out of the Simplon tunnel into unpretentious and uncantankerous Switzerland, my wife exclaimed, "Isn't it wonderful to be back again in this dear country, which God stroked ?"

But if God stroked the mountains which look down on the Escorial, He stroked them the wrong way. The angry outcrops of spiky crags on their crests suggest, not shade for hill lovers, but cover for hill fighters, and their forests bristle like the fur on the arched back of a spitting cat. All of which may be nothing more than an example of what Ruskin calls the "pathetic fallacy," the fallacy of reading our own sentiments into inanimate nature. Certainly, in that mood of Alpine nostalgia, the stern Sierras seemed to symbolise the uncompromising fanaticism of Spain. All or nothing, *Todo o nada*, is the key to Spanish history, but the Swiss mosaic of races would have disintegrated long since, had not the Swiss mastered the technique of "splitting the difference," a technique in which their only rivals are the British. Switzerland did not escape the backwash of Reformation and Revolution, but these spiritual cyclones had spent their force before they reached Switzerland. Switzerland produced no Torquemada nor Robespierre, and it is significant that the border town, Geneva, least Swiss of all Swiss towns, was the scene of Calvin's experiment in fanaticism. Even Swiss civil wars run true to type, for the Sonderbund war of 1848 caused fewer casualties than the months of so-called peace which preceded the outbreak of the Civil War in Spain.

Life is a choice of sacrifices, and great Art is the by-product not of tolerance but of uncritical faith. The age which produced the Escorial was an age of fanatic faith, feudalism, noble art, cruelty and dirt. The age which is coming to an end is one of growing scepticism, of democracy, humanitarianism, artistic decadence and admirable hygiene. Unfortunately, as Cnossos proved, good plumbing will not save a civilisation.

Torquemada was a high price to pay for the Escorial, but the Albert Memorial suggests that there is no necessary connection between architectural and ethical progress. Creative races are like bees. Remove their sting and they die.

If our world were less cruel than Torquemada's, and if the conviction that no price is too high to pay for peace had given us peace, we could resign ourselves to the decadence of art, but this is not the case. The soft pain-dreading temper of sceptical humanism has prepared the way for a new fanaticism and for an age of totalitarian wars. The cruelty of past ages is returning, but not their artistic glories. Though creative genius is often cruel, cruelty is not creative. As indeed was effectively demonstrated by the pretentious vulgarity of the exhibition of models and photographs of Nazi architecture which I visited in Lisbon.

I said good-bye to Europe at the Azores, and to the last outpost of Great Britain when the Clipper rose from Bermuda. For hour after hour we flew over a sun-tinted pavement of fleecy iridescent clouds, which reminded me of the Alpine *Nebelmeer*, but the monotony of these inane and empty realms, *vacua et inania regna*, was unrelieved by the thrust of cloud-piercing peaks, rising like islands above the foam of Alpine mists. And below these clouds there was no beloved Thun or Brienz or Lucerne, nothing but the dark solitudes of the sundering Atlantic.

I wrote the first words of this chapter in Lisbon on November 15th, 1941, and I am bringing it to a close in midsummer, 1942, but I have not spent six months polishing my paragraphs, for I am writing these lines in Lima, and, though it is midsummer, the date is January 12th, 1942.

I sailed from New York shortly after the United States entered the war. Electric lights were dimmed and all portholes hermetically sealed at night, with the result that life was unendurable below decks once we reached the tropics. I slept on deck and watched the Pole Star dip below the horizon and the Southern Cross climb above the southern wave, and I knew that not only the Atlantic, but the Equator, separated me from all that I love. Christmas in the Caribbean seas was a grotesque parody of Christmas at Mürren. Midnight Mass was celebrated in an airless lounge with dimmed lights and sealed portholes. Priest and congregation dripped with perspiration. I remembered the frosty stars of Alpine Christmas-tides, and the friends who will never see Mürren again.

I have just returned to my room after buying an evening paper which contains a great deal of unnecessary information about Axis designs on Malta. There are too many Lunns at Malta, Peter and Antoinette and grandson David and granddaughter Innominata. I call her that because I do not know her name. All I do know is that she is " most alarmingly like " her grandfather, to quote an irreverent telegram which I received on landing at New York. " Los bombardeos contra Malta han sido casi continuos en las ultimas semanas." I do not think I will buy *La Noche* to-morrow.

I landed in Callao, the port for Lima, on January 1st. And as I drove along the dusty road towards the " scorched earth " of rainless hills, I thought of Ernst Gertsch setting the " New Year's Slalom," which Peter won in 1932. If the Judgment Day were announced for January 2nd, Ernst would insist on running this Oberland classic before the last trump.

I could not but feel that something had gone wrong with the calendar, for the Peruvian January seemed as grotesque as Hitler's " New Order." I sighed for the song of powdery crystals as the ski dive into sheltered glades, and for snows flooded with the temperate light of an invigorating sun, very different from the molten globe whose relentless inquisition has liquidated every blade of heretical green on the coastal ranges of Peru.

It was not only the seasons which were reversed when I crossed the Equator. I moved forward into summer, and backward into the Colonial past. A new civilisation is being created in North America ; an old culture is dying in Peru.

What is left of Viceregal Lima is a fragment of the old Spain, abandoned and forgotten, on the far Pacific coast. The ruling families, mainly Spanish or of Spanish ancestry, are outnumbered twenty or thirty to one by the sullen Mestizos. Half-breeds and

Indians are dreaming of the day when they too can liquidate the white ascendancy.

The new civilisation which is coming to birth in North America has many enviable aspects, such as the high standard of living—the consequence of mass production. But it is not only in economics that revolutionary changes are taking place. American humanism has given us the sky-scraper, the Disney cartoon, the humour of the disillusioned (Thurber and Peter Arno), the Charleston, jazz, Negro spirituals, and a new philosophy of drink, the cocktail for a quick kick replacing the leisurely habit of wine. Nowhere is this new civilisation more bitterly criticised and more enthusiastically imitated than in Lima. A Spanish priest who had settled in Peru favoured me with a pungent variant of a familiar theme. " An American friend of mine took me to see the Brooklyn bridge and was pained because I was not very enthusiastic. But I can shut my eyes and think of a bridge five times bigger than Brooklyn, but I cannot shut my eyes and think of a painting five times more beautiful than a masterpiece by Velasquez or Murillo. The Americans judge all things by physical standards." This is widely false, but it is arguable that the mediæval emphasis on *qualitas* has been replaced, in America as elsewhere, by a new emphasis on *quantitas.* Yet the very emphasis on size, which disedified the Spanish priest, is really the expression of a romantic craving for *qualitas.* New qualities emerge in the course of a quantitative increase. The Mississippi is not only a very big river ; the Rockefeller building is not only a very big building. There is a new *qualitas* in the Mississippi and in the best sky-scrapers which is absent from the smaller rivers and buildings of Europe.

The economic interpretation of architecture is as inadequate as the economic interpretation of history. High ground rents only partially explain the architecture of New York. The craving for the transcendental finds expression in the stone of Gothic Cathedrals in an age of Faith, and in the steel and concrete of a sky-scraper in an age of disillusion.

To have raised the standard of living among the lower strata of society is the supreme achievement of this new civilisation of North America, a civilisation which, whether we like it or not, is the civilisation of the " brave new world " of to-morrow. This new way of life is as different from the dying culture of Europe as *The New Yorker* from *Punch*, as indeed the aristocrats of Lima realise only too clearly. It has an irresistible appeal to the under-privileged and is even making converts within the citadels of aristocratic conservatism, for the younger generation of the ruling classes enjoy American films, adopt American fashions, and read American papers such as *The New Yorker* and *Time*—" Time which antiquates antiquity and hath an art to make a dust of all things."* But the older generation dread the influence of America, the great Anarch, solvent of authority, the authority of the Church, the authority of tradition, the authority of the parent, the authority of the husband, and do not allow for the religious and cultural forces in the U.S.A. which are resisting the disintegrating influence of an industrial civilisation.

The conflict of cultures has left its mark on the outward appearance of Lima. The rising tide of progress has engulfed all save a few sad remnants of the gracious past. In Viceregal Lima it is the baroque Church or Colonial architecture which is out of place, lingering on like a nervous guest who has outstayed his welcome.

When the day's work is done I often wander into the Plaza des Armes, and loiter for a few twilight moments near the fountain while the westering sun lights up the façade of the Cathedral which Pizarro planned. My evening pilgrimage takes me to the bridge across the Rimac, near which stands a decaying palace modelled on the Ducal Palace at Venice. Smoke-begrimed by the railway, which runs between palace and river, this forlorn parody stabs me with nostalgic regret for the airy miracle of white and pink which floats above the blue shimmer of the Adriatic. Strange that any man should have thought it possible to recapture that phantom loveliness, but the old nobleman of Lima, who was guilty of this audacity, must have loved Venice, and across the years I salute his congenial ghost.

The contrast between the palaces which overlook the Grande Canale and the Rimac is no greater than the contrast between the Alps and the scorched hills above Lima. There are places on the Peruvian coast where rain has not fallen since the first world war, and even Lima measures its drought not in weeks but in months. San Cristobal, which dominates the view from the Rimac bridge, has a mummified appearance, and the smooth pock-marked rocks which break through the arid slopes of dusty earth are like the bones of a skeleton showing through the disintegrating shroud of an exhumed corpse. Bad mountains when they die go to Peru. San

* Sir Thomas Browne.

Cristobal should have been christened Dives, for it raises its parched lips to heaven vainly imploring the benediction of rain.

The Rimac river is like the cup of cold water for which Dives begged in vain. Its meandering journey to the sea is marked by a narrow strip of privileged earth, lush green grass beside the river bed, gay gardens near its banks.

The Rimac springs in the ice caves of the Andean peaks, and does not wholly lose the virtue of snow in its long, sad pilgrimage through parched and thirsty lands. It is not the Rhône nor the Reuss nor the Aare, but was conceived, as they were, in the womb of ice. It is of the same royal race of snow-begotten streams, and speaks to me in a language which I can understand.

I have only to shut out San Cristobal and to close my eyes for a few minutes to forget my surroundings. The tuneless chanties of the Rimac recall the half-forgotten melodies of distant and beloved rivers. The barriers of space dissolve, and I hear again the plain chant of the Lütschine floating up through the thin air to the open windows of our old home at Grindelwald. And the golden past is reborn, and I return home to face with renewed confidence the dark and difficult future.

LIMA.
January 12th, 1942.

CHAPTER II

Before Jonah Got on Board

"THE great popularity of winter sports," writes Neville Lytton in his Preface to the volume Winter Sports in the Lonsdale Library, "dates from the Grindelwald Conference. This was organised by Sir Henry Lunn in 1892; its object was to unite all the Christian churches; as Lord Lytton once said in a witty speech: 'Sir Henry Lunn is a courageous man—once he set out to convert the Pope of Rome to Protestantism.' Naturally the Conference failed, but *à quelque chose malheur est bon*—Sir Henry noticed that mid-winter in the high Alps is an earthly paradise—the gloom and fog and damp are left in the valley below, while up in the eternal snows the sun is often too hot to bear and the sparkling atmosphere is more of a tonic than the finest champagne. He soon turned his organising ability to propagating this important discovery."

Few skiers have had more influence on the development of ski-ing than my father who never skied.

My father's business career began in his early boyhood when he discovered that he could exchange mice at a profit through the paper called *The Exchange and Mart*. From mice he passed on to poultry, such as the Brahmaputra and Game Bantams, and from poultry to tennis rackets, for he was one of the first to realise the commercial possibilities of the new game Spharistike, which is now known as Lawn Tennis.

Before he was twenty he had taken his father into partnership, and laid the foundation of a promising business career.

"Promising," but the promise was never fulfilled. My father was a complex character—a born company promoter, and an ardent Christian crusader; a mystic and a merchant adventurer. He loved making money, but his conscience was always troubled on the rare occasions when he had a substantial balance in the bank. He was tormented by scruples. He believed that Jesus Christ meant what He said on the subject of wealth and its spiritual dangers; and as a result of this unfortunate "literalism" he was even more successful in dis-embarrassing himself and his heirs of superfluous wealth than in making large sums of money. At the time of his death his bank balance would have slid without friction through the eye of the narrowest of needles.

At the age of 20 he retired from business, and spent his capital training himself for a career as a medical missionary at Trinity College, Dublin. Unfortunately his health broke down in India. On his return he founded a paper called *The Review of the Churches* dedicated to Reunion.

My father had unlimited faith in the technique of the Round Table as a method of solving outstanding differences. He was convinced that if the representatives of the different churches could be persuaded to meet in pleasant, healthy surroundings many of the barriers to Reunion would disappear.

He therefore invited a number of ecclesiastics representing different churches to travel to Norway in mid-winter in order to discuss their differences in a little village called Vossevangen.

Accommodation was booked for the pilgrims in the *Fridtjof* which was wrecked, and then in the *Norge* which followed the *Fridtjof* to the bottom of the sea. A few days after it had been selected for the honour of conveying the Reunion pilgrims to Norway, the *Star* gave the pilgrims a paragraph headed "Before Jonah Went on Board," and my father decided that Norway was unsuited for ecclesiastic discussions, and booked accommodation at Grindelwald.

My father made the business arrangements for this party and the little group of 26 persons who left England on January 6th, 1892, for Grindelwald provided the nucleus of the travel business which my father founded.

This first venture was a success, and my father resolved to summon a formal Conference at Grindelwald to discuss Reunion. He wrote to Mr. Gladstone and to every Bishop on the Bench, and to all the leading Free Church divines inviting them to attend this Conference as his guests. He was confident that the galaxy of leading Churchmen who were to travel to Grindelwald at his expense would attract sufficient paying tourists to save him from bankruptcy.

My father was 32 years of age at the time. He was unknown outside of Methodism. He had no capital but his courage and his unbounded belief in himself and in his mission.

The Prime Minister replied with studied courtesy wishing the Conference every success, but regretted that the pressure of his political duties prevented his acceptance. Of all the Bishops who had been invited only one accepted, the Bishop of Worcester. The Free Churches were represented by many of their Leaders.

I have always regarded my father as the real founder of the *Freikarte* Club—an allusion which I will not explain because only the members of the Club in question would understand its significance.

It is odd to reflect that but for two shipwrecks I might have spent my holidays in Norway and become an ardent champion of Langlauf and Jumping. Instead of leading a successful campaign for converting Norwegians to the joys of downhill ski-racing, I might have wasted my time trying to persuade Englishmen to desert downhill racing for the jumping-hill.

A few days before the Conference was due to open half Grindelwald, including the Bear Hotel and Chalet in which we were living, was burnt to the ground. Undismayed by this setback, my father arranged to transfer the Conference members to such of the hotels as were still standing.

It was symbolic that my father's business career should begin with two shipwrecks and a fire. The *Argonaut*, which he chartered for his Hellenic Cruises, was shipwrecked a few years later, and the Palace Hotel, Mürren, which he had bought and of which he was the Chairman, was partially burnt in 1926. During the blitz the headquarters of the Firm, which had already survived two fires, three shipwrecks, and two wars, was badly damaged by a land mine. But the dynamic ghost of its founder will galvanise the Firm into life when once this war is ended.

The Grindelwald chalet, to which we returned every summer, was the social centre of the Conference. On Sundays our verandahs were crowded with a fine confused assortment of Reunionists ranging from an Anglican Bishop to Dutch Calvinists. As a boy I collected butterflies, and my ambition, which remained unfulfilled, was to capture a Purple Emperor, a variety which was very rare in the Oberland. My father was an ardent collector of ecclesiastical varieties, and never happier than when he had netted some rare and many-coloured specimen for his Conferences, which were resumed at Mürren after the first World War. I remember the enthusiasm with which he described the capture for one of his cruises of an Eastern Patriarch who had the unique privilege of wearing some peculiar vestment and of saying Mass according to some venerable rite.

My father's attitude to Rome was a queer mixture of resentment and respect. Respect because a Roman Bishop corresponded to the Purple Emperor which was missing from the collection, resentment because the missing scarlet hat of a Cardinal would have rounded off his collection so beautifully.

We did not collect the same butterflies, and his Grindelwald was not mine. Early in life I discovered that the Alpine Club had a great contempt for trippers in general and for ecclesiastical trippers in particular. Had not the great pioneer of modern rock climbing, Mummery, referred in scorn to Grindelwald as a place given over to religious conferences and prayer meetings? I wilted with shame when I read this contemptuous reference to my father's activities.

Sometimes the two Grindelwalds overlapped. I remember an expedition to the Great Scheidegg with my father, Hugh Price Hughes and an Anglican Dean. Hughes was a brilliant Methodist, a man of great eloquence, radiant goodness, disarming egoism, and inexhaustible energy.

My brother, Hugh Kingsmill and I tried to escape from the range of his voice, but in vain. The day was perfect; light clouds drifting across the sky cast faint shadows on the snow, but all the lovely sounds and rumours of sound, which are native to the hills, the music of snow-fed streams, the chorus of cowbells and the echoes of distant avalanches competed in vain with the Reverend Hugh Price Hughes. "No, my dear Dean. *No.* I am not opposed to Episcopacy *per se*, but I cannot subscribe to any theory which would confine God's grace within mechanical channels. . . ."

On our return to Grindelwald we were overtaken by two guideless climbers, tall bronzed men, sunburnt and happy, swinging down the road from the Wetterhorn Hotel, with their ice-axes under their arms. Hughes was still booming away. The Dean had long been silenced. "I am prepared, my dear Dean, to concede that Bishops may be of the *bene esse* but not of the *esse* of the Church. . . ."

I noticed a look of derision on the face of one climber as they passed us. He made some whispered comment, the nature of which I could guess. I looked after them with envy. I longed to assure them that mountains were not only the *bene esse* but the *esse* of the only Society to which I wished to belong, a Society for which I had already qualified by the baptism of desire.

My father was seldom guilty of the solecism of intruding his clerical friends on to our mountain walks, for though mountains meant little to him, his children meant a great deal, and he loved to lead us on the lower ranges which faced the great peaks of the

Oberland. I can see him, as I write, with the pith helmet which he had brought back from India, and the vast alpine stock on which were burnt the names of the Faulhorn, Scheidegg and other mountains which he had climbed. The Mettenberg was his nearest approach to a real peak, and he may, as my brother Hugh suggests, have given preference to the Mettenberg because it was the only big peak which could be climbed in one day. He could not spare two days from the Conferences for the Wetterhorn.

People may be divided into those who are more interested in people than in places, and the small minority who are more interested in places than in people. I have sometimes been accused, unjustly I think, of belonging to the second class, but I did not inherit this bias, for my father was supremely interested in people and wholly uninterested in places. He liked mountains as a background for animated religious (or business) discussions, but he never walked alone, either among the hills or elsewhere.

In 1931 my friend, Christopher Mackintosh, saved the Firm from liquidation and my father, in his last years, concentrated on the Hellenic Travellers Club. Every year he passed through Switzerland twice on his way to and from the cruises, but he never left the train to revisit Grindelwald of the Conferences or Mürren which he created as a winter sports centre. He adored the cruises because he liked to surround himself with learned men and with divines, and he was never happier than when presiding over debates on the future of democracy or on the lessons of Greece. But, if he were alive to-day, he would not be tormented by nostalgic longings for the Acropolis. His dreams would not be disturbed by memories of that little corner of the Erechtheum draped in the branches of olive which Minerva planted, or by the distant echoes of the wind sighing through the pines at Olympia.

He was the first to " open " in winter most of the great Alpine centres, Chamonix, Adelboden, Villars, Montana, Mürren and Wengen among others, but he never put on ski and, according to his fellow curlers, he can never be said to have curled. And yet few men had a greater influence on ski-ing. " Amongst other things," writes E. C. Richardson, " the application of the word ' Kandahar ' to ski-ing affairs originated with him. The first race bearing that name was held under his supervision in 1911. And since then in connection with the famous club of that name, the well-known binding and so on, ' Kandahar ' is probably better known to most people rightly or wrongly, in connection with ski-ing than with the late Lord Roberts and his victories in India. Not the least of the services which your father rendered to the sport was the fact that he was your father and that he gave you so free a hand. For where would British ski-ing be to-day without our Arnold? To which I may now safely add, without our Peter? Not everybody has always seen eye to eye with any of the three of you. But, well, I think I may leave it at that!"

I have struggled in vain against the temptation to quote this signal tribute to the Lunn dynasty, and my anxiety to avoid a charge of gross vanity would have prevailed but for the fact that my father deserves the compliment paid to him by the Father of British ski-ing. He certainly gave me a free hand. He had entered me for the Bar, and he was ambitious to transform me into a successful barrister and politician. I had no such ambitions. I wanted to play a part in the development of ski-ing and of ski-mountaineering, and the family business provided the very opportunities which I needed for the fulfilment of my hopes. My father let me have my way. He financed my ski-mountaineering, backed my various plans for the foundation of clubs, paid for the lunch at which the Alpine Ski Club was founded, and followed with lively interest and sympathy all my ski-ing activities. He never skied but as Richardson says, "Sir Henry was a great pioneer of ski-ing."

Though he never climbed nor skied, he had one quality without which it is impossible to achieve outstanding success, either as a mountaineer or as a ski-racer. He was one of the most fearless men that I have ever known. He combined in an unusual degree moral and physical courage. He faced financial ruin or a dangerous operation with the same composure. I remember being with him when he was awaiting an operation. He was nearly eighty at the time, and the operation, as he knew, would certainly be painful and would possibly be fatal. His last remark to me, as they wheeled him into an operating room, was a reference to a business scheme which he had been discussing with all his old fire.

And he had no sooner fully recovered consciousness than he resumed the conversation at the point where it had been broken off just before the operation.

He never struck sail to a fear.

He was over seventy years of age when he lost control of the business, and became a salaried servant instead of a dictator.

Christopher Mackintosh, who held the controlling shares, treated him with great tact and consideration, but the position was not easy. By sheer force of character he regained control of the Hellenic Cruises.

He died, appropriately, on the opening day of the Arlberg-Kandahar of 1939, the classic race which traces its pedigree back to the first Kandahar which my father founded. He had been taken ill on a cruise, and only retired from control when he ceased to be conscious of his surroundings.

His eclectic tastes would have been satisfied, I hope, by the arrangements which I made for his funeral. Edgar Stogdon, Vicar of Harrow, conducted the service. Benjamin Gregory, a leading Methodist, preached an excellent sermon. Bishop David Mathew, a Catholic, said Mass for his intentions in the hospital in which he died, and the prayers for the dead beside the coffin in the mortuary in which his body was lying. He had netted his Purple Emperor at the last.

Opposite: *GRINDELWALD AND THE EIGER.* *By kind permission of R. Schude.*

CHAPTER III

The Mountain of Youth

"I ENVY you," said my hostess, "I wish we could spend Christmas in Rome with you. Give my love to Rome. My father was Bulgarian Minister there for some years. Love of Italy is a tradition in our family."

"Yes, indeed," said her father. "I was a child of five when I made the first of many journeys to Italy. We travelled in the family coach from Sofia to Venice. This morning I said good-bye to an American friend at our Sofia airport. I watched the plane take off, knowing that it would cover the distance to Venice in a few hours. Americans can still travel, whereas we poor Bulgarians couldn't get the necessary foreign exchange even before this war began. My father may have taken three weeks on the road but at least he got there, whereas all I can do is to watch a plane take off which will get to Venice in a few hours. Meanwhile, like Luther, 'here I stay and can no other.' So much for science and modern speed of communications."

My heart sank. Would these travel restrictions, all but universal in Europe before the war, be extended to England after the war? Was my Balkan journey in those last months of 1939 the last of many wanderings in Europe?

I was born in 1888, in the Indian summer of that *laissez-faire* Liberalism which hoped progressively to remove all barriers which impeded the free movement of men, of goods or of ideas across national frontiers. I had crossed the Straits of Dover more than a hundred times before I applied for my first passport, an application which was necessary to comply with the tiresome view of the Turks. In those days there were no restrictions on the export of currency, and no money declarations to be completed at frontiers, and the French franc was valid in France, Italy, Switzerland, Belgium, Greece and other countries of the Latin currency union.

If only the "Four Freedoms" could be extended to include freedom from travel restrictions! But I fear that we senile survivors from the age of the magic carpet will astonish our grandchildren with stories of forgotten freedoms. "There was a time when a man who wanted to go to Switzerland just bought a ticket at a station or in any of the tourist agencies, as they were called . . . Yes, tourist agencies, not Government departments. . . ."

Opposite *SPRING DAWN*. *By kind permission of A. Pedrett.*

Between 1892 and 1940, when France fell, I missed two summers, and between 1899 and 1940, two winters in the Alps. Even the first world war did not interrupt this sequence for I was rejected by the Army and found work in Switzerland.

At Grindelwald my brother and I walked and scrambled in the Faulhorn range, but it was at Montana that we matriculated as mountaineers. Montana, where we spent many summers of our boyhood, lies on the southern slopes of the Wildstrubel-Wildhorn range, and is an ideal playground for novices who are ambitious to work out their own salvation without professional assistance. There were ice slopes long enough to tire inexpert step-cutters, and rock climbs which were difficult enough for beginners, a peaklet which was virgin because obscure, and which we climbed and christened. The name has since found its way on to the Government map. While still at Harrow I wrote a guide to Montana, and spent the money which I earned on guides for the Matterhorn. But guided climbs were few. We were self-taught, and learned by the old method of trial and error, which has many virtues but one drawback, for in the mountain school the first error may also be the last. As indeed our parents realised. I shall never cease to be grateful to them for the free hand which they gave us.

Those early adventures are described in my book, *The Mountains of Youth.* Samuel Butler said that he wrote books in order to have something to read in his old age which he knew that he would enjoy. I have just reread *The Mountains of Youth,* and I was pleased to find that it satisfied Butler's exacting test, for this book helped me " to beget the golden time again." It was not only the mountain days recorded in that book which came back to me like stars after a storm, but also episodes and adventures which I had not thought worth chronicling. One such episode would certainly have found its way into my book had Mr. Dunne's *An Experiment in Time* been published while I was writing *The Mountains of Youth.* Mr. Dunne, as we know, maintains that dreams are a preview of the future, and the interest aroused by his book has had the incidental effect of weakening the convention which condemns as a social solecism the infliction of one's dreams on other people. The unwisdom of ignoring convention is in that immortal classic, *The Diary of a Nobody,* the hero of which, poor Mr. Pooter, describes his family's abrupt and discourteous reception of the strange and singular dream in which he attempted to interest them.

However uninteresting other people's dreams may be, one somehow feels, like Mr. Pooter, that one's own dreams are exceptional, but 4 a.m. in an Alpine hut was, perhaps, an inauspicious moment to put this theory to the test. My brother and I had just sat down to an unappetising breakfast before starting out to climb one of the peaks in the eastern end of the Mont Blanc chain.

" I had a very interesting dream last night," I began.

" Pass the tea," said my brother.

" I dreamt that I was cutting steps down a steep ice slope . . ."

" Go easy with that potted meat. You're not dreaming now. Sleep-walking and sleep-eating are barred."

" And suddenly you slipped."

" I slipped ? " said my brother. " Sure it wasn't you ? "

" Quite sure. And I watched the rope running out, and I knew that I couldn't hold you, and I waited for the inevitable jerk, and then . . ."

" What then ? " asked my brother displaying his first gleam of interest in my dream.

" And then just before the rope tightened, I awoke."

" Is that all ? " said my brother.

" Yes, that's all."

" Lord ! What a damned silly dream. Pointless. Pass the cheese."

I should have replied by quoting the immortal Pooter. " I shall never tell my dreams again the longest day I live."

I gave no further thought to my dream once we had roped up. A prolonged drought had transformed into ice the long slope of snow leading up to the final easy rocks of our peak, and I decided to try a variation route up an ice slope which though steeper was much shorter, but the prospect of returning down a slope on which, at one point, I had been forced to cut handholds was not attractive, so we descended by the usual route. The dry summer had strengthened the defences of our peak by an unusually large bergschrund, spanned by one rather rickety snowbridge. From above it was difficult to locate this snowbridge, for the upper lip of the schrund was much higher than the lower.

My brother and I were standing side by side some little distance above the upper lip, wondering whether we should cut straight down or bear to the right or the left. While we were arguing about the exact position of the snowbridge, my brother slipped and shot down the ice towards the invisible crevasse. Instinctively I prepared to resist the shock, but I realised with crystal clarity that I should be whipped off the ice and sucked down into the unseen abyss below. And then just before the rope tightened my brother reappeared on the far side of the crevasse. He had hit off the snowbridge for which we were searching and had slithered harmlessly across. Those seconds, while the rope was running out, were unnerving, but infinitely less so than the grimmest moment in my Alpine career. The story of the bride whose honeymoon all but ended on the Jungfrau is worth telling for its moral, but I was too ashamed to tell it when I was writing *The Mountains of Youth.* I am shamed into this belated confession by the uncompromising candour with which a former president of the Alpine Club described in the *Alpine Journal* his own blunder which involved his friends and himself in an accident which might well have ended fatally.

I first met the lady, whom I all but lost on the Jungfrau, in the house of her uncle, my old ski-ing companion, Canon Savage. Mabel Northcote thought me odd and aggressive, and I did what I could to confirm this unpleasant impression. On the eve of my twenty-first birthday I lectured, at Canon Savage's request, to his parishioners.

T'were profanation of our joys
To tell the laity our love

and I therefore confined myself to the externals of mountaineering history, the epic of the Matterhorn, and the story of Mont Blanc. But there was one member of my audience, Mabel Northcote, to whom my slides revealed a new world of unsuspected enchantment. Long after the lecture we sat up talking mountains, and when I said good night I looked at my watch. It was five minutes past midnight, I had come of age.

During our engagement Mabel visited Mürren both in summer and in winter. She loved mountains, and with the egoism of the male I assumed that she must love them in the way that I did. But it is easy to adore mountains without wishing to climb them, and to enjoy ski-ing without any ambition to pass tests. Mabel had undaunted courage and perfect balance but she was never strong, and it was her spirit and not her muscles which carried her through the tests. She was the first woman to win the British Gold Medal, the standard of which was then more or less the equivalent of the modern Silver. But it was to gratify my ambition, not hers, that she entered for the tests. Our first rock climb was an Easter ascent of one of the easier of the Lliwedd buttresses. Wind and falling snow did not add to the amenities of the climb, and we were relieved to reach the summit.

Our next climb was the rocky tooth of the Lobhorn above Mürren, a steep and intriguing climb, but a very long day from Mürren. Mabel was very tired by the time we reached the forest above Grütsch, and, to make matters worse, we followed, as many have done before and since, a track which did not lead to Grütsch but to Lauterbrunnen three thousand feet below. I had struck my last match and thrown away the matchbox two or three hundred feet above Grütsch, and it was only when I realised that the faint track through the darkening woods was leading not to Grütsch, but to Lauterbrunnen, that I began frantically to search the rucksack for matches with which to light our lantern. There was no moon, and damp clouds obscured the stars, and as the light failed, I knew that once the Egyptian darkness had descended on the impenetrable forest, we could never hope to follow the elusive track without the help of a lantern.

From the depths of my rucksack I fished out a mouldy match, but no matchbox. Fortunately matches will strike not only on matchboxes but also on glass. The only glass available was the glass of my wrist watch, which I rubbed until it glowed with friction.

Mabel held the lantern open. With a beating heart I struck the last match across the face of the watch. I remember the agony of suspense as the match spluttered, the excitement as the wick caught, and the ecstatic relief when the lantern was well and truly lit.

Moments such as these have a place all their own in the mosaic of mountain adventure.

We were married on December 10th, 1913, and spent the first week of our honeymoon in the Pyrenees, and the remaining weeks in the Oberland. On a glorious morning in January, we caught the first train from Wengen to the Jungfraujoch (11,400 feet above the sea). Instead of spending a night at the Jungfraujoch to get acclimatised we left at once for the Jungfrau. That was my first mistake.

I was so preoccupied with the importance of attaching Mabel firmly to the rope, that I did not pay enough attention to my end. The noose round my waist was loose and worked looser. Normally this would not have mattered, for the odds are thousands to one that a noose could slip from one's waist over one's knees to one's ankles, without being caught on the way, and that the noose would reach one's feet at the precise moment when they were so close together that one could step clean out of the noose without tripping, without being aware that it was not still round one's waist. I know of only two cases where the leader has walked out of the rope, in the first of which the leader was one of the greatest climbers of my generation, and in the second was the author of this humiliating confession.

We left our ski at the bergschrund, and climbed on foot the steep snow slopes leading to the Rottalsattel, whence a steep ice ridge leads to the summit of the Jungfrau. About half-way between the saddle and the summit, I heard a startled exclamation from Mabel. I turned round to discover that I had stepped clean out of the rope. It was not only shame which censored this incident from my book, but also a reluctance to recall the worst moment of my life. Even now I feel faintly sick as I relive the devastating horror of that moment. I can still hear the angry hiss of the ice-swollen rope darting down like a snake about to strike. I can see the gleam of ice, and the shoulder curving over into the depths of the Rottal, the shoulder over which a falling body would plunge. . . . I can see a small fragile form as the rope jerked at her waist . . . swaying . . . swaying. . . .

We climbed the Mönch together before returning to Wengen, but the Mönch was Mabel's last big peak.

Many years later my wife and I motored over to Lauterbrunnen for the funeral of three young Englishmen who had been killed on the Jungfrau. One of them had slipped, near the point where I had walked out of the rope, and had dragged his companions with him. The Jungfrau had been less indulgent to them than to us. George Finch, of Everest fame, was leading another rope, and as he described the tragedy of which he had been an impotent spectator, I felt faintly sick. . . . I could see the gleam of ice, and the shoulder curving over into the malignant depths below, and a small figure swaying . . . swaying. . . .

The sad procession filed out of the church, and followed the coffins to the open grave in the churchyard not far from the foot of the smooth polished limestone cliffs above which lies Mürren. It was a perfect summer's day. The silver dust of the Staubbach stream seemed to hover rather than to fall, fluttering like a veil, ever changing and yet ever the same.

> Wenn in Unendlichen dasselbe
> Sich widerholen ewig fliesst.

Was it, perhaps, the Staubbach which inspired these lines, the Staubbach which fascinated Goethe on his visit to Lauterbrunnen?

Thousands of feet above the graveyard, the Jungfrau towered into a cloudless sky, serene, indifferent, capricious queen of an arbitrary tribunal which exacts from one the ultimate penalty for a moment's neglect, and allows others equally guilty to escape.

Dust to dust and ashes to ashes. The thunder of the falling rocks in the far distant Rottal echoed like a response to the words of committal, as if to remind us that mountains, like men, are born and grow to maturity and, like men, decay and die.

As we left the churchyard George Finch said, as if in answer to an unspoken question, "Of the undergraduates that I come into touch with the best find their way to the mountains or the sea. Some get killed, but it's the hard sports which breed men."

CHAPTER IV

"Yesterday—Many Years Ago"

. . . *ut ipse quodammodo mihi viderer in præterita redire, non ea quæ jam transacta et decursa sunt, recordatione revocare:*

. . . *so that I seemed to be living in the past, rather than recalling the memory of that which was gone.*—Minucius Felix.

It was at Chamonix that I first put on ski, in December, 1898, and it was at Grindelwald, two years later, that I made my first ski tour, the Kleine Scheidegg, in the company of the Bostocks.

Adelboden was first opened for winter sports in January, 1902. Only a small minority of the visitors skied, but this minority included two enthusiasts, Canon Savage and Percival Farrar, who invited me to join them on their exploration of the surrounding hills. In their company I was introduced to many of the now popular Adelboden runs, including the Elsighorn of which we made the first ski ascent.

In 1903 I discovered an enthusiast who was only a year my senior, a Sedbergh boy, Milligan by name. On many of our expeditions we had no other companions and no professional assistance, and had the fun of working out our own solutions to the problems of a new sport.

As there were no ski-lifts or funiculars in the Adelboden of those days, four thousand feet of downhill ski-ing was the most that we ever managed to enjoy in one day. The modern skier sometimes exceeds an aggregate of thirty thousand feet of descent in the day. Ski-lifts have not only multiplied manyfold the aggregate of downhill ski-ing on any particular day; they have also increased the number of days on which ski-ing is practicable. At Adelboden a snowstorm confined us to the practice slopes, and even when the snow had ceased falling it was often too soft and too deep for a long climb, but the modern skier is almost independent of weather. So long as his standard course is still plastered by a layer of snow, however thin, he can ski. The soft falling snow is soon trampled into the regulation hard-beaten surface, and even rain seldom renders the smooth polished standard course unusable.

The ski-lift is a good slave but a bad master. It enables the beginner to master hard-snow technique very rapidly, and can also be used for soft-snow practice, for an hour's climb from the summit of most ski-lifts will often open out soft-snow runs untracked by the downhill only addicts. The ski-lift is invaluable to the ski-racer and also to skiers with short holidays who are anxious to concentrate as much downhill ski-ing possible into a week-end. Thousands of skiers use them intelligently, but there are also the slaves of the ski-lift, the "Cresta skiers," who detest soft snow, who never stir from a standard course, skiers for whom ski-ing is nothing more than a glorified tobogganing down a run with every bump and curve of which they are as familiar as the Cresta riders with the banks of the Cresta ice run at St. Moritz.

The contrast between modern Cresta ski-ing and ski-ing in the age of the pioneers may be illustrated by comparing a day in the life of a Cresta skier with a ski tour which Milligan and I carried out at Adelboden in the winter of 1903–1904.

I doubt whether the contrast between modern and primitive technique is greater than between modern and primitive equipment. In my first Adelboden season I used the cane binding, a hoop of cane, the curve of which was kept in position round one's heels by a strap. There were no toe irons, nothing but a strap which was threaded through a hole in the ski just below one's toes. There was virtually no lateral, and very little vertical control.

The fashionable parallel turn is impossible without the most rigid control, both vertical and lateral, but there is loss as well as gain in all mechanical progress. None of the visitors broke their legs ski-ing during my first two seasons at Adelboden, whereas accidents are all too common with the modern bindings.

Even ski-ing boots were unknown in 1902. I used ordinary English boots, and the routine of every run included a pause to remove boots and to rub half-frozen feet. On one of the many occasions on which I was restoring circulation to my toes, a boot which I had removed shot down five hundred feet over hard frozen crust. I have often wondered how I should have descended had not my companion managed to retrieve it.

Instead of two light bamboo sticks, we used a large solid diskless pole which would often bury itself two or three feet in deep snow before finding purchase. Sealskins and climbing wax were unknown. Sometimes at the beginning of a climb we dipped our skis in a spring in order to cover the running surfaces with a rough surface, which would facilitate climbing. A modern skier with his two sticks and sealskins climbs twice or three times as fast as we did in the pioneering days.

Because there were no ski-lifts and no sealskins, and because we were so much slower both uphill and downhill, we could not afford to waste the best hours of the day in bed. The Cresta skier enjoys a late breakfast, and takes his place in the queue for the ski-lift long after the sun has flooded the valley, but in December, 1903, when Milligan and I started for the Laveygrat, we left the sleeping village while the morning star still disputed the dawn. The dusk still lingered in the arches of pine which vaulted the old wood path, now transformed into a motor road, but the day had won by the time we crossed the valley river. A trailing wisp of river mist, supercharged with frost, stung like a whip. Below the bridge the anæmic river drained of colour and music trickled sadly round ice glazed rocks. On the banks of the stream the hoar frost had conjured silverpoint effects out of the white tracery of shrub and tree. The rose of dawn, flowering on the white cone of the Albristhorn, offered no immediate promise of relief, for the valley leading to our pass was overshadowed by the eastern barrier of the Wildstrubel range. To the summer climber the hour before the dawn is often as delightful as the noonday heat is oppressive, and consequently the summer dawn is less welcome than the reappearance of the winter sun which restores to a frozen world not only colour and light but also the benediction of warmth. It was very cold in the Hahnenmoos Valley and I congratulated myself on the fact that I had acquired proper ski-ing boots. It was tantalising to watch the cold light radiating from an unseen focus behind the Ammertengrat, but at last a diamond point blazed from the rocky crest ; the point evolved into an arc, the arc into a semi-circle, the semi-circle into the complete burning majesty of the risen sun. Suddenly the flat toneless snows at our feet sparkled into a mosaic of glittering light and pearl-grey shadow. There was grace and vitality in the glowing slopes of sun-reflecting powder snow. Today you can reach the Hahnenmoos without climbing, and there is a standard course and a broad highway of that dead tired beaten stuff which is the by-product of mass-produced ski-ing. The shadows retreated and our bodies relaxed in the temperate flood of invigorating warmth. We drank in the golden sunshine as if it had been wine. We were serenely happy. We had broken the back of the climb.

We had come forth from the valley of chill shadows into the glory of the Alpine sun. A wonderful moment, but foreign to the experience of the Cresta skier.

Milligan and I were intrigued by two ski tracks descending from the pass. Few of the local Swiss or of the British visitors toured on ski, and it would have been impossible for any member of our little group to visit the Hahnenmoos without his fellow enthusiasts hearing of his experiences. In those days one could usually put a name to a ski track.

"There are no uphill tracks," said Milligan, "so those chaps must have come from Lenk."

"That means," said I, "that they're Swiss. Lenk hasn't been opened up for winter sports."

There was magic in the solitude of the Hahnenmoos and yet we were conscious of a sense of unwarranted intrusion. In summer Man was at home among the mountains. He had acquired rights of domicile in the long centuries during which he had occupied the higher grazing grounds. Even above the snowline he was tolerated. But after the autumn snows had dusted the green cattle alps with silver and the last of the cows had jangled her way down to the valley, the mountains resumed their suspended sovereignty and withdrew from Man his right of entry into their realm. The profane ski-runner, who disregarded this tacit compact between the mountains and Man often felt the need to conciliate the *genius loci*. The modern ski-runner must invade the remotest glaciers to experience a comparable sense of intrusion into a realm for which the human passport is not endorsed.

We lunched on the windless sun-kissed crest of the Laveygrat. It would be illogical, in this comparison between the past and the present to describe a view which, objectively at least, has not changed. And yet I am very sure that the ski-runner who unhooks himself from a ski tow does not see the same view as the man who has paid for beauty in the currency of toil. "We become what we behold," said Blake. It would, perhaps, be truer to say that what we become influences what we behold.

So far we had not broken new ground, but from the Laveygrat we continued climbing for an hour to the Thierberg, and cut what were, perhaps, the first ski tracks up what is now a popular run. In those far off days we did not regard the climb merely as a tedious but unavoidable prelude to a downhill run. Ski-ing was not only an exciting mode of sliding down snow, but also a branch of exploration. Ski gave one the right of entry to the deep untracked snows of the winter Alps. A new chapter in the history of mountaineering was beginning. Little or nothing was known of the ever-changing moods of winter snow. We soon discovered that even on the ascent summer routes were sometimes useless and sometimes dangerous. And, of course, summer experience was useless to the skier planning his descent. We had to solve our own problems with no help from books, guide books or guides. The first ski-ing guide to any part of the Swiss Alps appeared in 1909. It was published by a British Club, the Alpine Ski Club, and was written by an English skier. (*The Bernese Oberland*, Volume I, by Arnold Lunn.) What the exploration of the summer Alps on foot meant to an earlier generation, the exploration of the winter Alps on ski meant to us.

All that the ski-tourer of those days has in common with the modern Cresta skier are the skis. In all other respects the Cresta skier, who devotes his days to memorising a standard run, has infinitely more in common with the Cresta tobogganer than with the ski-mountaineer. The essence of ski-mountaineering is exploration. The essence of Cresta ski-ing is repetition.

After a brief rest on the summit of the Thierberg, we pointed our ski downhill. The Cresta ski-runner who is unloaded several times a day at the summit of his favourite run never tastes the happiness of those who buckle on their ski for the descent after long hours of climbing. Repetition stales the thrill of those moments when the skis gather speed on the first downward dive of the day.

In those days our technique was primitive, our style non-existent. We reduced speed by leaning heavily on, and we achieved long drawn out changes of direction by dragging ourselves slowly round on our single stout and sturdy pole. Poor fun, of course, compared with the thrill of linking telemarks and christianias in the free stickless style which Vivian Caulfeild was the first to introduce to British ski-runners. And yet because we knew so little, because we had everything to learn, and none to teach us, there was a genuine thrill in our clumsy experimental strivings for the elements of technique. A modern artist takes the laws of aerial perspective for granted, but Úcello was intoxicated by the excitement of his first experiments in perspective. "You cannot begin to understand," he was in the habit of explaining to his wife, "what a fascinating thing perspective can be."

Half-way down to the valley a tree loomed up suddenly in front of me, and in the crisis of the moment I achieved—with the aid of pole—a right-angle-turn. I shouted to Milligan who was just behind to take note of this marvel. "Look at my track," I exclaimed "I think I've just pulled off what the Norwegians call a christiania."

"Perhaps you have," said Milligan, for he was ever a generous soul.

The last descending slopes petered out into a flat meadow near the river bed. The hiss of powder snow, scattered by the ski, faded out into one last regretful reminiscent sigh. Gravity had done what gravity could do. The run was over.

We recrossed the little bridge from which we had watched the young dawn incarnadine the western hills, and already the eastern slopes were luminous with Vesper lights. As we came out of the wood path the first stars had re-occupied the eastern sky, and little lights twinkled from the village. But the serene sunlight of the heights still lingered in our minds. We clung to the day which was dying, as if loth to cross the frontier which divides vision from retrospect, things seen from things remembered. Meanwhile memory was already busying herself with her task of selection, choosing that which was to be secured against the rust of time, the vestal loveliness of the snows at dawn, the weather-stained rafters of an alp hut just clear of the white smother, the spectral calm of spellbound peaks, dreaming of the beginning of days when their foundations were laid in primeval seas, the transparent blue of light shadows cast by scudding clouds on distant snows, and snowladen pines on a western ridge aflame as the setting sun shone through their tracery of snow. . . .

And what of the Cresta skier as he returns to his hotel after completing twenty thousand feet of downhill ski-ing in the day? Well, he too has his reward, for modern ski-ing is an exacting test of courage, and there is pride and joy in the conquest of fear. And so, as the Cresta skier skies home through the twilight he relives the tense thrill of moments when the quivering ski touched sixty miles an hour, and the ecstatic relief as he swept out on to gentler slopes, triumphant, erect and unconquered. Or it may be that things have gone wrong and that he has had a bad day, and failed by three seconds to win the coveted diamond badge awarded to those who can run the Standard course in, say, 4 minutes and 30 seconds. "I'd have made it," he reflects sadly, "if I'd done a half turn above Funnybone Fir instead of a sharp christy just below Beelzebub Bend. And why did I put in a turn at the top of 'Roaring Forties.' I'm sure I can hold it from the top. I'll spend next week practising that *schuss*, and I'll win that diamond yet, or bust myself in the attempt. . . ."

Ski-ing has been revolutionised not only by ski-lifts, but also by schools, tests and races all of which were non-existent in my first Adelboden season. The first organised school at Adelboden was founded by Willy Rickmers in the winter of 1903–1904. Rickmers was a German, married to a Scot. He was an explorer, mountaineer and ski pioneer. He did not teach ski-ing professionally for he was a man of means, with a gospel to proclaim. He was a disciple of Zdarsky, a brilliant and eccentric Austrian who lived alone like a hermit among the woods of Lillienfeld. Zdarsky had heard of ski-ing and imported a pair of ski from Norway. He decided that the Norwegian technique, of which he knew nothing, was unsuited for the steep Alpine terrain. He rediscovered the stem turn, and his book contains the first lucid analysis in print of that basic ski-ing manœuvre. He invented a steel binding which provided good lateral and virtually no vertical control, and founded the Lillienfeld ski school, the basis of which was the stem turn helped out by the single diskless pole. His disciples soon acquired remarkable control on steep ground, but they tended to regard turning as an end in itself, and high speed as a temptation of the devil.

I was never a disciple of this school and never used the Lillienfeld ski and bindings, but I must bear witness to Rickmers' great services to British ski-ing. The Lillienfeld school is as extinct as the Dodo, but in its day it served a useful purpose, for a skier who had been taught to stem by Rickmers was a safer companion among the mountains than a skier who could not stem at all. Moreover, Rickmers by his enthusiasm enticed many British winter sportsmen from the ice rink to the hills.

The publication in 1911 of Vivian Caulfeild's *How to Ski and How not to*, which opened with a vigorous attack on the Lillienfeld school, revolutionised British ski-ing. Caulfeild accused British skiers of evading difficulties, and of preferring timid control to speed. The influence of the book was immediate. There were, of course, other pioneers of the Norwegian style, notably E. C. Richardson, but none whose influence was as potent in its effect as Caulfeild's. He practised what he preached, for he was not only a gracefu but also a daring runner. His impromptu *schuss* down the Blumenlücke at Mürren has never been repeated. The vertical drop is about a thousand feet. The summit slopes, which were wind touched powder when he ran them, have a gradient of 35 degrees. Near the outrun Caulfeild had to cross the detritus of an old avalanche, thinly masked by about six inches of powder snow. This exploit was a more exacting test of pluck and skill than any rehearsed *schuss* down the hard-beaten snow of a standard run.

Caulfeild is a teacher of genius, and I use the big word advisedly. When his book appeared, Carl Egger, a great Swiss pioneer, contrasted the futile attempts to explain the turns in current Norwegian literature with the brilliant and helpful analysis of ski-ing mechanics in Caulfeild's work. His son, Barry, the most graceful skier that I have ever met, inherits his father's talents.

Such readers as suspect that I am inspired by a desire to say something pleasant about an old friend may be recommended to compare the descriptions of the parallel turn in current ski-ing literature with the masterly analysis of that intricate manœuvre which appeared under the joint signatures of Vivian and Barry Caulfeild in the British Ski Year Book for 1938.

The oldest of all ski tests were inaugurated by the Richardsons at Davos at the beginning of the century. Tests were introduced to Adelboden in 1903. Unknown to each other Vivian Caulfeild and I passed the Third Class Test at Adelboden on the same day in January, 1903.

In 1903 I entered for a ski race which was part of a three-event competition for the Public Schools Alpine Sports Challenge Cup, awarded to the competitor who scored the highest aggregate marks in skating, ski-ing and tobogganning. The ski race in 1903 consisted of a climb of about 400 feet and an aggregate descent of about 1,000 feet, the course being about four miles in length. Some twenty skiers entered for the race which was won by the youngest competitor, the present writer. My climbing muscles had been developed by running up and down the paths round Grindelwald and by ski-ing expeditions in the Adelboden hills, and it was on the uphill sections that I ran away from my rivals. In view of my subsequent role as the protagonist of downhill racing, it was ironical that I should have made my début by winning a primitive "langlauf." In those days skiers had not begun to specialise. I have often thought with regret of the many hours which I wasted on the rink and the toboggan run, but it gradually became increasingly difficult to find competitors for a three-event competition, which was therefore discontinued, and separate challenge cups were awarded for what had been, in effect, the Club skating, ski-ing and tobogganing championships. The skating event became the Lytton Challenge Cup, and the ski race the Roberts of Kandahar Challenge Cup.

Earl Roberts of Kandahar, who was a vice-president of the club, took his title from his famous march, Cabul to Kandahar, and the cup which bears his name is today the world's senior challenge cup for downhill ski-racing. It was first competed for on January 6th, 1911.

On January 30th, 1924, the Kandahar Club, which took its name from the race, was founded at Mürren to raise the standard of British ski-racing and to promote downhill and slalom, neither of which had received international recognition, and it was with the same object in view that the Kandahar later founded at St. Anton the famous Arlberg-Kandahar race. The club subsequently founded the Quebec Kandahar in the Laurentians, the Scottish Kandahar, the Far West Kandahar on the Pacific coast of the U.S.A. and the Kandahar of the Andes in Chile. All these races stem from that primitive competition which I won in 1903.

During a recent visit to Canada I spent a week-end with Tom Wheeler at the Gray Rock Inn, and was driven over to Tremblant at the foot of the Quebec Kandahar course. Thanks to the enthusiastic co-operation of the Red Birds and of Percy Douglas, Doyen of Canadian ski-ing, the Quebec Kandahar has become a classic of Canadian ski-ing, ranking in public estimation, if not officially, with the Canadian championship. I asked a Canadian at Gray Rock Inn why the Quebec Kandahar was so called. "Because it was founded," he replied, "by a distinguished Englishman, Mr. Kandahar." It is gratifying to have some hope of posthumous

Opposite: *KANDAHAR TRAIL ON MOUNT TREMBLANT (LAURENTIANS)*
By kind permission of Romney Jaques Studio.

fame as an ectoplasmic wraith attached to the Kandahar races. Centuries hence some learned pedant may investigate the origins of the Kandahar legend. He will assume, as such pedants invariably do assume, that the traditional explanation of past events must necessarily be false, and he will have no difficulty in proving that "L" and "S" are often confused in ancient cursive scripts, and that the Kandahar legend is nothing more than a variant of ancient Sun myths. The sun travels from Kandahar in Afghanistan, gilds the Arlberg snows, disperses the shadows of night from the hills of Scotland, crosses the Atlantic to flood the Laurentians and the Andes with the rose of dawn, finally sinking into the sea beyond the Far West coast of America. Lunrise in Afghanistan, and Lunset in the Pacific. It all sounds quite plausible.

My trivial success in that primitive race, ancestor of all the Kandahars, had no influence on my ski-ing career. I had no interest in competitive ski-ing, and continued to regard ski-ing as a means to an end, and that end the exploration of the Alps in winter. Had I been interested in ski-racing or in ski-ing as an end in itself I should have founded the Oxford University Ski Club, while I was at Oxford, and inaugurated the Oxford and Cambridge ski race. I did neither, but I was responsible—by an irony of fate—for the inauguration of the Oxford and Cambridge ice hockey match. A scratch game which I organised at Beatenberg between Oxford and Cambridge ice hockey players was the seed from which the official match developed. Had I not broken my leg a few months later I might have played in the first of the Oxford and Cambridge ice hockey matches which was held at Wengen in December, 1909, for even I could have satisfied the modest standards of the selection committee.

A genial friend of my brother's, now dead, volunteered to collect a team. He was unaware of the fact that first-class players could have been discovered among the Canadian and American Rhodes scholars at Oxford, but he had no difficulty in making up a team from undergraduates who were charmed by the prospect of a free trip to Switzerland. In return for his services he was offered a place in the team, and the captious objection to his inclusion raised by a cantankerous critic based on the admitted fact that he could not skate was over-ruled when he pointed out that immobility

3

Opposite: *SCHUSS.* *By kind permission of Walter Amstutz.*

was a positive advantage to a goalkeeper. When the teams changed ends, he was assisted across the rink by two friends. His attitude to such shots as did not actually strike his person would have qualified him for membership of a non-intervention committee, and such shots as did strike him only failed to score when he fell forwards instead of backwards.

Though I did not found the Oxford University Ski Club, I founded, during my years at Oxford, two clubs which still flourish, the Alpine Ski Club for ski-mountaineers, and the Oxford Mountaineering Club, of which H. E. G. Tyndale, now Editor of the Alpine Journal, was the first president.

Our little club, with a membership of less than twenty, published a slim volume, *Oxford Mountaineering Essays*, which was very well received by the reviewers and the mountaineering public. After thirty years' experience of editing journals for skiers and for ski-mountaineers I have learned that it is extremely difficult to find writers who can interpret the emotions which mountains provoke in those who love them, but as editor of these Oxford essays I was not in the least impressed by my luck in discovering in our small group no less than seven mountaineers, Julian and N. G. Huxley, H. E. G. Tyndale, Norman Young, Michael Sadleir, Hugh Kingsmill Lunn and Hugh Pope, who could write exactly the kind of essay which was required. The reviewers were kind, notably *The Times*, which wrote of an " array of talent—all of them enthusiastic, all of them young, and all sufficiently interested in the art of writing to be qualified to tell as well as to experience. Some of them, if that had been their aim, are entitled to write as masters of the craft. They have chosen a loftier way. . . ."

In the summer of 1913 the club entertained three distinguished Cambridge mountaineers, Geoffrey Young, H. O. Jones, and George Mallory who died eleven years later on Everest. As we sat down to dinner somebody remarked that we were thirteen. Within the year Trev Huxley had died, H. O. Jones and Hugh Pope had been killed among the mountains and the rest of us had taken part in one or other or both of the search parties that brought down the bodies of our dead friends. A mere coincidence for of all baseless superstitions the " 13 " superstition is the silliest. I have often dined thirteen since that dinner party at Oxford.

Oxford Mountaineering Essays was dedicated to Geoffrey Winthrop Young to whose encouragement the project owed its inception, and to whose criticism the youthful essayists were indebted for suggestions both positive and negative. Geoffrey Young has always occupied a unique position among the younger mountaineers and the passing of time has only strengthened his hold on their affection. And this for many reasons. In the period which ended with the first World War no mountaineer could rival Geoffrey's record of pioneer Alpine ascents. He could not only climb but also write. He is the author of some of the best Alpine prose, and though many poets had worshipped mountains from below, Geoffrey was the first poet worthily to interpret the romance and enchantment of mountaineering. Finally, young men turned to him ıor counsel because he had a temperamental understanding of iconoclastic and impatient youth.

It was, for instance, characteristic of Geoffrey that though he never became an expert skier, and only used ski on two glacier expeditions, he was free from that peculiar prejudice against ski-mountaineering which was then prevalent in the Alpine Club. The Mother of all Alpine Clubs had played its part in the development of winter mountaineering, but the pioneers of winter mountaineering such as W. A. B. Coolidge and Colonel Strutt climbed on snow racquettes and regarded ski as only suitable for the lower hills, and it was not until eleven years after the German Paulcke crossed the Oberland on ski, climbing the Jungfrau in the course of the expedition, that the first ski-mountaineering expedition of any note was carried through by an Englishman who, at that time, was not a member of the Alpine Club. The Englishman in question was the present writer who in company with Professor Roget crossed the Bernese Oberland from Kandersteg to Meiringen in January, 1909, climbing the Finsteraarhorn on the fifth day of this six-day expedition. In those days there was no Lötschberg tunnel—the first two days of our expedition were spent in crossing the Petersgrat to the Lötschenthal—and no Jungfrau railway. The modern skier breakfasts at the Scheidegg, takes the train to the Jungfraujoch (11,400 feet) and skis in thirty minutes down to the Concordiaplatz, but in those days the Concordiaplatz in winter was some fourteen hours from the nearest railhead. The Alpine glacier world has nothing nobler than the incomparable sweep of glaciers which meet at the Concordiaplatz, but the "Place of

Peace" has lost much of its ancient quiet since the railway was built. In summer the surrounding snows are scored by foot tracks, in winter and in spring by the furrows cut by innumerable ski. It was otherwise in 1909. The winter snows had hidden all evidence of the commerce between mountains and man, and the Concordia had recovered the aloof and lonely majesty which was hers before man first troubled the high mountains with his presence.

Shortly after this expedition I found myself involved in a controversy in the columns of *The Field* with distinguished members of the Alpine Club, notably Mr. W. A. B. Coolidge, who enlightened the argument about ski and their value to the mountaineer by demonstrating that I was twenty years of age. Geoffrey Young, however, from the first, followed with encouraging sympathy the new phase of mountaineering and included a chapter on ski-mountaineering by the young iconoclast in his classic work *Mountain Craft*.

The prejudice against ski-mountaineering gradually succumbed to stubborn facts, but there is still less liaison between skiers and mountaineers in England than abroad mainly because few of our people can manage a winter and a summer holiday in the Alps. In Switzerland the World Ski Champions have been recruited from the ranks of mountaineers (*e.g.*, Otto Furrer, David Zogg, the brothers Steuri among guides and Walter Amstutz among amateurs) but in the English-speaking world I can only recall one skier who achieved outstanding distinction both as a mountaineer and as a ski-racer, Miss Betty Wolsley who was a member of the expedition which climbed one of the most difficult of peaks on the American continent, Mount Waddington. Miss Wolsley captained an American ladies' ski team in the World Championship, and after breaking a leg returned to the arena to win the American Ladies' Ski Championship in 1940.

A few months after my ski traverse of the Oberland, I fell from a Welsh cliff, and shattered my right leg. The wound did not heal for twelve years, and my right leg is still two inches short and deformed. It was two years before I began to climb again, one of my first ascents being the ridge from which I fell. As the result of my accident I was rejected by the Army and spent most of the war in Switzerland on work connected with the British and French prisoners of war. I spent the winter of 1915–1916 at Montana where the French were interned, and the two subsequent winters at Mürren which was a centre for British internees.

To those war years I am indebted for the memory of a perfect friendship. Three of the British officers interned at Mürren and I formed a ski-ing quartette, united by a love of mountains, of ski-ing and of passionate debate for we argued and quarrelled about a fine confused array of themes, secular and divine. And when we were separated we continued our discussions by letter. Tristram Carlyon was a Cornish squire who spent most of his time on his property in New Zealand. He lost an eye in the first world war and his life in the second, for once again he crossed the seas to fight for England and died in a military hospital. Ralph du Boulay Evans was a Wykeamist who was twelfth man for the Cambridge Cricket XI. He was a geologist and developed a variant of the *odium theologicum* when his pet orthodoxies, such as the erosive power of glaciers, were challenged. From his French ancestor he had inherited Gallic wit and fire. He was a scientist with the soul of a poet. I remember "Booly" pausing on a moonlight run as we crossed the little pass into moonlight glade. Drunk with the beauty of the radiant snows he threw back his head and recited Meredith's *Love in a Valley*. "Booly" was killed in a motoring accident in 1929, and a few years later Bob Middleditch, in some ways the most lovable of the three, died at the end of a long and painful illness.

We used to ski at Mürren while the snow held out, and then follow the winter into the glacier world. During those war years I completed my exploration of the Oberland glaciers and made many ski expeditions in other ranges, such as the first ski ascent on June 18th, 1916, of the Dom (14,942 feet) the highest mountain wholly in Switzerland.

The Austrian Colonel Bilgeri was the first to insist that ski-ing is a snow sport rather than a winter sport. He was the pioneer of summer ski-ing, but he had few disciples. Before the first world war I made some ski ascents in summer (Monte Rosa, Fiescherhorn and Jungfrau), but it was not until I made my home in the Alps that I realised that the real ski-mountaineering season does not begin much before April.

Meanwhile, there was a new and fascinating field for research, snowcraft and its problems with special reference to ski-ing. Paulcke and Rickmers had laid the foundations, but only the foundations of avalanche craft, but little was known and virtually nothing had been written about spring snow. Only a small minority realised the magnificent possibilities of spring ski-ing. The Tourist Agency, Alpine Sports, Ltd., coined the slogan " February is the best month " in order to persuade skiers that February was not the beginning of the end, but merely the end of the beginning. It was not until Fritz von Allmen opened the Scheidegg for spring ski-ing that the ski-ing world as a whole discovered that there were two ski-ing seasons, of which the second season which began in March is the better.

The ski-ing season at Mürren, as I have said, began in October or November and lasted till May. During the long Mürren winters I kept a daily careful record of snow conditions, and the determining factors such as wind, and temperature. I photographed the more interesting snow surfaces and by comparing the daily records over a period of months was able to discover the relationships between very different snowfaces as they evolved into each other. This accumulation of notes formed the basis of my essay which appeared in Young's *Mountain Craft* and which was subsequently translated into German, and also of my book *Alpine Ski-ing at all Heights and Seasons*.

Marcel Kurz, that eminent Swiss mountaineer, who has an unrivalled record as a ski-mountaineer, and who is the author of the ski-mountaineering guides to the Valaisian chain, reproduced entire sections of my book in his *Alpinisme Hivernale* and offered to the reader a perplexed apology for his dependence on the work of an Englishman. " It is a curious fact," he wrote, " that the English who were the first to explore our Alps and the last to explore them on ski, possess since 1931, the best work on this subject. . . . Arnold Lunn has lived for entire years among the Alps like Zdarsky among the snows of Lillienfeld."

Alpine Ski-ing was translated by Captain de Gennes into French and had a considerable influence in the development of ski mountaineering in France. The crack group of the French Alpine Club (G.H.M.) elected me an honarary member.

In more recent years Gerald Seligman, a former president of the Ski Club of Great Britain, has brought to the study of snow the training and the methods of a scientist. He has lived for months at the Jungfraujoch, digging tunnels in ice, and carrying out a series of experiments in the structure of ice and snow. His classic book *Snow Structure and Ski Fields* has no rival in any other language.

Seligman is the Tyndall of our day. It is a matter of congratulation that the author of the most authoritative work on snow and ice should be not a scientist from Alpine lands but a citizen of Great Britain. Many scientists have been elected Fellow of the Royal Society for far less original and less important research.

I was surprised and relieved to discover how well my empirical theories had stood up to the critical test of scientific investigation. If I were to rewrite my book today there is little that I should need either to add or to correct. I shall always be grateful for the chance of collecting the necessary data to write *Alpine Ski-ing*, but I am indebted to those long years in the Alps for something which I value more highly than an expert knowledge of the habits of snow. Only those who have made their home in one of the loftier of Alpine resorts can fully appreciate the wonder of the Alpine spring. I have known deep powder snow on the slopes round Mürren in the second week of October and have had perfect ski-ing down to the level of Mürren in May. But even skiers tire of the snow, if they make their home at Mürren or Davos.

In those war winters we welcomed the first snows of late October with passionate joy, but by mid-winter we had begun to weary of the uncompromising contrast between the steely blues of the winter sky and the dazzle of sun-reflecting snowfields, and to long for the polychromatic range of April colouring.

It is in March that winter relents and sound returns with colour to the mountain world. As the days lengthen the sun begins to thaw the frozen music of streams long muted by the frost. And then one morning one awakens to hear through the open windows a sound for which one has waited through the long months of silence, a fugitive tune borne upwards from the valley far below on the wings of hope, the opening bars of the river valley in the first movement of the Spring Symphony.

The undisputed triumph of May is less dramatic than the first difficult victories of March. The glory of Alpine valleys in May is less appealing than the *sursum corda* of the first emergence of colour and life from the frozen tomb of the wintry earth, the vivid blades of young grass piercing through the dead herbage, and the fragile soldanellas which follow the retreating snowline.

During those long war winters, my wife and I always escaped from

Mürren in April for a few days beside the lakes. I remember leaving Mürren after an exceptionally severe winter. As the funicular from Grütsch started its slow descent to Lauterbrunnen, the weary senile snow, pitted and lined and wrinkled, faded out into grey and dirty drifts beneath the shadow of the pines. As we came out of the station at Lauterbrunnen the spring welcomed us. The renascent Staubbach, which in winter is a pitiful trickle oozing down through fluted icicles, was a falling foam of triumphant water. The meadows were splashed with colour, and the air was fragrant with growing things. At Interlaken, where we lunched, there were violets in the woods, and there were gentians on the Brünig, and at Alpnach we could see the triple-crested Wetterhorn showing through a tracery of apple blossom.

The blossom falls, the violet fades, and even the mountains themselves will cease to be. And yet among the things that pass there are some which bear witness to the thing that remains. In the loveliness of the lakes in April there is something which is not wholly of this world. There have been moments beside the shores of Lucerne or Leman when I have seen quite plain in the beauty which dies the hope and promise of a beauty unshadowed by the doom which is the fate of all mortal things.

On the earth the broken arcs, in the heaven a perfect round.

From my room in St. Mary's Hospital, Montreal, I can see drifts of grey snow. Dirt has been defined as matter in the wrong place, and snow in a city street is dirt. But the eyes of the mind have windows other than those which open out on to the mere it is. Within a few hours I shall be on the operating table, but there are moments, and this one of them, when the golden past expels the grey present. The writing of this chapter has called for an effort to overcome lassitude and pain, but I have had my reward. My spirit has returned to the mountains of youth. The years dissolve and the beloved dead return. Once again four friends link their christianias down the dawn snows of the Oberaar. Once again they stroll down through the scented pines to Rosenlaui while a hundred strong streams fill the valley with song, the magnificat of spring. "Never the time and the place and the loved one all together." Well hardly ever, and it is vain to hope that perfect combinations will recur.

"Perhaps," wrote Evans from Mesopotamia, "the four of us will get together for another May run, when we have 'gone over to the other side,' as Lodge puts it. We shall never get all the conditions right in this life." In this life, no, for my friends are dead. But they will be there to welcome me when I cross my last pass to "the country of everlasting clearness."

St. Mary's Hospital, Montreal.
November 14th, 1942.

CHAPTER V

The Undiscovered Country

THERE is a country from which no traveller returns, but it may be that a fleeting glimpse of what lies beyond is revealed to those who have approached most closely to the frontier. I remember a conversation on this point with Frank Smythe. Smythe survived a long fall in the Alps, and he still retains a vivid memory of his thoughts while falling. The fall had hardly begun before he felt as if he were watching, with complete detachment, his own body somersaulting down from crag to crag. It was as if the real Smythe had escaped from the body, as if this thing, making feeble convulsive movements were something which had once been his, something which he had discarded, like an old suit of clothes or his first set of teeth. This thing did not matter. It could be scrapped without damage to the personality which had used it as a temporary habitation. And this experience, he added, convinced him beyond all need of proof that he would survive the death of his body.

There is a wide measure of agreement among mountaineers who have survived long falls that such falls are characterised by freedom from fear and by a quickened tempo of thought, so that the thinking of minutes is crowded into as many seconds. In support of this I can cite various experiences of my own. I remember, for instance, a brief but crowded crisis on the Matterhorn. I had been dragged off one of the steeper pitches by an absent-minded guide, who had been forced on me by an over-anxious parent. We were climbing upwards on a steep traverse, and I was, of course, completely unprepared for so monumental a gaffe. I was jerked off the rocks and the guide and I swung round like a pendulum. Our fate was decided within two seconds, for the leading guide held—a magnificent effort—and even before the rope had reached the vertical, the second guide and I had grabbed new handholds. But those two seconds were long enough for me to register wild surprise when the jerk came, indignant and impotent fury when I was pulled off the rocks, righteous indignation that I should suffer for the folly of a guide who had been imposed on me as an extra precaution, a rapid and pessimistic calculation of our chances, the dawn of hope as the rope tightened above me, instead of slackening as it would have done had the leading guide fallen, and ecstatic relief when my hands came to rest on a firm and adequate handhold.

It is not only what Sophocles calls " wind-swift thought " which registers its movements on the mind. Things seen are etched into one's memory with a sharpness of detail for which there is no parallel on the quieter levels of existence. I remember, one New Year's day many years ago, being caught on the crest of the Eiger by the most violent tornado in all my Alpine experience. I had inadvertently left my crampons (ice-claws) behind, and I was climbing in unnailed ski-ing boots. After struggling for eight hours through mist and driving snow we reached the summit during a momentary lull in the storm, and we had just started down the ice stairway which we had cut on the ascent when Hell broke loose. A stone whipped off the slope whistled past like a bullet, and out I went at ıull rope's length. If I could draw, which I can't, I could reproduce in detail two pictures, which are engraved on my mind, first of the roofs of Grindelwald, nine thousand feet below, showing through a rent in the black storm clouds, and secondly of my guide, straining against the rope, leaning back on the gale, perfect poise and perfect balance, his ten-pointed crampons grinding into the ice.

Though fear is in abeyance during a fall, one's mind is alert. One's first reaction is often one of indignation. Young climbers believe in their star, and are taken by surprise when their luck breaks. Accidents are things which only happen to other people. Even one's friends are deemed to be immune from the chances of sudden death. The first dead body that I ever saw was that of a friend, and as I followed the stretcher down from the Pyrenean peak from which he had fallen, I felt as if his death were a mischievous reversal of nature. That was before the first World War, and in that remote age young men still expected to outlive their elders.

Like other climbers I had had my bad moments, when the margin of safety had been cut too narrow, and was no stranger to the horror of a half slip while leading on rock or ice. But even so, when I first found myself dropping through empty space, I felt as if the mountains were taking a monstrous liberty. It was on one of the ridges of Cader Idris in Wales that I lost my illusions. Non-climbers sometimes commiserate with me on the indignity of coming to grief in Wales, but though our British hills are not high, they provide the rock climber with a magnificent arena for adventure, and the man who can lead the more severe of our native climbs ranks high in the mountain brotherhood.

On August 28th, 1909, I descended the Cyfrwy ridge of Cader Idris. I have seldom enjoyed rock climbing more. The sun flooded down from a cloudless sky. The climb though tricky was well within my margin of safety. There was sensuous pleasure in the feel of the warm dry rocks, and a mental stimulant in the contrast between the apparent threat of the drop below and the confidence born of firm rock and acquired skill. I was on the best of terms with the mountains. We understood each other. We were friends. I had descended the steep pitch above the pinnacle, on which the solitary figure is seen in the illustration facing p. 48, and had just lowered myself from the edge on the right-hand corner of the pinnacle, when suddenly the whole mountain seemed to quiver. I clung to the trembling cliffs in an agony of fear. A vast monolith liberated itself from the stony matrix of the cliff and heeled over on top of me. And I fell.

Fear vanished when the fall began. I struck the face of the cliff three or four times, and each time that I somersaulted off again into space, I felt the same angry disappointment that my fall had not been finally checked. But the basic reaction was one of righteous indignation. You can't do this to me. . . . You can't do this to ME. . . .

But Cader could . . . and did. One hundred feet below the point from which I fell I came to rest on a narrow sloping ledge, just above a vertical drop of two hundred feet on to the screes below. I tried to sit up, but fell back hurriedly on seeing my right shin sticking through my stocking. My leg was bent almost at right angles. I shouted and shouted and the twenty minutes which passed before I heard an answering cry were the longest of my life.

Cader left me with a shortened and misshapen leg, the balance of which has always been precarious, and this must be my excuse for tumbling off the Eiger some fifteen years later. Three Swiss friends and I had made the first ski ascent of the Eiger by way of the Eiger Glacier, and had left our ski on the Eigerjoch. As we started our descent from the summit to the Eigerjoch, the snow which masked the ice on this long ridge had begun to soften. We cut no steps and trusted to our crampons, which we drove through the snow into the underlying ice. My game leg was always painful at the end of a long climb, and I failed to drive into the ice with sufficient punch. I slipped, and my friend, who was above me, was taken unawares and jerked out of his steps. I saw him shoot past, head first, protecting his head with his hands. The ice slope ended some five hundred feet below in the glacier snows, and there was no reason to suppose that we should stop before we reached the bottom. My first reaction was intense irritation with myself for slipping, flavoured by milder annoyance with my companion for failing to hold me. Our friends were on another rope. There was nothing they could do to help, but as we shot past them I was faintly annoyed by their impassive attitude. They might at least, I felt, have indicated their sympathy by a gesture, such as the removal of their hats to prospective corpses. And then, as we continued to slide, I felt an odd sense of linking up with the fall on Cader, as if I had never really stopped falling, as if the intervening years had dropped out.

And then suddenly the rope tightened and we stopped. The foreground which had been rushing up to meet us at an ever accelerating speed gave a little jerk. The world came to rest, and we were alive and unhurt. The rope had caught on a tiny spike of rock, some three inches broad, protruding about an inch above the snow. The soft snow swept down by the rope had packed against the limestone wrinkle, and had acted as a buffer with the happy result that the rope was frayed, but not cut.

As on Cader, it was the odd chance in ten thousand that saved me, and yet I never felt that I was facing extinction. I knew that my body might shortly cease to function but the thought that I might shortly cease to exist never passed through my mind. Smythe's beliefs were profoundly influenced by his fall ; mine were not, but at least these experiences started a train of thought, and form the slender basis for a provisional theory to explain that freedom from fear which is such a perplexing characteristic of mountain tumbles. Provided that one does not blur the sharp distinction between beliefs which one can defend by rational argument and tentative guesses which are consistent with known facts but not an inevitable deduction from them, there is no harm in guessing.

I can best explain them by my own provisional solution to the problem which I have been discussing by means of an analogy. The unborn child may fear birth, as we fear death, and knowing nothing of the splendour of life may cling tenaciously to the only existence which it knows. Fear may be Nature's device for preventing premature birth and premature death.

Where the issue between life and death is still in doubt, fear often evokes a dynamic and superhuman effort, for man has unsuspected powers on which he can draw in moments of great emergency, but in the experiences which I have described no effort, human or superhuman, could have had the slightest influence on the result. One was as helpless as a falling stone, the toy of external forces. Fear could no longer perform any useful function, and because fear was useless fear ceased to be.

A war-time memory lends some slight support to what is admittedly only a tentative hypothesis. In the early summer of 1940 I crossed the Atlantic as the only civilian on board one of the small escort vessels which accompanied a large convoy. The *Bismarck* was at sea and just before we reached harbour we met a battleship escorted by destroyers sailing out for the battle which was joined a few days later. On one of our last days at sea I was aroused at dawn by the alarm signal, and came on deck to see an unknown battleship shaping itself out of the shadows. There was no response to our recognition signal, and we could take no chances, so while the merchant ships began to scatter our little escort vessel headed towards the dark invader. I stood beside a sub-lieutenant who was young in years, but old in war, for he had seen action off Norway, Dunkirk, Oran and Dakar. There was an eager expectant look on his face.

A few minutes later the unknown battleship gave the recognition signal, and the tension relaxed. "I'm immensely relieved," I said, "that it isn't a Nazi raider, but there is a faint flat feeling of anti-climax which reminds me of the first air-raid warning of the war, when the German bombers never came over."

"I know what you mean," said the sub-lieutenant, "if that ship had been a raider our delaying action would have been so ridiculously quixotic that one can't help feeling one has missed something rather splendid."

And I knew that had the ship been a Nazi raider, the inescapableness of death would have given to his last moments of active and defiant service a quality unattainable on the lower levels of existence.

"Armies," says Mr. Belloc, "fighting for a just cause are the happiest places for living." And perhaps, also, the happiest places for dying.

CHAPTER VI

. . . Deos Qui Novit Agrestes

MANY people, as Christopher Hollis remarked in one of his articles, were happier during the big raids than at any previous period of their lives, because they learned to their surprise that they were not demoralised by danger. It is exceptional for people to behave badly on sinking ships, or under fire ; indeed, the modicum of courage, which enables a man to acquit himself without discredit in time of peril, is so common that it is only its absence which calls for comment. None the less, until a man has been tested, there will always be a note of interrogation in his mind, and it is because the blitz enabled many thousands who had never previously been in grave danger to give an affirmative answer to the question, " Can I take it ? " that the mental climate of those days was one of pleasurable pride. " Freedom from fear," which is one of the freedoms which Mr. Roosevelt includes among our war aims, is of doubtful value. Freedom from the fear of fear, on the other hand, is an ideal which few attain and which all desire. Whatever may be our grievances against the period through which we are living, we must at least concede that it has provided most Europeans with ample data to discover their reactions to the peril of death, but if, as is possible, though by no means probable, this war is followed by a long period of peace, sports such as mountaineering will fulfil a valuable function, for they will provide that " moral substitute " for the ordeal of war, the importance of which was the theme of a famous essay by a great American philosopher, William James.

The more extreme Nazi exponents of the modern school sought in mountaineering not a " moral substitute " but a rehearsal for war, and the casualties on the various attempts to climb the Eiger Nordwand were far higher in proportion to those who took part than the casualties in the Dieppe raid. The layman who seldom hears about mountaineering except in connection with its more extreme exploits or with much publicised accidents, often entertains a grossly exaggerated conception of the real perils of mountaineering. History always tends to over-emphasise the exceptional, and Alpine literature naturally gives more prominence to unusual incidents, dramatic escapes and fatal accidents, than to the quiet commonplaces of uneventful climbs. It is as true of mountaineering as of war that people are "always awe-struck by the narrow escapes they have had and always forget what a much narrower escape they have had from complete non-existence." I am quoting from a letter in which my son Peter described a dive-bombing attack at Malta. "Think of all the odds against you and Father meeting and against both your parents meeting and so on. The narrowest escape one could have from a bomb can't compare with the narrowness of one's escape from not being born at all."

Mountaineers do not court danger for its own sake. They try, on the contrary, to reduce the risks of a given climb to the minimum. Mummery did not cross the Col du Lion because it was more dangerous but because it was more difficult than the Théodule. "My attention," he writes, "was rivetted by the Col du Lion, and it was brought to my mind that no more circuitous or inconvenient method of getting from Zermatt to Breuil could possibly be devised than by using this same col as a pass."

The essence of sport is the invention of a problem for the fun of solving it. Why did Mummery cross the Col du Lion? Because the crossing of the Col du Lion was a problem as yet unsolved by the mountaineering community. Why does a chicken cross the road? To get to the other side. If chickens were sportsmen they would wait until a car was approaching to complicate the crossing of the road by a problem of their own devising. As indeed some of them do.

An unclimbed peak is a problem, and once the peak has been climbed by its easiest route, mountaineers continue to explore its unclimbed faces and ridges in search of new problems. Guideless climbing, winter mountaineering, and ski-mountaineering all introduce new conditions, and thus create new problems, which are solved for the pleasure of solving them rather than for the intrinsic value of the solution. Difficulties, artificial difficulties, are deliberately created in order to maintain the reality of the contest between man and mountain, for a game in which the result is certain loses all interest.

The value of a sport depends on the qualities which are called into play in the solution of the peculiar problems of the sport in question. No sport is more exacting in its demands on mind and body than mountaineering. Rock climbing calls for qualities very different from those which are necessary for quick and accurate step-cutting on steep ice. The complete mountaineer must there-

Opposite: *THE EAST RIDGE OF CYFRWY* (see p. 44).
By kind permission of G. P. Abraham, Keswick.

fore master two distinct crafts, nay three for, unless he confines his mountaineering to the summer months, he must also master ski-ing. Mountaineering is an even more exacting test of mental than of physical qualities. The mountaineer must learn to interpret the language of rock, snow and ice, and the ski-mountaineer must carry the study of snowcraft far beyond the point where the summer mountaineer can stop. There are twenty clearly defined varieties of snow surface, each of which has been named and classified. The skier must not only be able to recognise these varieties when he sees them, but also to forecast the varieties he is likely to encounter under given conditions of weather and season.

There is virtue in any way of life which brings man into direct contact with Nature. The fact that sterility is so common among families which have lived for three generations in big cities is significant. I should be happier about the future of my own country but for the fear that this future will be increasingly shaped by good examinees who have spent most of their lives indoors. " The perfect State," writes Neville Lytton, " ought to contain a certain proportion of unlettered peasants. Unlettered persons are only behind the educated ones in the matter of mechanical knowledge—emotionally and artistically they are far superior." This may be a picturesque overstatement of an important truth, but I am not disposed to pick holes in any emphasis on the cultural importance of the free peasant in the life of the community. Plato believed that democracies must inevitably degenerate into tyrannies, and his prediction may well come true of those democracies in which the interests of the peasant are completely subordinated to those of the urban proletariat. The stability of Swiss democracy is, as I tried to show in my book *Come What May*, due to the wise balance maintained between town and country, and to the fact that no single party is more influential than the peasant's party.

The Swiss peasant is a democrat, but he is a Tory democrat. He believes in progress but, like Nature, he also believes in tradition. Virgil's *justissima tellus* encourages no Utopian illusions, for the " most just earth " gives nothing for nothing. The peasant who has learned in a hard school that man must sow to reap, realises that it is necessary not only to vote for but also to work for " the more abundant life."

The direct and continuous contact with Nature, which the peasant and the seaman enjoy, is impossible for most of us, but even

Opposite: *SPRING SNOW.* *By kind permission of A. Pedrett.*

intermittent contact with Nature has a healing influence on those condemned to city life.

I have been exceptionally fortunate, for I was free to choose, in preference to the Bar, for which my father intended me, a way of life which allowed me to live among the mountains, and so devote many years to the study of mountains in general and of snowcraft in particular.

I have yet to meet a man who, having dedicated the best years of his life to the study of Nature in any one of her many aspects, regrets his choice. It is impossible to explain the spiritual influence which mountains and the sea exercise on those who submit to their discipline, and who accept the risks which that discipline demands, but it is not difficult to trace the slow spiritual impoverishment which is the bitter fruit of an industrial and an urban civilisation. It has been said that the Greek civilisation will be remembered for its philosophy, the Middle Ages for their Cathedrals and our own age for its department stores. The foundation of the Alpine Club in the Mid-Victorian age was, perhaps, an unconscious reaction against the tendencies of that age, and the expression of a determination to seek among the mountains for an antidote to megalopolitan maladies. Many of its members were scholars who had discovered among the hills sources of knowledge which are not available in the best equipped libraries.

Every great culture is born within the economy of the small town, farm and village and dies in the sterile climate of Cosmopolis. The urbanised poets who carry the town with them even into the country may sometimes choose a country theme to demonstrate their virtuosity, but they have lost that power over the hearts of men which distinguishes inspiration from mere cleverness.

Fortunatus et ille deos qui novit agrestes.

It was because Virgil " knew the country gods " and because Wordsworth's " daily teachers had been woods and hills " that the author of the Georgics and the poet of lakeland belong to the ages.

It was characteristic of Martial that he could persuade himself that all we needed were rich patrons to produce a plentiful crop of Virgils (*Sint Mœcenates, non deerunt, Flacce, Marones*) but the world is indebted for the Virgilian magic not to the wealth of Mæcenas but to the woods of Mantua, not to the applause of city cliques but to that hard life of the plough of which Virgil is the supreme interpreter.

Nature is an exacting teacher and does not encourage her pupils to dogmatise on insufficient evidence. An historian or a literary critic only risks his reputation if he stakes it on a theory unsupported by adequate facts, but a mountaineer risks his life if his interpretation of the clues which snow and ice and rock provide is refuted. There is no room for irresponsible theorising in a game in which one's first mistake may be one's last. An analogous contrast distinguishes the light-hearted chatter of undergraduates debating communism from the realism of Fighter Pilots thrashing out in discussion some problem of combat technique.

I have written books on subjects of greater importance than mountaineering, but I find it difficult to believe that anything which I have written could have much influence excepting on people who are already in substantial or at least partial agreement with me. An author who hopes for a reading public which will study every word he writes with the utmost solicitude might do worse than specialise in the writing of Climber's Guides. In the preparation of such guides, and of the ski map which I edited, I have been haunted by the knowledge that the accuracy, or otherwise, of my work might have a critical effect on the fortunes of a guideless party. I could so well, from personal experience, envisage the kind of setting in which the absent author would be called into consultation. Failing light and rising mist and an outside chance of reaching the valley before darkness provided that all goes well. Out comes the dog-eared little guidebook from the sack. "Lunn says," mutters the leader, "that we should leave the glacier at the 2,700-metre contour, well my aneroid registers 2,700 metres, so that's all right." "You forget," says the sceptic, "that this nasty change of weather may have produced a drop in pressure, so perhaps we're nearer 2,800 metres than 2,700 metres." "Well, anyhow, Lunn says that on leaving the glacier we ought to bear east, aiming at a red tower on the south ridge of the Blauhorn. I can't see any red tower, can you?" "It may be behind that mist. Why can't Lunn mention a landmark which doesn't disappear at the first touch of bad weather?" "Well, let's hope the mist lifts," retorts the leader, "because the only gully down the belt of cliffs below the Blauhorn is near the base of that red tower. At least so Lunn says."

And then the mist rolls back, and the red tower emerges, and the guideless party find their gully, and link their stem turns down the last snow slopes into the village just as the evening star climbs into the sky.

I remember once trying to find, in failing light, a club hut which had not been built, when I was editing a map, which had just been published. " What's the trouble," said my brother, " the map's quite clear? There's the ridge below which the hut stands. It's marked on the map." " Yes, but it was *I* who put it on to the map." My brother's face fell. Fortunately his scepticism proved to be unjustified.

Othmar Gurtner and I were invited, some years ago, to edit a ski edition of the Government map to the Bernese Oberland glaciers. Of the many new ski-ing passes from the central glacier region to the Rhône valley which I had pioneered, there was one the possibility of which was revealed to me by an aeroplane photograph. This pass called for good leadership to pick out an intricate route down, which avoided slopes liable to be swept by avalanches, and which hit off the little gully, which was the key to the descent of the steep cliff just above the valley. The pass was attractive, and the ski-ing interesting, and we therefore marked the pass on our map, with a warning symbol to indicate the need of great caution. I had led a guideless party down this pass in bad light, without much difficulty, but two young skiers who followed the line shown on our map got into trouble and wrote a letter of bitter complaint, in which they alleged, not that the route had been incorrectly marked, but that the pass was so intricate that it should never have been advertised on our map. I gave far more anxious thought to this criticism, though I felt it to be unreasonable, than I have ever done to a hostile review of my non-mountaineering books.

A discipline which encourages exact thought and which develops in a writer a sense of responsibility is a useful apprenticeship for a author, whatever may be his other subjects, and I sometimes find myself wishing that the exacting standards of a Climber's Guide could be imposed on all those who are writing the guides to the brave new world of the future.

Memory lightly discards the inessential experiences and decorative knowledge, but is very retentive of facts which possess survival value. Of the books, which I have read many years ago, I remember only an occasional passage which has impressed itself on my imagination, but I could live for years among the plains without impairing my judgment of whether a particular slope is likely to avalanche. A few years after leaving school I could not have translated easy Latin at sight, and have had to relearn Latin in my scanty leisure, but the language of snow once mastered is never forgotten. I am always meeting new people and have a wretched memory for faces and names, but if I have once identified a peak, I can never fail to recognise it, even at a great distance, perhaps because this particular gift has survival value, since the ability to recognise a peak or buttress, revealed for a fleeting moment when the storm clouds pass may determine one's position at a critical moment.

I remember watching the sun set on the far distant Oberland from the Wartburg, a hill above Olten. I bought a postcard of this panorama, which showed the conspicuous landmarks in the foreground, and the Oberland rising beyond a sea of mist. The Wetterhorn showed on this postcard as a mere speck, yet there was something wrong with that speck. It was the aspect of the Wetterhorn as seen, not from the Wartburg hill, but from the Weissenstein, only a nuance but enough to convince me that the microscopic Wetterhorn on my postcard had been photographed from a slightly different angle . . . very puzzling, for the foreground was correct. . . . And then suddenly I realised that the photographer had superimposed the distant Oberland as seen from the Weissenstein on the foreground of the view from the Wartburg.

My father is not the only critic who has pointed out the chances which he alleged that I had missed as the result of an exaggerated devotion to the Alps. A discerning friend of mine has often scolded me for my failure to follow up my book *The Harrovians* by a determined siege of the literary world. An author, so I am assured, must take as much trouble to sell himself as his books. Instead of which I made my home in Grindelwald and buried myself in the Alps for sixteen years.

. . . flumina amem silvasque inglorius

There is something to be said, and Virgil said it, for preferring the love of rivers and trees and, in my case, mountains, to ambition, but I do not despise those " glittering prizes," to which Lord Birkenhead referred with such deep feeling in the course of a famous rectorial address, and I should have competed for them, if without success, at least not without determination, had I been able to resist the mountain spell. I should value the prizes which are not to be won " without dust and heat " in the contests of Cosmopolis, but I happen to like other things better. Such things for instance as the rebirth of colour in Maggiore when the sun unshadows the Simplon snows, or the rediscovery of the Spring when one looks down from some window among the glaciers on the beauty of the world which the sun has reclaimed from winter. I never knew " how green was my valley " until I saw Grindelwald in May from the crest of the Eiger, and not only green, for the cherry blossom showed as threads of silver and the buttercups as a shimmer of gold. The trouble with life is that it is such an absurdly short affair. There is a book which I have been wanting to write for years, a book which would need at least two years of research and concentrated reading, a book which I might have written had I not devoted all my spare time for so many years to the study of snow, to the organisation of ski racing, to the writing of books about ski-ing, and to the editing of over thirty annual publications devoted to ski-ing and mountaineering. That book, like every book which I have planned, and unlike every book which I have written, is a very good book indeed. But I would certainly not exchange the knowledge which I acquired among the mountains for the wisdom which I might have accumulated had I spent the corresponding years of my life in research at the British Museum.

CHAPTER VII

"... Who Needs Must Go"

Spirit of ice and snow,
  Goddess, whose hands are laid
Upon the brows of men who needs must go
Seeking thy loneliness, immortal Maid,
Within the fastness of Thy frozen place;
  Dost Thou their toil behold,
  Thine heart is dull with cold,
Cold is Thy shrine, and colder Thine embrace!

Maud Holland.

GENERALISATIONS are seldom convincing, and therefore the generalities of my apologia for mountaineering need to be reinforced by particular examples. This must be my excuse for retelling a tale which appears in *The Mountains of Youth*, but which seems to me to illustrate many of the points which I tried to establish in the last chapter.

More than thirty years have passed since my brother, Hugh Kingsmill and I wandered up the long white road of many memories to Bourg St. Pierre. We had been driven from the Oberland by persistent bad weather. At Bourg St. Pierre we found the great guide Maurice Crettex, who was to save my life two years later, on the Eiger, and learned that he had been forced to retreat from an easy pass. Two feet of fresh snow met us at the Valsorey Hut, and our spirits were still further depressed by a solitary entry in the Hut book registering a defeat on the mountain which we hoped to climb, the Grand Combin (14,164 ft.) the highest mountain in the Alps outside the immediate neighbourhood of Mont Blanc or Monte Rosa. On our ascent next day of the Valsorey Combin, we were perhaps the first to reach the 4,000-metre mark in that desolate July.

We left the hut at 4 a.m. The stars had a watery look. The night had been mild and the thin crust let us through every two or three strides.

The essence of mountaineering is, as I have said, the search for problems in order to have the fun of solving them. The first of the many problems which we were called upon to solve on that memorable day was a problem of snowcraft. Was the Valsorey hut somewhere near the critical altitude where lower temperatures might be expected to produce a solid crust? Or would the breakable crust continue right up to the Col de Meiten, two thousand feet above us? The look of the stars and the feel of the wind recalled those spells of foehn in mid-winter when rain sometimes falls on the highest peaks, and we therefore judged—correctly—that it would be best to try to reach the col by the southwesterly rock ridge. We did not know whether this ridge had been climbed before, or whether it was climbable under the atrocious conditions in which we expected to find it, but anything seemed better than an interminable climb in breakable crust.

By a tricky couloir we reached the ridge in time for the first movement of the dawn. A watery sun bleered through a smudge of dampness. Beyond the sullen snows of the Velan the Italian Alps burnt up, a violent and angry red, precarious splendour on the brink of impending calamity. Nothing could be less reassuring than the contrast between the flaming snows of Paradiso and the cupola of pitchblack cloud which hovered over the dome of Mont Blanc.

Es wechselt Paradieseshelle
Mit tiefer schauervoller Nacht.

Meanwhile the dialectic of storm and sunshine created a bewildering succession of changing effects. At one moment the intricate labyrinth of interlocking peaks hung suspended above the mists, flat and bodiless like painted mountains on a theatre curtain; at the next a sharp movement of wind opened a passage for the sun, and restored the third dimension, resolving the fusion of plane surfaces into successive and separate ridges, each distinguished from the next by a change of tone and texture. The weak light filtered feebly through the mists which concealed the valleys, but the issue was not long in doubt. The countries of the sky, which still admitted the entry of the sun, lost their transparency in a blur of indefinite gloom, the only surviving hint of colour being the copper glint of a thundery cloud. We looked down from our ridge into a seething cauldron of mist, which like an octopus wound its writhing tentacles around projecting pinnacles and sucked them down into the grey smother. In the hollows of the hills eddies of the snow circled round, and miniature whirlwinds chased each other down the gullies. Little puffs of snow volleyed off the crest of the pass, and the wind, still feeble and undecided, took on a new note of querulous shrillness. The clouds broke and a crepitating staccato of hailstones pattered down on such iceglazed slabs as protruded through the snow. And then the temperature fell sharply and soft clinging snowflakes began to fall.

A steep wall of rock, some three hundred feet in height, led to our pass ; an easy scramble, perhaps, in fair weather, but far from easy as we found it. The strata sloped downwards, and the ice-glazed slabs, masked by deep snow, provided the most precarious of footholds. We had no crampons. During an awkward traverse a stone shot out of the mist and cut our rope in two. I worked back across the icy slabs and looped up the broken strands. A short steep pitch of hard frozen snow crowned by a cornice gave us a lot of trouble. I battered down the cornice, and with a thrust from behind, managed to get my head and shoulders above the pass, but I was almost thrown back by the wind, and clung on breathlessly waiting for a lull before scrambling on to the pass.

We were caught in the very vortex of the storm, and our ice-swollen rope blew out between us, flapping like a sail. Bellying surges of black cloud broke on the ice-fretted bastions of the Combin, and disintegrated into long feathery streamers of icy particles. We looked with longing down the snowslopes leading downwards from our pass. It would have been so easy to hurry down those slopes to the Valsorey glen, and thence to the little inn where Napoleon slept on his way to the St. Bernard. Our fingers were numbed by contact with icy slabs, and our spirits depressed by the tumult of the storm.

With a sinking heart I listened to the rising temper of the hurricane, as it screamed defiance from the cliffs which we hoped to climb. Honour was satisfied, and we had only to retreat to find an excellent dinner and a good bottle of wine and a warm bed waiting for us in the valley, but we might well spend the night cowering beneath a rock if we persisted in the ascent. I longed to abandon the climb, but " the Spirit of ice and snow " hardened her heart like Pharaoh and " would not let us go,"

> Whence do the deep spells rise
> Which draw men still to Thee ?
> Thou hast no warmth of summer in Thine eyes,
> Like her who called across the Ægean Sea
> Grave wayfarers to quaff her foaming vine.
> Thou hast but frozen dew,
> Thy worshippers are few,
> But these, Thy chosen ones, hold Thee divine.

The flesh might yearn for the security of Bourg St. Pierre, but the spirit still demanded battle with the storm. Self-conquest rather than mountain conquest is the secret of our strivings. " Have we vanquished an enemy ? " wrote George Mallory, " None but ourselves." The happiness of the ascetic is enjoyed by all those who subordinate the body to the mind, the flesh to the spirit, and it is to merit and to win this happiness that men climb steep rocks and race down steep hills.

In fair weather the Valsorey ridge is a steep, amusing and by no means difficult climb. As we found it, the ridge taxed our powers to the utmost, partly because we were so often forced off the ridge by the storm, in search of difficult and dangerous traverses on the face. How we hated the malignant humour of the wind which seemed to time its outbursts of malice to coincide with the moments when the leader was most insecure ! On the other hand, when the leader paused for a few seconds on some broad and secure shelf, the wind would suddenly drop, or make a great show of having business elsewhere. Meanwhile the new snow poured down like water, silting up the footholds, gumming up our eyes and plastering our hair with clammy powder. At such moments it is tempting to scamp one's job and to take chances, and difficult to handle the rope with patient care, and to test every foothold for ice glaze. It is not easy to concentrate fiercely on the business of route finding when even mental effort hurts like physical pain. Our troubles were aggravated by the ice-swollen knot, where the rope had been mended. The knot kept on catching, and once all but dragged the leader from his holds. Meanwhile the temperature was falling and our finger tips had lost all traces of sensation. If happiness, like pleasure, were wholly dependent on physical well being, there would be nothing but unredeemed misery in experiences such as these, but even on the Valsorey ridge there were rare and fleeting moments of exaltation, moments whose spirit is finely caught in the well-known lines of Geoffrey Young :

Together on the ice-glazed wall
numbed by the slow snow-breath,
oft have we heard that instant pace,
and looked intent upon the face
of our rude comrade, death
and our clear hearts have leaped to feel
muscle and will brace tense as steel
to wrestle one more fall.

Eight hours after leaving the hut, we found ourselves on the last rocks of the Combin de Valsorey, some thirteen thousand six hundred feet above the sea. A narrow snow and ice ridge would have led us in half an hour to the Grand Combin, but it would have been madness to attempt it in the teeth of the gale. We had climbed one of the Combin peaks, and by descending the south face we should complete a fine traverse. With that we were content.

In fair weather the south slope is an easy scramble down broken rocks, but the rocks had been submerged by windswept snow down which we had to break tracks. The fight with the storm had, at least, been exciting, but there was no thrill to relieve the soul-destroying monotony of the snowslopes from which all landmarks had disappeared. One peered down into the unchanging foreground, nothing but a few yards of wind-driven snow, hoping for a clue and finding none. With guides one can at least give one's brain a rest, but it is difficult to contend not only with physical but also with mental fatigue, yet to have surrendered to mental ıatigue would have been disastrous, for our only hope of escaping a night in the storm was to solve the last and trickiest problem of the day's climb.

The south slope leads down towards the icefall Glacier du Sonadon and I had little hope of avoiding a night out in the storm unless I could hit off a small shoulder, some ten feet in length, which enables one to escape from the south face on to the slopes down which one could glissade in safety to the Valsorey Hut. It would have been only too easy to have continued the descent of the south slope far below the shoulder which provided the only feasible exit from our perplexities. It seemed a reasonable assumption that this shoulder would correspond to an ill-defined belt of gentler gradient running more or less horizontally across the south slope. I therefore decided to turn sharply to the right directly the slope eased off. Driving snow obscured all but the immediate foreground, and I had to depend on the sense of touch rather than of sight ıor the solution of our problem. I felt my way down and, at last, the slope relaxed from some thirty degrees to ten. I turned sharply to the right and suddenly the grey white of a snow shoulder loomed up against the darker grey of the mist. I shall never forget that moment. I had been sustained by a reasoned faith in my plan, and in my ability to reach the haven of our hopes. But there is a world of difference between faith and sight. Heaven, I suspect, is full of newcomers delightedly prodding the cherubim in the ribs, and of Popes murmuring with happy surprise, " I always said I was intallible."

The pleasure of solving a problem depends on two things, the qualities which the problem tests and the penalties for failure.

A genial Bavarian professor whom I had met at Garmisch challenged me to solve a problem, in some ways more difficult than the problem of the Combin shoulder. "You must discover a formula," he said, "to enable us to determine a number, which is by definition less than 100, given that its remainders are a, b, and c, when divided respectively by 3, 5, and 7. I have given this problem to my mathematical colleagues and they all begin by thinking it is easy, and they all become very cross when they cannot find the formula."

More by luck than judgment I found the formula—the number in question equals the remainder when $70a + 21b + 15c$ is divided by 105. Had I failed I should have been faintly mortified and, because I succeeded, I was mildly tickled by the professor's ingenuous surprise. I was less proud to have solved the problem than to have found the miniature shoulder on the Combin face, less proud and of course infinitely less relieved, for my rapture when the shoulder loomed up through the mist was provoked not only by intellectual vanity but mainly by the most primitive of emotions, overwhelming relief after oppressive anxiety.

The shoulder was crested by a cornice and the slope underneath was very steep and windblown. I cut through the cornice and Hugh lowered me on to the slope below where I anchored the rope round the axe head. It was not too easy to descend without a rope from above, but Hugh did not slip. We repeated this process several times, the leader advancing only when the rope had been carefully belayed round the axe. And then the slope eased off once more and nothing remained but a succession of glissades through the greyness.

I have sentimental affection for Combin, the last Alpine peak which I climbed with two legs of approximately the same length. A few weeks later I crashed on Cader, and it was two years before I climbed again. My first big peak, the Dent Blanche, was a humiliating experience, for until then I had refused to concede that my accident had demoted me several grades in the Alpine hierarchy. There was only one way to restore my self-respect, to dispense with guides and companions and settle my trouble with the hills by the solitary ascent of a great peak. I chose the Combin for this experiment in re-integration, mainly because I had been haunted during my long illness by the memory of that uncompleted link, the ice and snow ridge from the Combin de Valsoret to the Grand Combin.

I was joined in the Valsorey Hut by a young Swiss, whose companions had returned home, and who had remained on for one more night on the offchance of attaching himself to another party. He was enchanted to discover a solitary climber, and I had not the heart to decline his suggestion that we should join forces, but I made one stipulation. I was to be allowed to lead the Valsorey ridge. The arrangement had one advantage. I never feel happy on snow-covered glaciers without a companion, and the accident of a chance companion made it possible to descend the great north face of the Combin, which was new to me and to reach the Val de Bagnes *via* the Chanrion Glacier.

The Combin made noble amends for its scurvy treatment. The sky was cloudless and the touch of warm dry rocks was all the more delightful because my finger tips still tingled reminiscently at the thought of that earlier climb. But though the objective difficulties of the climb were infinitely less, the subjective factor reduced the discrepancy and the physical readjustments imposed upon me by the result of my accident kept me very fully occupied. But I had insisted in leading the Valsorey ridge, and I did not ask to be released from a condition which I had myself imposed. I was on the best of terms with the reconciled hills by the time I had sunk exhausted on to the little plot of icy snow where the Combin ends and the sky begins. I could still climb. I could still lead.

> I have not lost the magic of long days :
> I live them, dream them still,
> Still am I master of the starry ways
> And freeman of the hill.
> Shattered my glass ere half the sands were run
> I hold the heights, I hold the heights I won. *

All the high company of heavenly peaks were there to welcome the exile returning to his mountain home. Finsteraarhorn and Monte Rosa and Mont Blanc. And there was a softness somewhere behind Paradiso which could only be Italy, and in the north a Germany which had not lost her soul. A blue mist resolved itself into the waters of Lake Leman and I remembered a corner on the railway near Lausanne, where the gleam of Combin snows suddenly shows beyond the embattled turrets of the Dent du Midi, and I

* G. W. Young

knew that when next I took the train from Vevey to Lausanne I should be waiting at the windows to salute, beyond the liquid distances of golden air, the beloved enemy which holds something of my past life in his possession, for the mountain which one has climbed is a bank in which one deposits the currency of memories which no inflation can diminish nor destroy.

It was one of those perfect days when the vast circumference of earth marches with a sky whose distances are unveiled even by the silver dust of unco-ordinated mist. The ground swell of the Jura melted into trembling margins of translucent and infinite blue. There is a timeless quality in such views which helps me to understand something which otherwise I could never hope to comprehend, the possibility of eternal happiness in a timeless and unchanging state. But the serene loveliness of this foretaste and preparation for the beatific vision would have meant far less to me had it not been for the foil of earlier memories, the passion and tumult of the angry dawn from the Meiten ridge, and the ordeal of the storm-tormented rocks. Even the frustration of that first attempt, which ended on the secondary summit was a perfect preparation for the joy of consummation. " To have attained a summit too readily," writes Geoffrey Young, " is to neglect most of its opportunities."

Twenty years after I climbed the Combin I motored up the St. Bernard and stopped for an hour at Bourg St. Pierre. I wandered up the bridle path which leads to the Valsorey glen and thence to the beloved mountain of many memories, of a defeat which was not inglorious and of a victory which was the symbol of Risorgimento from crippledom. And the mountain torrent sang the same song which it had sung in the days of long ago, a wordless *Te Deum* to the Lord and Giver of life, who fashioned the mountains for our discipline and for our delight, an arena of splendid adventure in our youth and a treasury of incorruptible memory " when the evening comes and our work is done."

CHAPTER VIII

" ANYWHERE, ANYWHEN "

Perfecta est sapientia creaturam creatori pie subdere ; discernere conditorem a condito, artificem a operibus. Quis commiscet artifici opera, nec artem intelligit, nec artificem.

Perfect wisdom piously subordinates the creature to the creator, distinguishing the builder from the building. Whoever confuses the Artist and his art understands neither the art nor the Artist.—ST. AUGUSTINE.

THE stout little man, lurching along the narrow pavement of a street in Lima, had been celebrating Peru's rupture of relations with the Axis, and he was looking for Germans to insult. His technique for identifying German citizens was to thrust two fingers, extended in the symbolic shape of a " V " into the face of passers by and to study their reactions. Mine failed to satisfy him, but when he finally realised that I was English he melted into a flood of tender remorse. " *Tu es mi amigo*. All English my friends." " *Muchas gracias*," I replied, " *A Dios*." But he would not let me go. " You are my friend. Anywhere, anywhen." His heart was in the right place, but his feet were not ; and by the time I had rescued him from a passing car, his affection was dynamic in its energy. Seizing me by the arm he propelled me through the front door of his own shop. I disengaged myself as the champion of the democracies collapsed on to the sofa. " You are my friend. Anywhere. Anywhen." I looked up and my eyes came to rest on an advertisement for the Leica, an enlargement of a Leica snapshot of the Wetterhorn from Grindelwald. And, for one vivid moment, I had a sense of bilocation as if part of me was in Grindelwald, and part in Peru. " My friend. Anywhere. Anywhen." Fifty years have passed since I first saw Grindelwald, and few indeed are the human friends whose company I should prefer to the Wetterhorn. And yet what, in the final analysis, is the Wetterhorn ? A lump of limestone plastered with snow and ice. Could anything be less rational than to claim friendship with a rock ? " These men are really atheists," said Clement of Alexandria, " who with a silly pretence of wisdom worship matter." But do mountain lovers worship mountains ? And, if not, what is the explanation of this sense of communion with a shadowy personality or, with the shadow of a Personality, which we experience among mountains ?

I think it was St. Thomas Aquinas who said that it was the province of theology to explain, not God but the world, and if this be so, theology might explain the Wetterhorn. There was certainly no shortage of theologians at Grindelwald during those early summers of my boyhood, but the theologians who met every summer to discuss Reunion at the Grindelwald conferences were too busy explaining themselves to have any leisure for explaining the Wetterhorn.

Unlike many of those who are surfeited with religion in their youth, I did not react violently against religion, I was not sufficiently interested to be attracted or repelled. My own interior life was unaffected by my father's ecclesiastical enthusiasms. For me the Fathers of the Church were the pioneers of the Alps, the Alpine Club was the body of the faithful, and the Alpine Journal my variant of Migne's Library of patristic literature. Leslie Stephen's *The Plavground of Europe* was my breviary, a selected portion of which I read every evening.

I preferred Stephen to Whymper or Mummery, because his *Playground of Europe* is no mere record of adventure. It was indeed the quasi-religious note in his finest essays which attracted me. This agnostic who had left the Church in which he had taken Orders to write *An Agnostic's Apology* had tried to find among the mountains a substitute for his lost faith. To Leslie Stephen the mountains spoke " in tones at once more tender and more awe-inspiring than that of any mortal teacher." He was the interpreter for whom I was searching.

I developed a cult of Leslie Stephen, and by the time I reached Oxford I had read all his literary criticism and most of his philosophical works. His portrait had a place of honour in my rooms at Balliol, and when his nephew, the late Mr. H. A. L. Fisher, read a paper in my rooms to a society of which I was the secretary, his uncle's portrait attracted his attention, and, long after the meeting had ended, we continued to talk " Stephen." On his return home he told Mrs. Fisher that he had met an undergraduate who knew more about Leslie Stephen's work than he did himself. Mr. Fisher was the editor of the Home University Library, and it was to this chance meeting and to my knowledge of his uncle's work that I owed the invitation to write the volume on " The Alps " for that series.

I not only read Leslie Stephen. He was my model and my inspiration when I tried my prentice hand at mountain writing.

Opposite: *MOUNTAIN LAKE. By kind permission of C. Schildknesht.*

Essays of which the headmaster thought highly were copied by their proud authors into a morocco-bound book, kept in the Vaughan Library. My father was proud of the fact that an essay of mine, on "Snow," was honoured in this fashion, and he insisted on showing the essay to a friend of his, Father X, a fine judge of literature. "Father X," said my father, "has no future in the Church of Rome. His Bishop doesn't trust him. He's not submissive enough. He is suspected of modernism."

A few days later Father X came down from London and had tea with us. After tea he took me into the garden. "Your father," he began, "has shown me your essay. You seem to have a great admiration for Leslie Stephen. Have you ever read his book, *An Agnostic's Apology*? You can get it for sixpence in the cheap reprints issued by the Rationalist Press Association."

I took his advice, invested sixpence in Leslie Stephen's apologia, and embodied some of his more mordant remarks about Jehovah in an essay which did not find its way into the morocco-bound volume of choice Harroviana.

My father, of course, was very angry with Father X, but Father X was unmoved by his reproaches. "Arnold's real religion is a kind of mountain idolatry, all that Leslie Stephen has done is to eliminate the faint Christian flavour which he has acquired from his environment. He can now start from scratch in his search for truth, unhampered by any Protestant prejudices. He will end a Catholic."

"I used to think," said my father, when he told me this story some years later, "that Father X's Bishop did not make proper use of his brilliant gifts. But maybe the Bishop was right. He was a bit too brilliant. And I've never met a Roman priest who wasn't profoundly shocked by his recommending you to read that book."

Leslie Stephen had convinced me not only that I could no longer believe, but also that I had never really believed. I discarded Christianity with no fuss and with no regrets, but a curious experience among the mountains helped me to understand, by analogy, the tragic sense of loss which many of the great Victorians experienced when they faced life without the sustaining power of the ancestral creed.

I was eighteen at the time, and I was returning with my brother from a climb in the Wildstrubel range. I had not slept well in the hut, and I had forgotten to protect my face against the sun, and the scorching snows of the Plaine Morte exacted the full price for my

Opposite: *THE LAKE OF THE FOUR FOREST CANTONS*
By kind permission of Franz Schneider.

carelessness. By the time we reached the rim of the glacier, I was tired, sleepy and slightly feverish as the result of severe sunburn.

We sat down and rested. From our lofty outpost we looked on to one of the noblest panoramas in all the Alpine chain. I looked at the shapely pyramid of the Weisshorn and there was no beauty in it. Far away in the West the silvery dome of Mont Blanc floated like a cloud above a canopy of sun-tinted mist. " It's ugly . . . it's all ugly," I muttered despondently.

I tried to reason my way back to the threshold of faith by analysing the form and colour of this noble mountain view. In vain. My doubts hardened into sullen negation. The beauty of the mountains was a myth, their loveliness an illusion. " But even if mountains are ugly," I persisted, " it would still be fun to climb them." " Fun ?" sneered the Spirit that denies, " why ? " " Why is it fun to climb ? Oh, because . . . because . . ." I tried to remember what Leslie Stephen had said, but his apologetics for the mountain faith seemed as unconvincing as Paley's apologia for Christianity. " But even if mountains are ugly, and even if there's no point in climbing them, life is still worth living ; it still has a meaning." " A meaning ? what meaning ? " asked the Spirit that denies. I could not answer. I was overwhelmed by the sense of dereliction. I felt as if the Universe had lost its soul.

I hated every step of the downward tramp to Montana. Once home, I went straight to bed and did not awake until the dawn. I got out of bed, and went to the window. The morning star still lingered in the thinning darkness, and then suddenly Mont Blanc saluted the sun. The mountains had never seemed so lovely. Nothing remained of the darkness of doubt, nothing but a shadow which only served to intensify by contrast the shining splendour of faith restored. Wonder had returned to the world, and life again had a meaning.

Leslie Stephen converted me to agnosticism. Haeckel, whose *Riddle of the Universe* was also issued as a cheap reprint by the R.P.A., all but converted me to materialism. Materialism, an old heresy, had a special appeal to Victorian Escapists from the complexity of life. The dynamic energy of the great centuries had spent itself, and an age which was mentally tired was in search of short cuts, such as the oversimplification. Marx attempted to simplify history by eliminating all factors save the economic, Darwin tried to simplify Evolution by ignoring all agents save Natural Selection.

Freud explained all philosophy, excepting, of course, Freudianism, as a mere by-product of sex. The Materialists denied the reality of spirit ; the Christian Scientists denied the reality of matter.

True simplicity has an æsthetic quality, and even false simplicity has a certain meretricious appeal, but it did not take me long to discover that Haeckel had failed to solve the problem which interested me beyond all others. He had not explained the Wetterhorn.

I remember, as if it were yesterday, the moment when I threw aside materialism for ever. I was nineteen at the time. My brother and I were returning from a great climb, and we were smoking a quiet pipe on a pass a few thousand feet above the valley, plunged in the rich gloom of an Alpine twilight.

The evening breeze served as a soft pedal to the music of a glacier stream which faded into piano when the wind rose. Sixty miles away the white bar of the Oberland responded to the farewell of the sun. The golden glow subdued the massive ranges, and dissolved the solidity of rock and earth into a succession of luminous planes melting into a background of ever deepening shadow. A white speck that was Chillon stood out against the deep purple of the lake. The whole vast shadowed landscape was haunted by something of which visible beauty is only the sacramental expression. I thought of Haeckel's dusty nonsense and laughed aloud, and from that moment I discarded materialism for ever. An experience such as this helps one to understand by analogy the sudden passage from doubt to faith which is the essence of evangelical conversion. These moments of spiritual intuition are valuable not only because they are completely convincing to the individual concerned, but also because they should encourage one to continue one's search for the objective and the impersonal arguments which are independent of personal intuition.

It is, of course, easy to refute Materialism without that appeal to personal experience which as I know (by personal experience) only serves to exasperate those who have never shared the experience in question.

Materialism is a disease of the great cities and does not flourish among men who are in close touch with Nature. I remember a night on an East Coast Convoy, when we were expecting an E-boat attack, I asked the Captain, as he peered out into the star-reflecting waters of a calm but sinister sea, whether he had ever met a sailor who was an atheist. " No," said the captain, " not one. Sailors have time to think." Mountaineers, like sailors, have time to think, and like sailors they are in close touch with that Nature which is "the art of God." And though some mountaineers incur the reproach of St. Augustine by failing to distinguish between the Art and the Artist, there are many more who are only restrained by shyness from admitting that they have felt among the mountains, and perhaps only among the mountains, a sense of communion with the Lord and Giver of life. Let me recall an experience which every true mountain lover could parallel. An April sunrise on the shores of an Alpine lake, set among hills which rose through a gradation of tone from the glory of vivid green near the water's edge through the parched browns of the higher slopes from which the snow had just retreated to the gleam of the summit ridges where winter still resisted the sun. In the west the last lingering stars surrendered. In the east the finite and the infinite met where the clear-cut lines of the summit ridges showed sharp against the unending distances of pure space. At noon the sky is a roof, at dawn an emptiness without end. There was promise rather than revelation of colour in sky and in lake, and the silence was only ruffled but not broken by the little wind which goes before the dawn. The solitary chirrup of an impertinent bird was suddenly suppressed as if by an unseen baton. Nature was waiting. Hill and lake and every feathered thing seemed poised in expectancy.

Then the wind began to make patterns on the lake, and the water darkened where the breeze touched it.

Suddenly the rocky crest of an eastern peak burnt up into a halo of flame. Rays from an unseen sun radiated into the eastern sky. The grass stirred to meet the dawn, the flowers opened a little wider and the mountains seemed to stand at the salute.

At such moments one knows beyond all need of proof that a veil has been drawn aside, and that the barrier between the things which are seen and the things which are unseen has been lowered for an instant:

> Such harmony is in immortal souls,
> But whilst this muddy vesture of decay
> Doth grossly close it in, we cannot hear it.

Among the hills we wear our muddy vesture with a difference and hear the distant notes of immortal harmony.

If the essence of mystical experience be the certitude that the world of sense is only a veil which masks the ultimate reality, the mountain lover is I suppose a mystic of sorts, even though he be confined with the catechumens to the atrium. For myself I would not claim ever to have had any religious experience, in the usual sense of the term, other than these moments of intuition among the hills. But such moments have given meaning to the passages in which the great mystics have struggled to communicate the incommunicable. It is a pity that many of those who have written of mountain mysticism have never studied the subject of mysticism in general, for it is only lack of knowledge which tempts people to imply a contrast between mystical and institutional religion. It is precisely within the framework of rigid and dogmatic systems that the greatest mystics have developed their genius.

Some people are content to feel; others cannot rest until they have accounted for their feelings. In the Victorian age scientists were emotional about science and unscientific about their emotions, and the interpreters of mountain mysticism were the victims of a bad tradition. And it was because mountaineers had failed to explain the Wetterhorn that I finally turned to the theologians and philosophers and sought in their works a key to the mystery of mountain beauty and to the influence of mountains on the mind of Man.

CHAPTER IX

Alpine Mysticism and "Cold Philosophy"

> Do not all charms fly
> At the mere touch of cold philosophy?—Keats.

SUDDEN changes in æsthetic fashion are often difficult to explain. Our ancestors, as we know, were all but unanimous in regarding the mountains with mild distaste or active disgust. There were outstanding exceptions, such as Petrarch and Gesner, but it is not in their works but in the writings of men like John de Bremble that we discover what mediæval man thought of the mountains. "Lord, restore me to my brethren," exclaimed de Bremble on the St. Bernard, "that I may tell them that they come not to this place of torment." Now, of course, it is easy to understand why de Bremble, who crossed the St. Bernard in 1188, should have felt less at ease than a modern tourist who is driven over this classic pass in a charabanc, but there is no necessary connection between detesting mountain travel and disliking mountain scenery. The Alpine passes, which were often infested by brigands, may well have seemed "places of torment" to the early travellers, but there is nothing alarming in a distant view of the Alps, and yet there is no mediæval tribute to the ethereal beauty of the Oberland as it appears from the Jura or Berne.

The Alpine dawn as seen from the roof of Milan Cathedral inspired the loveliest quatrain that Tennyson ever wrote:

> How faintly flushed, how phantom fair
> Was Monte Rosa hanging there,
> A thousand shadowy-pencill'd valleys
> And snowy dells in a golden air.

Generation after generation of the gifted and artistic race which inhabited the North Italian plain saw what Tennyson saw, not once but many times, and left no trace in prose or poetry to prove that they were not blind to the enchanting loveliness of Monte Rosa rising beyond the foothills of Lombardy.

The dome of Mont Blanc reversed in the blue of Lake Leman challenges comparison with Monte Rosa from Milan, but Voltaire and Rousseau, who lived for years in Geneva, never mention Mont Blanc. We need not be surprised that Voltaire, whose æsthetic standards were those of his century, never refers to Mont Blanc and its Gothic aiguilles. Rousseau's failure to praise this glorious view is more surprising, and casts some doubt on his sincerity as the high-priest of Nature worship; but in spite of this lapse, Rousseau must be regarded as the forerunner of the Romantic revival, whereas Voltaire, in his attitude to the mountains, was as characteristic of his period as John de Bremble was of his century.

The standards of taste which determine our attitude to scenery fluctuate with æsthetic fashion. The eighteenth-century humanist who enjoyed the artificial extravagances of Baroque gardens regarded natural beauty as uncouth. The fashion for mountain scenery makes its appearance with the Gothic revival. The æsthetic fashion which provides a criterion for the appreciation of scenery is itself very largely determined by the dominant philosophy of the age, for every culture is the expression of a creed. From the humanism of Greece is derived the bodily perfection of the Hermes of Praxiteles, the earthbound Doric temple, massively set upon the landscape, and an attitude to Nature which finds Nature attractive in proportion as Nature is disciplined by man. To the neo-humanist of the eighteenth century, "Gothic" was a term of abuse, mountains were uncouth, and religion faintly ridiculous. The æsthetics of the century were moulded by the prevailing philosophy of an age in which institutional religion was fighting a rear-guard action. It was "an agreed point," wrote Bishop Butler of his contemporaries, "that Christianity should be set up as the principal subject of mirth and ridicule." Man cannot rest content with negations, for he requires some integrating principles to give significance to life. The inevitable reaction against the arid deism of the eighteenth century was the pantheistic nature-worship of Rousseau, Wordsworth and Shelley. The Gothic revival, the discovery of mountain beauty and the Oxford Movement were different aspects of the same Romantic movement.

It was no accident that the Gothic revival coincided with the new-found enthusiasm for mountain scenery. The trite comparison between a Gothic spire and an Alpine aiguille is not so shallow as it seems, for both spire and peak suggest that upward soaring movement of the spirit from which the Greek humanist shrank. The entablature of the Greek temple binds the column firmly to earth. The Gothic spire and the Chamonix aiguille rise from the earth into the blue infinity of heaven. If the Gothic revival coincided with the discovery that mountains were beautiful, why did not the men who built the great Gothic cathedrals love mountains? Perhaps because the old cathedrals expressed in stone a supernatural faith so secure against doubt that it did not require to be buttressed by the revelations of God in nature. Petrarch, the first of the Romantic mountaineers, tells us that he opened the Confessions of St. Augustine on the summit of Mont Ventoux. "The first place that I lighted upon, it was thus written: 'There are men who go to admire the high places of mountains, and who neglect themselves.' . . . I shut the book, half-angry with myself that I, who was even now admiring terrestrial things, ought to have learned from the philosophers that nothing is truly great except the soul."

The greatest exponent, in its later phases, of the Romantic revival was John Ruskin. He had more influence than any of his predecessors (or of his successors) in converting contemporary England to a love of mountains and to a love of Gothic architecture. Few people realise how much the new attitude to mountain scenery owed to Ruskin, and how completely he revolutionised architectural taste. Gibbon visited Venice on April 27th, 1765. "Old and, in general, ill-built houses," he wrote, "ruined pictures, and stinking ditches, dignified with the pompous denomination of canals, a fine bridge spoilt by two rows of houses upon it, and a large square decorated with the worst architecture I ever saw." This view prevailed until Ruskin wrote his *Stones of Venice*. "The architecture of St. Mark's at Venice," wrote the *Daily News* reviewer of Ruskin's book, "has, from of old, been the butt for students . . . but Mr. Ruskin comes and assures us, etc."

Few men have loved mountains more passionately than Ruskin, and few have attacked mountaineers more bitterly.

"The Alps themselves, which your own poets used to love so reverently, you look upon as soaped poles in a bear-garden, which you set yourselves to climb, and slide down again, with 'shrieks of delight.' When you are past shrieking, having no human articulate voice to say you are glad with, you fill the quietude of their valleys with gunpowder blasts, and rush home, red with cutaneous eruption of conceit, and voluble with convulsive hiccough of self-satisfaction."

The love of mountains, of which Ruskin was the greatest prophet, developed as an important phase of a general revolt against the narrow humanism of the eighteenth century. The beginnings of systematic mountaineering, which Ruskin hated, date from the decade in which Darwin published *The Origin of Species*. The devastating effect of the materialistic philosophy, which had deduced from Darwin's hypothesis conclusions which Darwin had explicitly disowned, was described in a notable passage by a great scientist, Romanes.

" I am not afraid to confess," he wrote, " that with this virtual negation of God, the universe to me has lost its soul of loveliness, and though from henceforth the precept to work while it is day will doubtless but gain an intensified force from the terribly intensified meaning of the words ' that the night cometh when no man can work,' yet when I think, as think at times I must, of the contrast between the hallowed glory of that creed which once was mine, and the lonely mystery of life as I now find it, at such times I find it impossible to avoid the sharpest pang of which my nature is capable."

Many of the early mountaineers were orthodox Christians, but there were many more who in a greater or lesser degree recovered among the mountains that " soul of loveliness " which the universe appeared to have lost, and of these the greatest was the mountaineer who had left the Church of his baptism, in which he had taken Orders, to write *An Agnostic's Apology*.

" If I were to invent," wrote Leslie Stephen, " a new idolatory (rather a needless task) I should prostrate myself, not before beast, or ocean, or sun, but before one of those gigantic masses to which, in spite of all reason, it is impossible not to attribute some shadowy personality. Their voice is mystic and has found discordant interpreters ; but to me at least it speaks in tones at once more tender and more awe-inspiring than that of any mortal teacher. The loftiest and sweetest strains of Milton or Wordsworth may be more articulate, but do not lay so forcible a grasp upon my imagination."

This confession will surprise readers who only knew Leslie Stephen as the high-priest of a somewhat arid and unimaginative agnosticism, and Leslie Stephen himself would certainly have disclaimed any attempt to base conclusions, however tentative, on his own emotional reactions to mountain scenery. Leslie Stephen was a mystic *malgré lui*. A man's half-beliefs are often not only more interesting but more illuminating than the beliefs which he is prepared to defend at the bar of reason. *Der Aberglaube*, as Goethe somewhere says, *ist die Poesie des Lebens*. Leslie Stephen's Victorian agnosticism is already a little dated, but his essay on Wordsworth and his *Playground of Europe* have outlasted the mental fashion of the Victorian Age.

The interpretation of Alpine mysticism has been the work of poets, using the word in its widest sense. It would be easy to compile an anthology of essays and long passages which deal either explicitly or by implication with such themes as "the religion of the mountain" or the "philosophy of a mountaineer," and so forth, but I have not yet discovered a serious attempt to formulate a scientific explanation of our reactions to mountain beauty, or to discover a philosophic basis for mountain mysticism. The diagnosis of mountain emotion is often inhibited by the distaste for the emotional, for we forget that emotion can be discussed unemotionally. The limestone of which the Wetterhorn is composed and the emotion which that limestone inspires have at least this in common. Both the limestone and the emotion are facts of which philosophers and scientists may be invited to offer an unemotional explanation.

So far, however, the philosophers and the scientists have not come to the assistance of the mountaineer, and the Alpine poet has had the field to himself. I have no desire to belittle their achievements in this field, for the intuitions of the poet provide the philosopher with valuable data. There is no reason why those who try to explain the things which the poets feel, but which poets make no attempt to explain, should not collaborate with the poets in a common enterprise. "*J'ai remarqué*," writes Anatole France, "*que les philosophes vivaient généralament en bonne intelligence avec les poètes. . . . Les philosophes savent que les poètes ne pensent pas ; cela les désarme, les attendrit et les enchante.*"

I shall use the word "mystic" and "mysticism" in their popular rather than in their technical sense. The Greeks, to whom we owe the word "mystic," described as *mystæ* the initiates of the mysteries who believed that they had received a direct vision of God. To the *mystæ* God was not an object of academic belief, but a Being experimentally known by direct intuition. The great mystics were fully conscious of the immense difficulty of communicating what is incommunicable—one remembers St. Augustine's: "Si nemo me quaerat scio . . ." "If nobody asks me I know. If I desire to explain, I do not know"—but, none the less, they never ceased in the attempts to illuminate the obscure, and to discover the apt word, phrase, analogy or metaphor which at least suggests that which can never be accurately described.

In Alpine literature, on the other hand, the word "mystic" is often used as if it were the equivalent of "misty," and as if obscurity rather than illumination were the essence of mystical experiences. The vagueness of Alpine mysticism is partly due to those paroxysms of shyness which overwhelm the average Englishman in any discussion of religion. The Greek *mystæ* claimed without embarrassment that he enjoyed a direct vision of God, but this useful monosyllable is unfashionable to-day—excepting as an expletive—with the curious result that Alpine mysticism might be described as an attempt to construct the corpus of Alpine theology without mentioning Theos. Are mountains cathedrals among which we worship or idols which we worship? That is the basic question, and until a man has the honesty to ask and answer this question, he had better confine himself to recording the physical aspects of a climb.

It is foolish for those who believe that strong emotion is a substitute for exact thought to cross the frontier which separates physics from metaphysics. Characteristic of Alpine religiosity is the following passage: ". . . the solemn dome resting on those marvellous buttresses, fine and firm above all its chasms of ice, its towers and crags; a place where desires point and aspirations end; very, very high and lovely, long-suffering and wise. . . . *Experience*, slowly and wonderfully filtered: at the last a purged remainder; such is the law. . . . We've only been obeying an old law then? Ah! but it's *the law* . . . and we understand—a little more. So ancient, wise and terrible—and yet kind we see them; with steps for children's feet."

This is Alpine mysticism at its worst. Is Mont Blanc a god or the creation of God? The author of this passage has evaded this basic question, perhaps because he was too shy to introduce the monosyllable "God" into a paper destined to be read before a meeting of the Alpine Club. His description of Mont Blanc as "long-suffering and wise" is, one suspects, half poetic licence and half a confused pantheistic idolatory of matter. "Mountains," as Mr. Michael Roberts rightly says, "may be symbols or images of some other reality, but the worship of symbols as if they were something more than images is a form of superstition."

"La religiosità è vaga," says Croce, "la religione è precisa."

The vagueness of Alpine religiosity may be contrasted with the precision of Alpine religion, the religion which Mr. Belloc saw " as it were " from the height of the Weissenstein :

" Here were these magnificent creatures of God, I mean the Alps, which now for the first time I saw from the height of Jura ; and because they were fifty or sixty miles away, and because they were a mile or two high, they were become something different from us others, and could strike one motionless with the awe of supernatural things. Up there in the sky, to which only clouds belong and birds and the last trembling colours of pure light, they stood fast and hard ; not moving as do the things of the sky. They were as distant as the little upper clouds of summer, as fine and tenuous ; but in their reflection and in their quality as it were of weapons (like spears and shields of an unknown array) they occupied the sky with a sublime invasion : and the things proper to the sky were forgotten by me in their presence as I gazed.

" To what emotion shall I compare this astonishment ? So, in first love one finds that *this* can belong to *me*.

" Their sharp steadfastness and their clean uplifted lines compelled my adoration. Up there, the sky above and below them, part of the sky, but part of us, the great peaks made communion between that homing creeping part of me which loves vineyards and dances and a slow movement among pastures, and that other part which is only properly at home in Heaven.

" These, the great Alps, seen thus, link one in some way to one's immortality. Nor is it possible to convey, or even to suggest, those few fifty miles and those few thousand feet ; there is something more. Let me put it thus : that from the height of Weissenstein I saw, as it were, my religion. I mean, humility, the fear of death, the terror of height and of distance, the glory of God, the infinite potentiality of reception whence springs that divine thirst of the soul ; my aspiration also towards completion, and my confidence in the dual destiny. For I know that we laughers have a gross cousinship with the Most High, and it is this contrast and perpetual quarrel which feels a spring of merriment in the soul of a sane man.

" Since I could now see such a wonder and it could work such things in my mind, therefore, some day I should be part of it. That is what I felt.

"That it is also which leads some men to climb mountain-tops, but not me, for I am afraid of slipping down."*

Every poet, Hilaire Belloc among others, accepts, consciously or unconsciously, the Platonic distinction between αὐτο τὸ καλὸν (beauty itself) and τὰ πολλὰ καλά (many beautiful things); that is, between beauty as a universal and beauty in its particular manifestations. The loveliness which Hilaire Belloc saw from the Weissenstein is a reflection in time and space of that timeless loveliness which is uneroded by change. "Natural beauty," as St. Thomas Aquinas says, "is but the similitude of divine beauty shared among things." On these great issues there is a generous measure of agreement among poets. "These, the great Alps, seen thus, link one in some way to one's immortality" can be compared with Baudelaire's "It is the immortal instinct for beauty which is the liveliest proof of immortality."

Leslie Stephen would have rejected, perhaps with regret, Hilaire Belloc's interpretation of mountain beauty. "The mountains," writes Leslie Stephen, "represent the indomitable forces of nature to which we are forced to adapt ourselves. They speak to man of his littleness and his ephemeral existence." This is true, but that is only part of their message. "*La nature a des perfections*," says Pascal, "*pour montrer qu'elle est l'image de Dieu ; et des défauts pour montrer qu'elle n'en est que l'image.*" Mountains only "speak to man of his littleness" if he is so foolish as to accept a yard measure as the criterion of his status. Shakespeare's mind is neither greater nor smaller than the Wetterhorn, for mind and matter are incommensurable. "All our dignity," says Pascal, "is born of thought." What, then, is the origin of the thoughts which mountains inspire in the minds of mountain lovers? Can science and philosophy add anything to the intuition of the poet?

Scientists assure us that there was a period when life was non-existent on the surface of the planet, from which it follows that life was potentially present in the molten crust and gases of the primeval planet, or alternatively some cause external to the planet must be invoked to explain the origin of life and the origin of a sense of beauty. Darwin's attempt to meet this difficulty was characteristically evasive. He assumed the existence of the sense of beauty, and, instead of explaining its origin, discussed its influence on evolution. According to Darwin's theory of sexual selection, beauty has a

* From *The Path to Rome*.

survival value. The female is attracted by a beautiful mate, with the happy result that beauty is passed on to the next generation, whereas the uglier examples of the species fade away and pass their days in forlorn bachelorhood. No doubt; but our problem still remains unanswered. I am prepared to believe that the peahen's reaction to a peacock's gay colouring influences the evolution of peacocks, but what we want to know is why the peahen thinks the peacock beautiful, and whence is derived the æsthetic sense which manifests itself throughout the animal kingdom. This is a question to which the materialist has no reply. "When the materialist," writes J. B. Mosley, "has exhausted himself in efforts to explain utility in nature, it would appear to be the peculiar office of beauty to rise up as a confounding and baffling *extra*."

The impotence of the scientist to reconcile a sense of beauty with a purely mechanistic interpretation of evolution provides a negative argument in support of the Platonic doctrine of beauty. The philosopher reinforces these conclusions with the positive argument that nothing can be present in an effect which was not present in the cause. It is fantastic to suppose that our reaction to mountain beauty could be potentially present in the lifeless rock, sea and mud of the primeval planet. You cannot get plus out of minus:

*Nihil quod animi quodque rationis est expers, id generare ex se potest animantem conpotemque rationis.**

It is not necessary to climb in order to accept the Platonic interpretation of mountain beauty, but the mountaineer has a great advantage over the non-mountaineer. He has chosen the ascetic way to mountain understanding, and among the hills, as elsewhere, asceticism is the key to the higher forms of mystical experience. One need not question the sincerity of Ruskin's condemnation of those who had transformed the mountain cathedrals into arenas for athletic feats, but I have sometimes suspected that the peculiar venom of his attack may have been due to the fact that the mountaineer provoked an uneasy and unformulated doubt as to the quality of his own life, which was essentially non-ascetic and soft. He had been privately educated and thus deprived of the ascetic experiences which the Victorian public schools so generously provided. He played no games, took part in no sports. He inherited a comfortable income from his father, which insured him against the necessity of

* "Nothing which is devoid of life and reason can give birth to a living and rational being." Cicero quoting Zeno, De natura Deorum *ii* 8.

uncongenial work. His life from birth to death was a stranger to the discipline of pain, danger or discomfort.

Asceticism is often confused with puritanism. The Puritan condemns pleasure as wicked, and the ascetic abstains from certain pleasures, which he admits to be innocent, as the price to be paid for the higher forms of happiness. An ascetic may confine his drinks to water, but he does not deserve to be branded as a Puritan so long as he makes no attempt to prevent other people from drinking wine. An ascetic might be defined as one who sacrifices pleasure to happiness, for pleasure and happiness are not identical. A candidate for the Oxford " Greats " Schools was once invited to comment on Aristotle's dictum, " A good man can be perfectly happy on the rack." He answered : " Possibly, if it were a very bad rack, or if he were a very good man." Good men have been happy even on good racks, for, as that puzzled pagan Seneca observed, men have been known to laugh, and " that right heartily," under torture.

The greatest thinkers, Roman, Greek, Muslim and Jew, agree that pain and happiness are not necessarily opposed. Whymper aptly quoted on the frontispiece of *Scrambles in the Alps* a sentence from Livy : " Though pain and pleasure are in their natures opposite, they are yet linked together in a kind of necessary connection."

" How singular is a thing called happiness," exclaimed Socrates, " and how curiously related to pain, which might be thought to be the opposite of it ; for they are never present to a man at the same instant, and yet he who pursues either is generally compelled to take the other : their bodies are two and they are joined by a necessary single head. . . ."

The famous saying of Mohammed, " Hell is veiled with delights, and heaven in hardships and misery," finds an echo in all great philosophies, Christian and non-Christian.

Indeed, the very word " ascetic " comes to us from the pagan world, and once meant no more than " exercise." To the Greek the athlete was the typical ascetic, for he exercised his body by sacrificing the pleasures of self-indulgence to the happiness of self-discipline. He was, as St. Paul said, temperate in all things to win a corruptible crown. No illustration, as St. Paul knew, was more calculated to impress his hearers with the reasonableness of Christian asceticism ; for where institutional religion declines, as in the pagan world, the ascetic instinct finds expression in strenuous sport.

If it were not for this peculiar form of happiness, which is the reward of the ascetic, there would be no boat-racing and no rock-climbing and no ski-racing. No ski racer can reach the international class unless he is prepared to risk fall after fall when practising or racing, at a speed which often attains to sixty miles an hour. There is no pleasure in such ski-ing, but there is a queer kind of happiness.

" The racer's mind must overcome the physical reactions, which shrink from the fastest line on steep slopes, and must keep the body under the control necessary for performing turns with complete precision.

" When the racer is ski-ing well there come moments when he knows that his mind has won, and for a few brief seconds he has complete control over his body. Such moments are rare, but it is for them that men endure the physical discomforts attendant upon all ascetic sports, for they then experience a happiness, almost an ecstasy, which has nothing in common with pleasure or enjoyment as these terms are normally understood.

" It is this spiritual, perhaps almost mystical, thrill, this fleeting glimpse of the paradise of Eden, which causes men to encounter gladly the dangers and hardships of mountaineering, to endure the acute physical agony of rowing and long-distance running, and to overcome the physical difficulties attendant on all sports."*

The happiness of the rock-climber is derived from the same source as the happiness of the racer—from the dominion, that is, of the mind over the body.

" The great peaks," says Mr. Belloc in the passage I have quoted, " made communion between that homing creeping part of me which loves vineyards and dances and slow movement among pastures, and that other part which is only properly at home in Heaven." Had Mr. Belloc been a climber, he would have discovered that the dominant theme of mountaineering is not the communion but the contrast and perpetual quarrel between " the homing creeping part " and the part which is " at home in Heaven."

It is the part which is at home in heaven that forces the creeping part which loves vineyards up the steep and rocky mountain side, and with every foot of ascent the protest of the creeping part becomes more pronounced. For though the result is the same whether one

* From *High Speed Ski-ing*, by Peter Lunn.

falls two hundred feet or two thousand, the downward drag of the earth below varies with the aerial distances which separate the body from its natural habitat, the gross and comfortable security of the horizontal. There is no sport which illustrates more perfectly the ascetic principle that happiness must be paid for by pain, and that the degree of happiness is in proportion to the price paid. Few sports offer their devotees a wider range of disagreeable moments. The agony of the half-slip when one is leading on an exposed climb, the desperate struggle to regain balance, a struggle which is a matter of infinitely small readjustments on a battle-ground measured in inches, are the price which the cragsman pays, not only for the exquisite relief of safety after peril, but also for the quasi-mystical happiness of those moments when his mind has established complete dominion over his body, moments when the effortless rhythm of the upward movement transforms the accident of crack and ledge into an ordered sequence of harmonious movement.

Many mountaineers who have lost all contact with institutional religion have discovered among the hills the satisfaction of certain aspirations which others have fulfilled within the framework of the religious life. They have caught the reflection of eternal beauty in the temporal loveliness of the hills. They have been initiated into the secret of the ascetic, and have found the happiness which is the by-product of pain and danger. But when we have said this we have said all that can usefully be said on the relation of mountaineering to religion. Points of contact do not suffice to establish their identity. Boxing involves asceticism, but no one has yet claimed that there is a religion of the Ring. It is a pity to make exaggerated claims for our sport.

There is something to be said for the view that the better type of young men gravitate naturally towards the ascetic sports, such as mountaineering, which involves the discipline of danger; but though the individual mountaineer is entitled to claim that he is a better man than he would have been if he had never climbed, he should not imply that he is a better man than those who do not climb, or even than those who detest all forms of active and dangerous sport. Samuel Johnson was no ascetic. He disliked mountains and detested solitude, and was seldom happy outside the congenial atmosphere of London, but he was a better man than most mountaineers. "If there is one thing worse," wrote Mr. Chesterton, "than the modern weakening of major morals, it is the modern strengthening of minor morals. Cleanliness is not next to godliness nowadays, but cleanliness is a convention and godliness is regarded as an offence. . . . A man can get used to getting up at five o'clock in the morning "—as mountaineers do—" a man cannot very well get used to being burnt for his opinions ; the first experiment is commonly fatal."

Is the man who detests crowds necessarily more spiritual than Samuel Johnson, who detested solitude? Epictetus, the greatest of the Stoics, addresses the same admonition to those who hate solitude as Johnson hated it, and to those who hate mobs : " If you are fated to spend your life alone, call it peace. . . . If you fall in with a crowd, try to make holiday with the crowd." If we could acquire this Stoic detachment we should all be serenely unaffected by our environment, whether this environment were a bank-holiday crowd or the severe loneliness of the Arctic regions. The Chinese proverb reminds us that " noise is not in the market-place, nor quiet in the hills, but in the ever-changing hearts of men."

The man who despises the routine of office life, and who escapes into unexplored mountain ranges to find his soul, may be less successful than some mystic of the suburbs who catches the 9.5 train to his office and the 6.30 train back to his home. Mountain worship began when institutional religion declined. It is the " estranged faces " that need the dramatic stimuli of mountain beauty. The true mystic hurrying from his office to the tube can see

> The traffic of Jacob's ladder
> Pitched between Heaven and Charing Cross.

It is not a sign of a spiritual but of a materialistic nature to over-emphasise the importance of material environment. I remember a discussion on this point with a great modern sculptor, Eric Gill. I was charmed by his picturesque hand-made smock. " It has many conveniences," he remarked. " My nice friends feel ashamed of me, and therefore don't ask me to lunch in their clubs." The talk then turned on the ugliness of our machine-made civilisation, and the supreme importance of surrounding oneself with hand-made furniture. I conceded that it would be easier to live a good life if one dined off a table carved by one of Eric Gill's disciples, but this seems to me evidence of the frailty of human nature. The true mystic could enjoy the beatific vision while sweeping out a latrine.

I am not working up to the paradoxical conclusion that a man's spirituality varies inversely with his appreciation of beautiful surroundings. There is, indeed, the highest of precedents for the choice of mountains for a spiritual retreat, but these withdrawals serve as a preparation for the life among men. " He had compassion on the multitude."

It is foolish to invite the ridicule of the discerning by making claims for mountaineering which cannot be substantiated. Mountaineering is neither a substitute for religion nor a civic duty. It is a sport ; for we climb, not to benefit the human race, but to amuse ourselves. In so far as mountaineering is something more than a sport we must base this claim on the fact that it is carried out in surroundings which suggest spiritual truths even to the unspiritual. Ruskin compared mountains to cathedrals, and the comparison is sound ; for one does not worship cathedrals, though one may worship in the cathedrals of man or among the cathedrals of nature.

All evil, as a great mediæval thinker remarked, is the result of mistaking means for ends. Mountaineering is not an end in itself, but a means to an end. " For it is true," as the first mountaineer to ascend the throne of St. Peter (Pius XI) remarked :

" For it is true that, of all innocent pleasures, none more than this one (excepting where unnecessary risks are taken) may be considered as being helpful mentally and physically, because, through the efforts required for climbing in the rarefied mountain air, energy is renewed ; and owing to the difficulties overcome the climber thereby becomes better equipped and strengthened to resist the difficulties encountered in life, and by admiring the beauties and grandeur of the scenery as seen from the mighty peaks of the Alps his spirit is uplifted to the Creator of all."

CHAPTER X

THE GOLDEN AGE OF BRITISH SKI-ING

I

THE mountain lover who has been tempted to read this book because of its title may perhaps throw it away in disgust when he discovers that it contains reminiscences of ski-racing, but this, I unhumbly suggest, would be a mistake. For there are lessons which can be learnt in one sport and applied in another, and both mountaineering and ski-ing were infected by the same malady in the latter years before the outbreak of this war.

Details of interest only to ski-racers will be found in my forthcoming *History of Downhill Racing*. In the chapters devoted to ski-racing in this book I shall confine myself to those aspects of the Golden Age which, I hope, may prove of some interest even to readers who have never skied, much less raced on ski.

The English have invented more than a fair share of the world's best games, and have usually ended by being soundly defeated by their pupils. The story of downhill racing is no exception to this rule. But at least we who sponsored the Downhill and invented the Slalom had the fun of racing when racing was young. There is a spontaneous and light-hearted quality in the spring-time of a sport which vanishes as the sport matures.

Let me illustrate the contrast between the sport in its natural youth and artificial maturity by describing two races: the first race for the Roberts of Kandahar Challenge Cup at Montana, 1911, and the World Championship in Downhill Ski-Racing at Engelberg, 1938.

Competitors for the Kandahar Race left Montana early in the morning of January 6th, 1911, and climbed slowly for some eight hours to the Plaine Morte Glacier. They spent the night in the Wildstrubel Hut and left next morning at 10 a.m. They raced for two miles across the glacier, and down from the Col de Thierry to Montana 5,000 feet below. The names of the competitors in the first Kandahar race deserve to be recorded. They are as follows :—Cecil Hopkinson (the winner), H. Collins (who finished second), E. Russell Clarke, President of the Alpine Ski Club (third), and M. C. Baggallay (fourth). The order of the remainder is not recorded, but their names are as follows :—Captain Buzzard, Captain Collis Brown, M. Collis Brown, and Brian Lunn (who cracked a collar-bone near the start, but none the less finished—and did not finish last).

Let us contrast this race with the World Championship at Engelberg, 1938.

At Montana all the competitors started together, the so-called *geschmozzel* start. At Engelberg the competitors started at minute intervals. The *geschmozzel* start had been abandoned for two reasons. First, because the high speed of modern racing and the substitution of steel for wooden edges gravely aggravated the risk of serious injuries resulting from accidental collisions. Secondly, because the increasing importance of downhill racing necessitated reducing the elements of luck to a minimum. It would be just too bad if a chance collision between two Nazi aces allowed the representative of a democratic country to demonstrate on the snows the value of his decadent political system. Still further to reduce the element of chance I invented the modern group draw under which all competitors of the same group start before competitors of a lower group.

The attempt to eliminate the role of luck was responsible not only for the substitution of an artificial for a natural start, but also for the substitution of artificial for natural snow. If the race is run on soft untracked snow No. 1 has a great advantage over No. 30 or No. 40.

At Engelberg competitors practised over the course for days, and in some cases for weeks. What little soft snow remained was diligently stamped hard by groups of workmen.

At Chamonix in 1937 the disaster of a snow-fall on the eve of the race was to some extent offset by mobilising a labour battalion who stamped hard, but not hard enough to escape the censure of a critical Nazi who wrote as follows :—" Wehmütig flog ein Gedanke hinüber nach Garmisch zu Hanni Neuner, dem ersten Spezialisten der Welt für parkettebene und glasglatte Abfarhtstrecken."*

No sentence could convey more clearly the extreme artificiality of modern racing.

Of the competitors for the first Kandahar few had been over the course before, and none had been over it more than twice. They climbed for eight hours to the point from which the race started,

* Regretfully one thought of Garmisch and Hans Neuner, the first specialist in the world for parquet-level and glass-smooth racing courses.

whereas at Engelberg the competitors travelled in a few minutes from the valley to the start in a cable railway.

At Engelberg the competitors knew every bump and turn on the course ; whereas the first Kandahar was a magnificent test of that essential quality of cross-country ski-ing, the power to travel at high speed over *unknown* ground, and over ever-changing snow surfaces.

At Engelberg the snow was artificially hard beaten crust. At Montana the competitors raced over deep, powder snow, wind slab and snow crusted by the sun.

Finally, there is the question of speed. Cecil Hopkinson's time was 61 minutes. If we allow 30 minutes for the "langlauf" over the glacier, this leaves about 30 minutes for 5,000 feet of vertical descent, say 6 minutes per thousand feet.

In the 1942 World Championship at Grindelwald, Heinz von Allmen raced down the extended Tschuggen course from the Männlichen summer path to Grund, a vertical drop of just under 4,000 feet (1,100 m.), in the fantastic time of 4 minutes 24.6 seconds, which works out at rather over a minute per 1,000 feet of descent.

Cecil Hopkinson, who was killed in the first world war, was a fine runner of the Alpine School, and the member of a famous mountaineering family. He met his match in 1912, when John Mercer, the first British racer of the modern school, defeated him at Mürren. Mercer won the cup outright by three successive victories. In those days he was as fast downhill as the best Swiss.

To-day when Downhill races are won by tenths of a second it is amazing to read a contemporary account of Mercer's third Kandahar. "Eventually Mercer got home with less than a minute to spare."

The British were not, of course, the first to discover that it is amusing to start at the top of a hill and race down to the bottom. But organised downhill racing is a British development, and the slalom a British invention. Ski-ing comes to us from the north where the terrain is gentle and where the traditional races are long distanced, beginning and ending at the same spot.

The first appearance in print of a plea for the Downhill race as the only reasonable criterion for downhill ski-ing was published in my book, *Ski-ing*, which appeared in 1913 ; and the first rules for Downhill and Slalom racing are those which I drew up in 1923, and which include the veto on stick-riding which I only carried against great opposition.

In the first post-war season we decided to award the British Ski Championship not, as in Norway, on a long distance race and a jumping competition, but on a Downhill race and a Style competition. The Style competition proved unsatisfactory.

A few days after Leonard Dobbs, a magnificent runner, had won the first Downhill Ski Championship in the history of ski-ing, E. C. Pery, now the Earl of Limerick, lost the Roberts of Kandahar race by an eccentric display of chivalrous scrupulosity. He had established a comfortable lead, but lost a ski some three yards short of the winning post. In those days there were virtually no laws, written or unwritten for Downhill racing, and Pery could have won easily had he struggled through the posts on one ski. Being, however, in some doubt as to whether it was justifiable to finish on one ski he wasted precious time collecting the errant ski, with the result that the race was won by Chilton, Pery finishing fourth.

His attitude should be compared with Inge Lantschner's at the World Championships described in a subsequent chapter.

Pery was primarily a ski-mountaineer, and many of my happiest days among mountaineers have been spent on the Oberland with him and Hugh Dowding. In those days I still regarded ski-racing not as an autonomous sport, but as a school for, and criterion of, cross-country ski-ing. But I was beginning to see that the Downhill race alone was not a wholly satisfactory test of Alpine ski-ing. I therefore founded the Alpine Ski Challenge Cup which was awarded in a competition decided on novel lines. Competitors were taken a full day's tour over difficult ground and on various types of snow and tested thoroughly in wood-running. Their performances were marked by two judges. Pery was outstandingly the best competitor, and won the Cup.

This type of competition proved extremely difficult to judge, and I was impressed by a chance remark of Joannides, who suggested that I should substitute a slalom. I did not like the existing Norwegian Slalom, which was a style competition. Competitors were required to turn at particular points, and were marked for style.

The modern Slalom, which I invented, has nothing but the name in common with the Norwegian Slalom. It consists in a race down a course defined by flag-pairs. Competitors have to turn through each pair of flags, and the flags are arranged to test every conceivable type of turn ; long, fast, and fluent, or short and abrupt, as the case may be.

It is odd to reflect that the Alpine Ski Challenge Cup, the oldest Slalom Cup in the world, should have evolved out of something as natural and as unsystematised as an untimed cross-country run.

II

January, 1924, was a memorable month in the history of ski-ing. The first Winter Olympic Games were held at Chamonix in January, 1924, and it was at Chamonix in that same month that the *Fédération Internationale de Ski* was founded.

The Olympic Games were confined, so far as ski-ing was concerned, to the "classic events," langlauf and jumping. The founders of the International Federation for the control of ski-ing knew nothing of certain momentous events in another part of the Alps, events destined to exercise far more influence on the course of ski-ing than the Winter Olympics.

It was in January, 1924, that the British carried through to a successful conclusion at Grindelwald the first international event decided on the combined result of a downhill race and a slalom. A few days later F. W. Edlin founded at Davos the Parsenn Derby. Finally it was on January 30th, 1924, that the Kandahar Ski Club was founded at Mürren, under the presidency of Major L. L. B. Angas, to promote downhill racing, and to raise the standard of British racing.

The Kandahar Ski Club takes its name from the Roberts of Kandahar Challenge Cup, the World's Senior Challenge Cup for downhill racing. I was once asked in St. Anton whether I was the famous general who had won the great battle of Kandahar. I replied that I was, for the battle of Kandahar was the battle for the recognition of downhill ski-racing.

My friend, Toby O'Brien, felicitously described the Kandahar as the "Jockey Club" of ski-ing. It is certainly the best known ski-racing club in the world. It has founded races which have become classics in two continents, the Arlberg-Kandahar in Austria, the Quebec Kandahar in Canada and the Far West Kandahar on the West Coast of America, and there is every reason to believe that the Kandahar of the Andes will prove one of the classic races on the

South American continent. I am even prouder of the fact that the Kandahar races are famous for their friendly and good-humoured rivalry.

The Golden Age of ski-ing was golden not only because the sport was young, but also because, in those days, skiers skied for fun. Racing for fun does not exclude a healthy interest in results, whether individual or national. Nationalism in sport is only to be condemned when it is uncontrolled and hysterical. It is very right, just and proper that an English skier should be pleased when British teams distinguish themselves in international events ; and there is no reason to apologise for the fact that all British mountaineers still continue to hope that Everest will be conquered by a British party.

Abusus non tollit usum. The abuse of a thing does not invalidate its use. Love of country, like other loves, is only wrong when uncontrolled ; and the defective who feels no pride in his country's triumphs whether in war or in sport deserves our sympathy like other defectives, such as those who are stone-deaf or colour-blind.

It is possible to be extremely serious while racing, and yet light-hearted when beaten. Alan d'Egville, usually known as Deggers, was as keen as I to win the first roped race for the Scaramanga Challenge Cup. But you have only to contrast his story of the race in the *British Ski Year Book* with articles written by Nazis after Nazi teams have failed to win, to realise what ski-racing means under Nazi influence. Here is a passage from d'Egville's article.

"Apparently Lunn and Allinson had decided to get down Hindmarsh Gully with about three turns, for it is exceptionally steep—over 30 degrees in parts—and has a narrow opening at the bottom through which you shoot after a quick left-handed turn followed by a quicker right-handed one. We even calculated on these three turns and, having gained the gully first, spread ourselves out therein and descended, or were about to descend, as gentlemen should, when Arnold Lunn throwing all decency and self-restraint to the winds and dragging the helpless Allinson like a sack of potatoes, shot straight down the gully like an avalanche. We could see Allinson's lips forming themselves into some sort of prayer, and said 'Amen.' I still think it was one of the finest sights I have seen. Allinson was marvellous, for he had no warning that Lunn was going to take it straight."

True enough, and it was thanks to Allinson that we won.

In later years by exercising a kind of ski *droit de seigneur*, that is by picking the best available partners, I contrived to win the race again with Christopher Mackintosh, and also to win two second prizes. But I was never a racer in any proper sense of the term.

Even more characteristic of the spirit of the golden age is "Deggers'" account of the first Inferno race in the 1928 *Ski Year Book*.

The Inferno course includes three short climbs and three flattish sections, the aggregate length of which is about 7 kilometres. The aggregate vertical descent including six climbs cannot be far short of 8,000 feet.

The course includes two extremely steep sections, the first of which extends from Kandahar Gully to the Egertental, and the second, which is even steeper and more difficult, from Grütsch to Lauterbrunnen.

The idea of the race originated with Harold Mitchell, Viscount Knebworth, Pelham Maitland, Dudley Ryder, "Patsy" Richardson and Bunny Ford.

The Inferno race was an attempt to recapture the spirit of the first Kandahar, that is of natural as opposed to artificial racing. The height of the starting-point above the nearest funicular was in itself a guarantee that the snow would not be beaten hard and tracked. The veto on stick-riding was suspended, for this veto is an artificial concession to an æsthetic criterion.

"The less artificial is ski-racing," wrote Antony Knebworth, "the better fun it will be. As the thing is less or more civilised so it is more or less good. Those who doubt that a thing is more noble as it is less civilised must have at the back of their minds the curious idea that the world is actually improving."

On January 29th eighteen competitors,* of whom four were ladies, caught an early funicular to the summit of the Allmendhubel. "True to Club traditions," writes d'Egville, "we carried no rucksacks, maps, compasses, or theodolites. Lunch was stored in the roomy pockets with which all right-minded ski-runners are provided."

All the competitors, save one, were members of the Kandahar. The exception was dis-edified by our very un-Alpine appearance.

* Their names are as follows: Mrs. Harvey, Miss Doreen Elliott, Miss Sale-Barker, Miss D. Crewdson, Messrs. Mitchell, Maitland, Ryder, Allinson, Arnold Lunn, d'Egville, Humphreys, Harbidge, Eaton, Pembroke, Cadbury, Heaton and Captain Brierly.

Under the impression that I was a " Downhill only " skier, he remarked that he himself was a mountaineer rather than a racer. The second statement was true for he finished last. I was impressed, and asked him what peaks he had climbed. He mentioned two easy expeditions in the Engadine, of which the Diavolezza was one, and then he asked me if I had ever skied on the glaciers. I made a non-committal reply ; but somebody must have told him my name, because he seemed readier to treat me as an equal, when next we met.

We climbed for four hours, and in spite of noisy protests from d'Egville who suffers from vertigo, we decided to start the race from the actual summit of the Schilthorn. Those who like Deggers refused to start from the Spitz, were told to hang about on the little col just below the summit and join in the hunt as we swept gaily by. As the oldest competitor I claimed the right, not only to pick the best position on the narrow summit crest, but also to start the race at the moment most convenient to myself and least convenient to my friend Deggers. I could see him from the summit just about to photograph the view, so I shouted " Go ! " and swept past him as he was jumping into his bindings.

Many a time at World Championships, with all their paraphernalia of electrical timing, and the tense atmosphere of a decisive battle ; my mind has travelled back to the first Inferno which was everything that a race should be—friendly, informal, impromptu.

Deggers soon overtook me, but I had a trump card up my sleeve. Not for nothing had I ridden my stick for many seasons, in the palæozoic age of British ski-ing. I had registered to the Half-way House station a stout and reliable pole in order to discard my light bamboo sticks before the final grim descent to Lauterbrunnen. I collected my pole at the Half-way House, drank a cup of coffee, and did not resume the race until I was adequately rested, by which time I was somewhere near the tail of the procession. Once arrived at Grütsch I whistled down the Wood Glade riding my pole like the most expert of witches.

Deggers and Audrey Sale-Barker introduced a variant of their own into the course by sliding 400 feet down the icy wood chute ; but Audrey, in spite of cracking a rib, continued the race. Deggers seemed a little shaken when I overtook him, and I had just bumped my game leg against a stone wall ; so we agreed to call it a day, and passed the finishing posts hand in hand—an equal sixth out of sixteen.

The race ended as all good races ended in a glorious beer party near the finish—all of us proud to have competed in the world's longest downhill race, and equally happy irrespective of where we had finished. Indeed, the most significant fact about d'Egville's spirited account of the first Inferno in *The British Ski Year Book* is that he was so occupied with recapturing the happy-go-lucky atmosphere of the first Inferno that he entirely forgot to mention who won.

Let me repair this omission. The race was won by Harold Mitchell in 1 hour and 12 minutes ; 2nd, F. Pelham Maitland ; 3rd, A. Dudley Ryder ; 4th, Miss Elliott and A. Allinson ; 6th, Arnold Lunn and A. H. d'Egville ; 8th, A. J. Humphreys.

It may well be that the light-hearted gaiety which characterised British ski-ing in those early days was one of the factors which helped us to do well in competition against Alpine skiers. For the odds against us were tremendous.

There is no Alpine valley which is not potentially capable of producing ten times as many first-class racers as the Ski Club of Great Britain. In the Alps ski-ing is a people's sport. British ski-ing is the sport of that privileged class which can afford the time and money for a winter holiday. Again we were handicapped by the fact that we could so seldom put our best team into the field. The principal races were usually held during the Oxford and Cambridge terms, and most of the racers were undergraduates.

To illustrate the difficulties with which we had to compete I may mention the World Championship of 1935. At that time there were exactly twelve first-class racers in the Ski Club of Great Britain, who were good enough to compete in an event of this importance. Of these racers four could not get leave of absence. Of the remaining eight four injured themselves seriously in training and were unable to compete. That left exactly four. But there was no Alpine country which had less than 500 crack racers from which to select their teams.

The handicap of numbers was aggravated by the disparity in the training of members. The German team began their training for the Olympics on the glaciers in August. Many of our best racers had a month at Christmas and no more.

The British University team, which won the University Ski

Olympics in 1935, had coaxed a week's leave from the College authorities and travelled straight out from England to compete. In 1933 my son Peter was working in Coventry. Fortunately his chief, Captain John Black, was an enthusiastic skier, so he granted him an extra week's holiday. After three weeks on the snow Peter finished 16th out of 64 competitors in the World Championship, and then returned to Coventry. A month later Captain Black sent him out to Switzerland for the week-end. He arrived on Friday, and on Saturday finished 10th in the Arlberg-Kandahar Downhill Race, beating every member of the Arlberg Club.

Mr. T. D. Richardson, the eminent skater, described the record of British racers during this period as " one of the most remarkable achievements of modern British sport." If we consider the odds against which British skiers had to compete I am inclined to think that their record in International events fully justifies Mr. Richardson's verdict.

CHAPTER XI

"A Round or Two Before"

THREE men who played a great part in the adventure of the snows, before the war wrote finis to the Golden Age of British ski-ing, died in the sunlit years between the two World conflicts. Of these, Andrew Irvine and Antony Viscount Knebworth, were original members, and Dick Waghorn, an honorary member of the Kandahar.

Andrew Irvine was primarily a mountaineer, but he loved Mürren and he adored ski-ing. "When I am old," he wrote to me from England, "I will look back on Christmas, 1923, as the day when to all intents and purposes I was born. I don't think anybody has ever lived until they have been on ski."

Andrew Irvine was one of the most remarkable beginners that I have seen. He passed the Second Class Test and won the Strang-Watkins Challenge Cup within three weeks of putting on ski. In the middle of January he left Mürren to cross the Oberland glaciers. I never saw him again.

Irvine was the youngest member of the Everest expedition, but his lack of self-assertion combined with a certain seriousness of purpose made him seem older than his years. I remember the grave courtesy with which he listened to the eager questions of a small boy, who finished second to him in the Strang-Watkins. Peter cross-examined him about oxygen, and Irvine answered with as much care as if he was giving evidence before an Alpine Club Committee. From the Himalaya he wrote three long letters to Peter, including his last letter from the base camp, before setting out on a journey from which he did not return. "The English," said an old chronicler, "love rather to live well than to live long." Irvine did not live long, but in his last year he rowed in a winning Oxford boat, explored Spitzbergen, fell in love with ski-ing and assaulted Everest. Somewhere near the summit his body lies—*coelo tegitur qui non urnam habet*—thousands of feet above the loftiest of human graves.

> Here let us leave him, for his shroud the snow,
> For funeral lamps he has the planets seven
> For a great sign the icy stair shall go
> Between the stars to heaven.

Flight-Lieutenant Henry Richard Danvers Waghorn was one of the founders of that great club, the Downhill-Only (D.H.O.)

the name of which is an unending provocation to sensitive mountaineers. In 1929 Dick Waghorn achieved world fame as the winning pilot in the race for the Schneider trophy.

He was one of the most ardent skiers that ever lived. In 1930 he was third in the British Championship, and won the Army, Navy and Air Force Ski Championship. In the same year he led the D.H.O. to victory against the local Wengen Club, which contained many of the best Swiss runners. On that occasion Dick won both the Downhill and the Slalom races. He raced for Britain in the first World Championship.

Waghorn served on the Council of the Club during my term of office as President, and died as the result of injuries sustained in a flying accident on the day of our Spring Dinner, 1931.

Waghorn and I used to lunch together before Council meetings to discuss the more controversial issues. I found myself relying more and more on the judgment of this young man, sixteen years my junior, and grew to regard him with ever increasing affection and respect. He did not intervene very often in debate, but he never intervened without effect. He was a slow starter. He disliked airing any opinion until he had walked round the subject, and had a good look at it from all possible angles. He was fearless in support either of a friend or of a policy in which he believed. And where his personal loyalties were concerned he did not rest content, as I had good reason to know, with registering an academic protest. Where he believed an injustice to have been committed he went on hammering away in long, typewritten letters, until he had extracted a withdrawal. He had a habit of selecting the right nail, and of continuing to hit the aforesaid nail with maddening persistence until the opposition succumbed through sheer weariness.

He was curiously impersonal in his attitude to himself. On one occasion an onlooker disapproved of Waghorn's judging in a First Class Test and put his criticism in an official letter to the Technical Committee. Waghorn listened with grave attention to the arguments put forward in the letter, and to the criticisms of his own decision, nodded his agreement and announced that he was convinced that he had been at fault, and that he proposed to vote for disallowing the test in question. He was, as Squadron-Leader S. Don wrote in *The Times*, "clear-cut and ruthless in regard to all thoughts and actions that did not measure up to his standard of right", all actions, including his own.

He inspired one of the most felicitous obituary notices that I have read, an anonymous tribute in the columns of *The Times*. A friend wrote : " His attitude to his own achievements was one of careless indifference which was more real than modesty and more serious than pride. He did not care about heroics. He was neither brave nor afraid. If he ever felt emotion he did not care to show it to the world. His home, his work, his play, his loyalties, and his affection—all these things were natural and simple to him. He accepted them without question and he loved them without saying so. There was never a man bred on English soil in whom were more perfectly combined those qualities which, when known, are universally adored. And there was never a man more determined that those qualities should not be known."

When I first met Antony Knebworth he struck me as a charming but rather soft, spoiled and self-indulgent young man. I remember him making an appalling fuss because his concierge had failed to book him a sleeper. I did not suspect the reserves of toughness on which he could draw, when he pleased. He was not a natural boxer but he won his blue, and after breaking one thumb, and dislocating the other, went on to win his fight against Cambridge.

He loved life and Dick Waghorn's death opened his eyes to the risks of flying. He and Mackintosh attended Waghorn's funeral. " This settles it," said Antony, " I shall never fly again." " I have enough faith in immortality," said Mackintosh to me, " to smile when I think of Dick's greetings to Tony on his arrival in the other world. ' Well, Tony, so you came here by air, after all.' "

He crashed on May 1st, 1933. The Kandahar, of which he was an ex-president, was just sitting down to dinner when the news came through on the tape machine.

Antony was a confirmed Mürrenite. Here are some extracts from his letters to his father : " . . . Gosh, I'm longing to get back to Mürren ; this is a damned awful place, but it is only for two nights. . . . It was like coming home getting back to Mürren. There are some awfully nice people here and I adore this place."

Antony was a true amateur in the best sense of that much abused word. " Amateur " is defined by the dictionary as " one who cultivates a thing as a pastime." The true amateur is one for whom a game is an end in itself and not a means to an end. It is easy to cite instances of men who are professionals in the narrow sense of the term, but who none the less play the game because they love it, and it is even easier to quote instance after instance of athletes who, though they were technically amateurs, were less interested in the game than in the prestige for which they were contending.

The true amateur is never at his best when forced to play the game in a serious spirit. At Eton Antony made runs freely when he was playing cricket for fun, and failed again and again when he was trying for a place in the Eton XI. I think he loved ski-ing more than any other sport because ski-ing, like Antony, was young, and because, in those days, nobody took ski-ing terribly seriously.

Our friends come back to us in their most characteristic attitudes, for memory is very selective. Sometimes when I am watching a modern race Antony's ghost intrudes itself into the procession of young men with grave, tense and anxious faces. I see him, as I saw him in one of the first Anglo-Swiss races, sweeping past with a cheery grin on his face. His capacity for laughing when he was racing flat out always amazed me.

There were times when he shocked serious-minded folk. I remember an early race for the Roberts of Kandahar. The snow was vile, breakable crust and ice, and Antony, who skied for pleasure, decided that on this particular occasion it was not pleasurable to ski. He therefore abandoned all attempt for the cup, sat on his ski and tobagganed comfortably downhill. " It isn't ski-ing," some people said, in the solemn tone in which other solemn people say, " It isn't cricket."

I have a good deal of the fundamental public schoolboy prig in my composition, but my comments on his performance merely made him laugh. This was annoying, but what was more serious was that the low opinion I formed of his ski-ing cost me money, as I laid ten to one against him on the next Kandahar and lost.

Not content with toboganning in the Roberts of Kandahar, he behaved very badly in connection with the Lady Denman Cup, which might be described as the Roberts of Kandahar for ladies.

" Martha Mainwaring " was only a name to me when I drew the entries for this race. I was told that Miss Mainwaring was a skier who had come over from St. Moritz to compete, but she did not turn up at the start, and I made some caustic comments on the unpunctuality of lady skiers, and told the starter to allow Miss Mainwaring thirty seconds grace and no more.

I skied down the course before the race started. Miss Betty

Schuster established a comfortable lead, and suddenly from behind a rock a dreadful apparition emerged, a rouged and powdered Antony in wig, jumper, scarf and skirt. Miss Mainwaring set off in pursuit of Miss Schuster, who was entirely put off by the sudden intrusion of an unknown female ski-ing as no woman skied in those days, and lost the race in consequence.

I went down to the finish and tackled Antony. I was very angry, but he seemed quite unabashed by my protests. He asked me whether I recognised his jumper and skirt. I told him that I was not interested in his young women or in their skirts. There was a glint in Antony's eye which made me feel vaguely uneasy, and not without cause. The jumper and skirt were my wife's, and my failure to recognise them resulted in my rapid transference from the judge's bench to the dock.

The memory of Antony's prank is perpetuated on the Kandahar course in the name which is now attached to the slopes near the finish—Martha's Meadow.

It is pleasant to be reminded by Antony's letters of that Eolithic age of British ski-ing when Antony used "to look at Arnold or Caulfeild as the goals of a skiers' ambition. . . . They were our idols, roughly speaking." This period did not last long. "Well, I've tried to show you the change. . . . I think the whole situation is best described when I say that the best skier in Switzerland is now an attractive and reckless young man of 20 instead of a reliable and cautious old one, of 35 or so." I was the "cautious old one," and Christopher Mackintosh was the iconoclast. I am proud of the fact that my ski-ing should have been mentioned in the same sentence as his.

Antony raced in the first World Championship in Mürren, which was held in a blinding snowstorm. Many of the cracks ran off the course. Antony finished seventh, beating, among others, the famous Zogg. When I told him that he had beaten Zogg, he threw back his head and the furniture rocked with his laughter. I have never heard a laugh like Tony's.

He was great fun to race *with*. He was my partner in the Scaramanga roped race of 1928, for which there was a record entry of twenty-four (twelve pairs). The conditions were execrable, breakable crust and ice. One of our rivals tore open his face on first slope. Antony and I followed a line of our own suitable for the timid and middle aged. I was both, and Tony who was neither was kind to me. Shrub Slope when we reached it seemed curiously empty of competitors. "I expect we're last," I said. "All is lost," said Tony, "save beauty. Our faces aren't scratched." But to our intense surprise we found that we were second when we sailed past the finishing posts.

In 1925 he tried glacier ski-ing. I am sorry for the guides who had the job of pacing his party down the glaciers, Mackintosh and Cyril White and Tom Fox and Tony and Andrew Irvine. "We had the most enormous fun. We were all unanimous that the ski-ing was rotten, but we were equally unanimous that the *vin du pays* in the first pub we came to was *goot*. Come down here when you come to England and we'll have the hell of a blind."

I always rejoiced when a bulky manuscript arrived from Tony for the *Year Book*, for he could not only ski but write as, indeed, the readers of his published letters have discovered.

The irresponsible gaiety which is associated not only with Antony but also with the Golden Age of British ski-ing died with Antony, for his death coincided with the end of a period. Sports like Civilisations have their life cycles. The early British ski-racers were "contemporary" in the Spenglerian sense with Gothic gargoyles, whereas modern racing is "contemporary" with Wren or Palladio. I thought of Spengler's thesis during the ski races at the Garmisch Olympic Games in 1936. How I longed for a Martha Mainwaring to break through the military cordon and gate-crash into those solemn races! But Martha could have been as out of place at Garmisch as a Gothic gargoyle on the classic façade of the Farnese Palace at Rome.

Antony was a period piece. His irresponsible gaiety lingers in our memory as a symbol of the days when men still raced for fun. He will not grow old, as the sport he loved grows old, and in our memory an ageless Antony will continue to frolic down the Martha's Meadow of his youth.

. . . . .

I wish that Antony and Dick could have lived to take part in the battle of Britain. They were pre-war casualties whose names should be inscribed on our Club's roll of honour, for they died, as many pilots died, in manœuvres which were an integral part of the preparation for that great battle which saved the world.

When peace returns let us hope that our country will continue to produce men like Irvine, Dick and Antony, who are prepared to prove, if need be, by dying that there are worse things than death. The mountains, the air and the sea are great avenues of adventure, not in spite of but because of the toll of young lives which they exact. *Sicut cursores vitai lampades tradunt.* The torch of a life more abundant than mere existence is passed on by those who risk death to prove that there are lessons to be learned in the school of danger which are never mastered in sheltered security.

CHAPTER XII

Les Neiges D'Antan

RUMOURS reach me of a highly personal and very entertaining history of the Mürrenites during the golden age, which is being compiled by Major Lindsay of the Irish Guards. In the faint hope of setting a standard for Tommy Lindsay I shall begin this chapter by quoting a nostalgic letter from Kingsmill Moore.

30, Burlington Road,
Dublin.
Xmas Eve, 1941.

My dear Arnie,

It is Christmas Eve. Outside the sky is sombre and the first snowflakes are already twisting down through the branches of the almond. I know I owe you a letter for many months, and the date and weather combine to turn my thoughts to you and to Mürren. Mürren, as seen from exile and in retrospect. "By the waters of Babylon we sat down and wept when we remembered thee, O Zion."

Somehow it is not easy to focus Mürren life as a whole. The "accidents" keep thrusting forward, jostling out of the way any attempt at synthesis. A wild rush to stop you going into an Anglo-Swiss dinner with a ski boot on one leg and a slipper on the other: woof and dunch of snow parting from the church roof: Doreen falling elegantly to encourage nervous candidates: "Achtungs" from microscopic village urchins on luges (very upsetting to the balance): the mountains under a full moon: a toy that made cow-noises: bacon and eggs at midnight. Sight and sound chase each other across my memory, the trimmings of the dish but not the dish itself.

"Mürren, geologically a narrow shelf above a glacier valley, became in turn a cow alp, a hamlet, a climbing village, a tourist centre and finally, in the twenty years of peace between the two world wars, reached to European fame as the Mecca of ski-ing. Here the technique of downhill racing was evolved, the Kandahar founded, the racing rules of the world drawn up and a new standard of ski-running created." That, or something like that, our grandchildren will read in the Baedeker of the future. But of the men and women who were Mürren, of the rivalry and comradeship which stimulated and bound them together they will have no hint except perhaps in the records of old races and old controversies tucked away in forgotten copies of the Ski Year Book. *Comradeship! I know now why my mind has been dodging the substance and taking refuge in the accidents, subconsciously*

endeavouring to avoid the sense of home sickness which any vivid recollection of that comradeship was inevitably to arouse. Home sickness is no false expression. Mürren was a home and each new visit a homecoming. The indiscriminate welcome of the concierges at the station, the tour of the shops after tea and finally the great hour of the day, the Palace lounge with the old familiar pictures and notice boards and trophies and all my friends, grown almost to brothers and sisters from long acquaintance, seated at the tables or drifting to and fro on their lawful occasions. A long roll call and many who will not answer again! Shaw Stuart has worn his last disguise; Squire will never again stump through the door with his skates on, his legs bandaged like racehorses' telling an Irish story in an accent only he imagined was Irish; Tony Knebworth's voice is rollicking through the corridors of another world. Before this war is over there will be other absentees.

Mürren, the real Mürren of those who returned with the snows of every year, was a microcosm. Not so cosmopolitan as some other centres, not so full of fashionable notorieties, it seemed to attract men of real eminence from every walk of life. I come from a people and a city famed for good conversation but the best and the best-informed talk I have ever listened to was at Mürren. In the Palace lounge I first heard of the inevitability of the Anschluss from a British minister, the intricacies of modern banking from Jakobsen, the extent of modern diabolism from Allinson, and the philosophic basis of Catholicism from you. And the arguments, the never-ending arguments starting between a couple of people (of whom you were usually one) and collecting a gradually growing circle of auditors and intervenients! Where but in Mürren could you have found a group of anything up to twenty young men and women listening with deference and attention to a debate on Thomist fundamentals? Where but in Mürren could you get first-hand information on any subject by walking a few yards across a room. Artists, lawyers, doctors, diplomats, business men, schoolmasters, generals, admirals, every branch of human activity and everyone in an expansive holiday mood which produced the best that was in them.

Some, of course, were what the ornithologist would call rare and exceptional migrants, but the number of regular winter visitors grew each year. Mürren was selective. Brains, athletic powers, social position came not amiss and served at least for an introduction. But none of those was an open sesame. Character and individuality, and nothing else counted in the long run. Not necessarily a very engaging character. It might be bubbly and aggressive; or again it might well be quiet and retiring. One of the most popular of Mürrenites did very little except sit in the sun and be lordly to everyone.

But genuine it must be and not assumed or second-hand. Think over all the persons who were most associated with Mürren and you will find that their characters were unusually clear cut and distinctive.

Mürren had many detractors. It was, said one young gentleman in a Wengen train, "lousy with Royals." It is an age of easy superciliousness towards those who come of ancient and royal blood, but when I think of courage in adversity, of devotion to duty, of reckless gallantry, of humour, of sane, tolerant judgment and of acts of rare courtesy I find my exemplars of those virtues among the "Royals" I got to know at Mürren. And I like to think that those men and women chose Mürren, among other reasons, because there they could meet with persons whose characters had something, at least, in common with their own.

Another stock jibe was that Mürren was an overgrown public school, with the public schoolboys' attitude to athletics, and their insignia in the form of badges, carried on into adult life. There is just sufficient truth in this to make it worth while to confute. Undoubtedly ski-ing and ski-racing was a large part of the life, and one of the avowed objects of Mürren organisation was to improve the ski-ing standard; and undoubtedly as outward marks of distinction have always proved an incentive to effort (why otherwise should you have the red cord of the Legion of Honour) good use was made of the wish to sport a Silver or Gold K. But before you condemn these things it is worth considering why thev are fostered at public schools, and if you find that the athletic cult produces courage, endurance, decision and initiative (as I believe it does) there seems no valid reason why even adults should not receive a refresher course in those virtues. If athleticism had been forced down everybody's throat, or if the non-athletic had been made to feel unwelcome, there would have been grounds for complaint. But this was not so. Let me confess that at first, as one of the unathletic, I did not appreciate, and indeed rather opposed, the prevalence of the public school attitude and that even now I think that in the earlier period it was occasionally exaggerated. But I have come to recognise its value and I write this as a palinode. The spirit of the Kandahar was the spirit that was the Battle of Britain, and the man that directed that battle and many of those who fought in it were members of the Kandahar.

Memories of the great skiers are pursuing me to-night. Bracken rippling down a slope like a snake, Joannides who attacked the snow almost as if he hated it, Mackintosh superb in his strength and recklessness, Peter strung up to a very fury of tenseness, Durel who "moving seemed asleep," and Doreen, in telemark position, leaving her faultless furrow straight down the steepest course. But it is for you, who raced among them and knew them so much better, to sing their praises, and some day I hope you will write a book on those figures of the heroic age of ski-ing.

Before I finish I must say a word about the 1940 Year Book, *in many ways the greatest you have produced. When I opened the envelope I was amazed and said to my wife, " What is the reason for this," and then, as I turned over and saw the large advertisement of* Come What May, *I added, " unless the explanation is on the back cover." I apologise. I have read it more than once, and not altogether with dry eyes. I was supposed to be a classic and you were a mathematician, but it has remained for you to interpret the classics to me in the fullness of their application to real life, and to make me see, as I never saw before, the glory that was Greece, and is still Greece, and is now also England.*

Meet me on the Schiltgrat after the war is over and I will race you to Kandahar Finish for a bottle of champagne.

Ever yours,

Kingsmill Moore.

" Those figures of the heroic age of ski-ing." Kingsmill Moore demands a book of which they shall be the theme, and perhaps even the most anti-Kandahar of mountaineers will forgive me devoting a few pages to the men (and women) who put British racing on the map.

Leonard Dobbs, Christopher Mackintosh, Bill Bracken and Peter Lunn. These four have a place all their own in the story of British ski-racing.

The first British racer to win an important international event was Leonard Dobbs, son of a ski pioneer, Mr. G. C. Dobbs.

Leonard was three times British ski champion. But his greatest triumph was his victory in the Downhill race of the second of the Anglo-Swiss University matches. In this race he beat Mackintosh and Amstutz, and laid the foundation of British victory.

In my *History of Ski-ing* I wrote :—

" Nobody who saw Leonard Dobbs moving uphill at the start of a big race would suspect his ski-ing genius. As a rule, he arrives five minutes late, having borrowed just before the train started a pair of ski from a younger brother. As the competitors line up for the start, Leonard Dobbs examines his bindings thoughtfully, and discovers that the string with which one of them is mended is wearing rather thin. He then casts his eyes over the running surfaces of his brother's ski, borrows a piece of wax from a spectator (wax which often turns out to be climbing wax, not running wax) and rams it thoughtfully into the largest hole in his ski. He then places on his head the woolly hat which has been such a godsend to d'Egville. Nobody knows the history of that hat, nobody dare inquire.

" A few seconds before the referee gives the word to start a look of absent-minded melancholy settles on Leonard Dobbs' face. The referee says ' Go,' Dobbs leaps forward, parks his ski into the steepest and iciest tracks that he can find, and while resting at the winning post studies with melancholy interest the technique of the various other competitors as they arrive.

" Leonard Dobbs is the best racing strategist that I know. He never loses his head, has a marvellous flair for country, and a very exact knowledge of the limits which he can safely exceed. He seldom falls, and when he falls he keeps his head and keeps his ski together. He is the telemark king, and never uses any other turn on soft snow, and he falls into the telemark position on steep slopes."

Mr. Leonard Dobbs, in the course of some captious remarks provoked by this tribute, informed me that he had " never seriously considered string as a material suitable for bindings," and that he did " not advocate the use of climbing wax for use in downhill races."

But in spite of this disclaimer I maintain that my pen picture was substantially accurate.

In the Palæozoic age of British racing, when races were timed, if at all, on wrist watches, some 15 racers might have been observed toiling upwards towards the Seelifuren Hut on the Schilthorn. It was snowing, and the competitors—there was no starter—decided that they had climbed high enough for glory. Somebody remarked that nothing had been done about the finishing posts. Someone else added dubiously that as A.L. was in bed with a mastoid, it was highly doubtful whether anybody else had concerned himself with such details. Two Swiss porters who had accompanied the expedition were therefore instructed to run down to the Egertental and post themselves and their sticks near " Menin Gate." " The finish will be between the porters," remarked a competitor who had been informally elected official in charge. The porters were given ten minutes' start, and the official in charge began to make arrangements for the start. " I shall say," he began, " Three, Two . . ." but by this time a tall, sturdy young man had already leaped down the snows in pursuit of the porters. This " dark horse from Wengen," to quote a contemporary account, overtook the porters in Kandahar Gully, and then wisely decided to act on the principle of " Every man his own finishing post." A few minutes later an old man with a grey beard who had lost his way in the snowstorm was startled by the sudden appearance of a human meteor. " Hi, there," shouted the meteor, " don't move. You're a finishing post." And that is how Christopher Mackintosh won his first Kandahar.

January 10th, 1924.—Prelude to a great international race. Myself much perplexed standing at the summit of what is known as " Mac's Leap." Fierce argument. Should the slope be controlled ? Yes, say some, because (*a*) anybody who took it straight would be killed. No, say others, because (*b*) nobody would be such a fool as to take it straight. " But what's wrong with taking it like this ? " said Mackintosh, who had suddenly appeared from nowhere. Whereupon he put his ski together and pointed them down the slope. Where the steep slope steepens abruptly he shot some 10 metres through the air, landing in a soft pocket. Rattling across a wood-sleigh path he struck the fierce and abrupt outrun, shot up the steep fronting slopes and finished with a cheerful christiania.

He had run from top to bottom without the faintest suggestion of a crouch. There was something very attractive in this refusal to make the least concession to speed. The incident lives in my memory as the most sensational and yet at the same time the most carefree bit of ski-ing that I have ever seen. Its only rival is Sigmund Ruud's wonderful performance in the Arlberg-Kandahar race.

Ten years later : *February 18th, 1934.*—A small group standing at the top of the Flying Kilometre. Mackintosh, who had been lunching at Corviglia, appears over the horizon on ski on which he had just slalomed in the FIS. " Are you," I asked by way of a jest, " going to take the Flying Kilometre straight ? " " *Am* I going to take your kilometre straight ? " replied Mackintosh, who had only seen the famous slope from afar. He came punting down the in-run and with a final thrust sent himself hurtling over the take-off. Guttural cries of terror from two Swiss workmen who had been stamping down the course, and who had leapt for safety as Mackintosh thundered past.

And as I saw him swing to rest far below, the ten years that had passed since I saw him take Mac's Leap fell from me, and I was back again in the glorious dawn of downhill racing.

It is one thing to take the Flying Kilometre when you have tried it out from half way. It is one thing to take it on jumping or specially built ski. It is another matter to launch yourself down it just because you feel like shifting.

Mackintosh is a natural athlete. He represented Scotland and Oxford at Rugby, and Great Britain as a jumper in the Olympic Games. As a ski-runner his chief assets are great strength and courage. No more fearless, indeed no more reckless, ski-runner has ever lived. His technique is rough and instinctive, but it is noticeable that his instincts are sound. He adopted naturally the well-sprung semi-erect position to which all leading racers have now reverted. And he had the sense to use both the telemark position for straight running and the telemark turn when these manœuvres were condemned by the fashion of the moment. He was not a pretty nor a graceful runner, but the tremendous impression of strength which his ski-ing conveyed had its own æsthetic appeal. Had he bothered to train systematically he would have been almost unbeatable. He would have been more successful had he enjoyed ski-ing less and winning more. Again and again he threw away races which he should have won. In the Championship of 1926, for which the Dobbs brothers and Bracken were competing, he treated the slalom flags as skittles and was disqualified in the first part. He then proceeded to win the second part with ease, and the straight race by the fantastic margin of 1½ minutes. In 1930 he won the first part of the Downhill race by a comfortable margin, and he had every chance of establishing a winning lead on the Schiltgrat. It was clearly wrong to take unnecessary risks. I explained all this to him as we lunched together on the Allmendhubel. I can still see him looking longingly at the absurd "Mac's Line" which he has only once held. "Don't take it," I pleaded, "you can't hold it." "But it would be such fun," he murmured. He took it, fell heavily, lost a stick, and though he still managed to win the Downhill race, his margin was not enough to set off against his defeat in the Slalom. Still, he had had his fun. No man enjoyed racing more. No man bothered less about the actual result.

In spite of this insouciance he won the Roberts of Kandahar on the four occasions on which he entered for it, and even in slaloms he has as good a record as any British racer. He captained two winning B.U.S.C.* teams in the annual Anglo-Swiss matches, and has captained the British team on three occasions. His finest effort, which just missed doing full justice to his reputation, was his effort in the first FIS† downhill race meeting at Mürren. In the Grütsch-Lauterbrunnen race he finished second to Lantschner, and beat, among others, such famous runners as Otto Furrer, David Zogg, Walter Amstutz, Ernst Feuz, Seelos of Austria and Paumgarten.

We who watched the crude beginnings of British racing and the sudden dawn of better days, must be forgiven if we feel that Mackintosh has a place all his own in this epic story. Younger runners may beat his best " times," but there is a legendary glamour about his ski-ing which belongs, and properly belongs, to the pioneer phase of the sport. The younger racers have learned that they can attain fantastic speeds and stand, but Mackintosh had no such fund of general experience to hearten him when he pointed his ski down Mac's Leap. And it is for such light-hearted impromptus that he will be remembered, for a certain gaiety in his ski-ing which we recall with regret in the modern phase of intense and serious specialisation.

Christopher never gave a conscious thought to technique or style. Bill Bracken is a ski artist, proud of his craftsmanship and ever seeking to perfect it. A supreme stylist, he is a joy to watch on ski.

Bracken won the British Ski Championship three years running, and the Kandahar Championship on three occasions. This championship is awarded by the Kandahar committee to the best British runner, if a member of the club, on a general review of the entire season's racing. If the best British racer of the year is not a member of the club the Kandahar Championship is not awarded, and this has never happened in the case of the men's championship and only once in the case of the ladies'.

Bracken never did himself real justice in the world championship but he won many events with a first-class international entry, such

* British Universities' Ski Club.

† The Fédération Internationale de Ski is usually known as " the FIS," and the World Championship which it controls as " the FIS meeting."

as the Lauberhorn Cup at Wengen. His greatest triumph was his victory in the Slalom of the Arlberg-Kandahar of 1931. He finished third on the combined result, one of the finest, perhaps the finest, performance by a British racer in any of the classic race meetings.

Bracken raced against Peter Lunn for the last time in 1932. Bracken beat Peter in two Downhill races, and lost to him in three Slaloms. The Committee which rightly attaches more value to Downhill than to Slalom racing awarded the Kandahar Championship for the season to Bracken.

Peter held the Kandahar Championship from 1933 until 1937, when he retired from racing and during these years he was the outstanding British racer. He raced for Britain eight times, and captained five teams. His most outstanding characteristic was his unruffled calmness in all conditions. He holds what may well be one world record in ski-ing. He entered for six consecutive No-fall races, in which one fall disqualifies, won the first five and finished second in the sixth.

It is not easy for me to write about Peter, and I was just preparing to reread old numbers of the *British Ski Year Book* in search of tributes to Peter by Othmer Gurtner and Dieterlen when I received a most opportune letter from Phyllis Holt-Needham, who writes :—

" Since I saw you I have been beguiling my waiting hours turning over my ski-ing memories, which has of course sent me to back numbers of the *Year Book*. I wonder if the people who used to write and say they didn't want the *Year Book* filled up with descriptions of people of whom they had never heard, turn now to those pages when they want to fill in the background to their own memories of those vanished winter seasons. Because I do find, and I expect other people do too, that it is the descriptions of the skiers themselves which make one able to live the time again.

" But in doing this I have been surprised to find how dim the portrait of Peter appears to be, considering how immensely outstanding his racing achievements were. Of course, I remember how extremely difficult you found it to write about Peter's ski-ing. The effect of this is that only a detailed comparison of results really shows that Peter's racing career was unique among British skiers, and I can't help regretting that we have not got those pæons which would have been his—and ours—had his name been Mackintosh or Bracken.

"But even my own memories of Peter in Switzerland are vague and shadowy. I think this is partly because he took his racing so quietly that it seemed less of an effort for him than for anyone else, and therefore in some curious way less deserving of enthusiasm. One took it completely for granted during the seasons I was at Mürren that Peter would inevitably win any race restricted to British competitors, and that he would finish at least in the first half of any international race. He was, in fact, so consistent a runner that his best results never had the necessary element of surprise to make them in any way spectacular.

"Then, too, the fact that one expected him to beat all British competitors made one always compare him not with other amateurs or lowlanders but with the best international skiers of the season. He never was among the very best of these, and the result of this has been that instead of remembering him as the most outstanding British racer we have ever had, one tends to think of him as an also-ran among the international 'Kanone'.

"And then he could not, would not, or at any rate did not play the part. One never heard him doing up his boots according to the latest hint from Furrer, nor did one hear other racers lacing theirs the same way as Peter. If he had theories about technique or wax they never stood a chance against his theories about Blake and James Joyce. He never told one just how many times he had been sick on the way to the start.

"He never looked the part. He had apparently had no new ski clothes since just before he stopped growing, and he never seemed to have more than one pair of ski. You remember the story of the girl who asked him how many 'stars' he had got in the Mürren School Tests, and when he said four, protested 'Oh, rot! You don't look as if you'd got two.'

"Vicarious pleasures have become so precious nowadays that I can't help feeling a slight grudge against Peter for being so apathetic towards his own legend. His portrait, which should stand out from our other racers, is monochrome and misty. But he can't *always* have raced in a blizzard."

In 1938 Roland Palmedo published a magnificent volume, *Ski-ing, the International Sport*, to which many of the most famous skiers contributed. Alice Wolfe, now Alice Kiare, contributed a brilliant chapter on the Women Ski-racers of Europe, in which she paid a generous tribute to the Kandahar ladies.

"In Mürren," writes Mrs. Kiare, "the Kandahar Club was developing an extraordinarily fine group of girl racers. They were the first girls to have *esprit de corps*, courage and grit. Also, thanks to Mr. Arnold Lunn, they were the first girls in the world to have training in the Slalom. Other countries, such as Switzerland, Austria and Germany, might have an individual girl here and there who loved to ski. There were girls in Austria who went ski-mountaineering with their brothers and friends in genial groups up from Innsbruck and who fundamentally skied very well in all kinds of deep powder and breakable crust. But nobody had ever taught them to race. It was the English girls at the 1929 races at Zakopane, Poland and St. Anton-am-Arlberg, who first put racing for women on the map.

"What a flutter they caused in central Europe! Incidentally, they were the first girl skiers in the world to be well dressed. Their long straight legs encased in even longer beautifully tailored, flapping dark blue trousers, caused the most open-mouthed wonder and astonishment in Mittel-Europa. And when these slim creatures could also ski it was really too much! Up till then, women skiers had been baggily clad, khaki figures with cold cream streaked across their sun-burned noses, and rucksacks on their strong backs. Ski clothes for women with any chic or style were completely unknown.

"And there were so many good English women skiers in 1929. First, Audrey Sale-Barker, surely still the most famous British lady skier running her first Arlberg-Kandahar, second in the Swiss championship, and best lady* at the first international races at Zakopane, beating forty-five men. When she and the other English girls came into a restaurant after the race, all the Polish skiers stood up and cheered. Audrey Sale-Barker made an extraordinary impression on everybody who saw her ski. Very tall, extremely slim, her height accentuated by trousers so long that they touched the ground around her boots, pale honey-coloured hair, a vague dreamy expression, and when she skied I can only describe her as a sleep-walker. She stood very erect, with both arms slightly lifted in front of her, she had little or no reserve strength in a race, gave everything she had, and often collapsed and fainted when a race was over. She had incredible courage, and I

* No. Miss Sale-Barker finished just behind Miss Elliott.

will never forget seeing her take the last steep slope of Dengert at the finish of the 1929 Arlberg-Kandahar absolutely straight, with lifted arms like someone in a trance.

"Doreen Elliott that same year won the Swiss championship, and skiers like Lady Raeburn, and Diana Kingsmill (now Gordon-Lennox) and others were excellent team mates.

"The English girls' ease and aplomb in the slalom was also a cause of admiration and despair to other nations. Austrian girls who knew they could ski well shied away from the red flags and sat down between them in a way to wreak havoc and disaster in their ski racing-rating. The year 1929 was an eyeopener in what courage and racing experience could do. There were plenty of good women skiers who were terrible cowards when it came to a race. The English girls were the first to do or die on any slope. The credit for this fine showing goes to Mr. Arnold Lunn and the Kandahar Ski Club. The girls raced over and over again against one another on the steep slopes of Mürren before they went out to other parts of Switzerland, Austria and Poland. If it had not been for Mr. Lunn, ski-racing for women would not have come into its own until several years later."

Like many other famous ski-racers, Audrey Sale-Barker was also an enthusiastic flier. In an attempted flight from London to the Cape, on which her only companion was another girl, she crashed in the African wilds. Fortunately she was found by friendly natives who carried to the nearest white colony a message which Audrey had written with lip stick on a stray piece of paper.

Audrey was awarded the Pery Medal, which is the highest distinction in the Ski Club of Great Britain. This medal is awarded for outstanding achievements in any branch of ski-ing, touring or competitive, and also for contributions to ski-ing literature which add substantially to our knowledge either of snowcraft or of technique. Foreigners are eligible for the award. There have only been eight recipients, and so far the medal has only been twice awarded to ski-racers—to Audrey Sale-Barker in 1935, and to Peter Lunn in 1937.

Doreen Elliott finished just ahead of Audrey on the memorable occasion at Zakopane. Her racing record though brilliant was less brilliant than that of Audrey, but she was by far the better runner across country, equally at home on all types of snow.

Our ladies soon lost the advantage of being the first in the field.

But long after the Alpine countries had begun to turn out women racers by the score and even by the hundred our girls still continued to hold their own.

There are two Downhill Race meetings which tower above all others in importance—the FIS or World Championship and the A-K, or Arlberg-Kandahar. In the 1931 FIS Esmé Mackinnon won every race for which she entered. In the 1936 FIS Evie Pinching won the World Championship. Audrey Sale-Barker won the Ladies' A-K twice. Esmé Mackinnon and Jeanette Kessler won this race in 1933 and in 1934 respectively. In the last pre-War winter Marion Steedman who, like Evie Pinching, had been taught ski-ing by Bill Bracken, won the Ladies' A-K at Mürren. Lady Raeburn led the British Ladies' team to victory in the first three races against Swiss ladies. Doreen Elliott, Audrey Sale-Barker, and Jeanette Kessler all won the Swiss Open Ladies' Championship.

I was always being badgered to enter our girls for international events. They were much sought after, and not only because they could ski well. "In Italy," said Count Bonacossa, "our girls have either strong legs, or nice faces and weak legs. How do you manage to find so many ladies who look so charming and who ski so fast?"

Our ladies had not only strong legs but wills of iron. Racing speeds sometimes touch sixty miles an hour even in women's races, and few indeed were the champions who escaped injury. But even those who had broken their legs returned to the arena, and raced with undiminished courage. Jeanette Kessler broke a leg in the 1935 FIS, and in the very next year won the coveted gold A-K medal and finished seventh in the Olympic Games. Doreen Elliott put her hip out at the very beginning of her racing career. Nell Carroll won the Gold A-K after breaking an ankle. In the last pre-war winter the British Ladies' Combined Championship and the British Ladies' Downhill Racing Championships were both won by ladies who had broken their legs in the previous winter (Isabel Roe and Helen Palmer-Tomkinson).

No attempt to reconstruct the Golden Age would be complete without some reference to "the Beetles." These aggressively nimble little creatures had a maddening habit of finishing far ahead of their elders and betters. I still possess a small cup inscribed "For the best performance by a father against a son." I had finished among the "also rans" in the Cuthbert-Savage Slalom, which Peter won at the age of ten.

In the early years after the first World War many parents brought their children to the Alps. No less than 24 junior skiers competed in the first Hewitt Competition which was restricted to junior British skiers, and which was held at Wengen in 1927. The Kandahar entered two teams of five and took the first eight places in the Downhill Race. A member of the second team, R. C. Dunn, finished first, much to Peter's annoyance.

Peter had an unfair advantage over his great rival, Digby Raeburn, for Eton went back one week later than Winchester, and Digby used to find Peter's complacency difficult to endure during the last melancholy moments on the departure platform at Mürren. And, indeed, on one occasion Peter's parting taunt, "Good luck, Digby, in your Greek proses," produced a last-minute sortie from the train, and a final scuffle on the platform.

It was a tradition of the Junior Kandahar that the Junior Championship should reverse the results of the leading races. Thus in 1930 Digby, aged 14, who finished second in the Roberts of Kandahar and third in the Downhill Race for the British Ski Championship for which there were 35 entries, was beaten in the Junior Kandahar by Peter.

In 1931 Peter, aged 16, was good enough to win the Roberts of Kandahar, and to finish in the first half of a World Championship Downhill Race, but not good enough to retain the Junior Championship. He was the youngest competitor in five of the seven World Championships in which he competed, and the youngest member of four of the six British teams which he captained.

Esmé Mackinnon was the Queen Beetle with no rivals. She won the Ladies' Ski Club Championship at the age of 13, the British Championship at the age of 14, the World Championship at the age of 15, and the Ladies' Arlberg-Kandahar at the age of 17. On all four occasions she was the youngest competitor. I doubt if this record could be equalled in any really tough sport. And though northern racers were at first inclined to regard Downhill ski-ing as a soft substitute for Langlauf they changed their opinion after watching the race from Grütsch to Lauterbrunnen at the first FIS meeting.

Not only the Norwegians and Swedes, but their hangers-on in Central Europe, such as Luther, Editor of *Der Winter*, of Munich, insisted that this course was far too steep for men, and a brutal ordeal for women. Yet Esmé Mackinnon, aged 15, sailed down the course to victory without turning a hair.

Luther could never forgive the British for having pioneered this new development of ski-ing. He had been a good langlaufer in his day, and resented the introduction of a new criterion of ski-ing skill, for he was a poor downhill skier. I remember overtaking him on the Grütsch run in one of the steepest and narrowest wood glades. He had come to a full stop and seemed harassed and uncertain how to tackle the next slope. As I passed him I quoted the saying of another and more famous Luther: "Hier stehe ich und kann nicht anders." ("Here I stand and can no other.")

Many and many a time have I held up my thumbs for my Beetles when they were racing, and when the Spitfires went into action in the skies above my house I often thought of those old struggles, and wondered whether any of the Spitfires were piloted by men who learned to "take it straight" on Lone Tree. Certainly *Sicut sagitta sagittante* (As an arrow from a bow), the Kandahar motto, would serve equally well for the Air Force.

Of the Mürren Beetles some have already fallen in this war. William Rhodes Moorhouse won a D.F.C. in the Battle of Britain, and was killed in one of the last great daylight raids of 1940. Hector, in his last farewell to his wife, pointed to his son and said, "May men say of him when he returns from the battle, he was a braver man than his father." It would not have been easy for William to be braver than his father, awarded a posthumous V.C. for a gallant exploit in the early days of air fighting, but William, who was awarded the D.F.C. shortly before he died, gallantly maintained the family tradition.

David Wilson, who was killed in 1941, met his death on a return flight after bombing the German submarine base at Lorient.

He was a delicate boy and consequently never went to school. Instead he spent a great deal of time in Europe with his mother, Lady Nunburnholme, and, when I met him at Mürren as a boy of 16 or 17, he struck me as far more mature, and more balanced in his judgments, than most undergraduates many years his senior.

A friend of David's wrote: "Labouring all his life under the burden of ill-health, it was incredible that he could become so expert in these two activities, as both need a strong physique, and an ability to stand up to an intense strain. What carried David through was his incredible courage, and his will-power. Never would he give in, not even though his body well-nigh refused to go farther, and how often at the end of a long race did he arrive white with exhaustion, only to laugh at one's anxiety, and take the next train up to practise for the slalom."

Lieut.-Colonel Geoffrey Keyes, V.C., M.C., was the youngest Colonel in the British Army when he was killed in a desperate Commando raid on Rommel's headquarters. He knew that he was going to almost certain death, but resisted every attempt to dissuade him from the raid. I remember him as a boy of thirteen, one of the most fearless novices that I have ever seen on ski. He only spent one short season, his first, at Mürren and did not qualify for the Kandahar of which his father, Sir Roger Keyes, is an honorary member. He was awarded a posthumous V.C.

Major John Lytton, Viscount Knebworth, who was awarded the M.B.E. in 1941, was killed during the Battle of Egypt on July 4th, 1942.

To-day the Beetles who learned to race at Mürren or on the Wengen Bumps or the Parsenn have given a good account of themselves on land, on sea and in the air.

Max Aitken, whom I first met on a Kandahar test for which he entered at the age of 15, is now a Wing Commander and D.F.C. When I last met him I reminded him of a remark which he made to me some time before the war. He was off for a week's training with his squadron. After explaining that he seized every opportunity for extra training, he added, "When the war comes I don't intend to be shot down."

"Yes, I remember," said Max, "and those extra hours of training were the best life insurance that I have ever taken out. Flying has something in common with ski-ing. One's natural instincts are all wrong. Unless one's acquired instincts are, so to speak, more instinctive than one's natural instincts one is asking for trouble. I'll give you an example. The other day I was returning from France and a Hun got on my tail. I was within a minute or two of England. I could see the cliffs of Dover and my instinctive reaction would have been to try to beat it for home. Fortunately acquired instinct was stronger. I turned sharply back towards France, shot through the Ack-ack on the French coast and holed out the Hun on the ninth hole at Le Touquet. The point is that one turns into the Hun, when one is in a jam just as one leans forward on ski. Neither movement comes natural."

Bill Clyde, who left Eton because he was too delicate to live in England, who learnt to ski in Switzerland, who raced in two World Championships, and in innumerable World University Championships, one of which he won, is to-day a Wing Commander and a D.F.C. "Mouse" Cleaver, who raced for England at Innsbruck, lost an eye and won a D.F.C. in the Battle of Britain.

Patricia Raeburn drove a van through the worst blitz unperturbed by the fact that the soles of her boots and the skin of her hands were scorched by the flames.

John Lunn won a mention in despatches in the battle of Flanders.

Peter Riddell, one of the caste in "Target for To-night," has fought in the Battle of Britain.

I am writing these lines just after the fall of Tobruk. Two Beetles, who were fierce rivals in bygone days, are both affected by recent events.

Major Digby Raeburn, M.B.E.—it seems only yesterday that he was one of the smallest of the Beetles—fought in Greece and in Sollum. "Digby had leave," writes his mother, "and spent it in Syria, hired skis and boots in Beirut and went up to the Lebanon for four days. Jimmy Riddell was there teaching people to ski. Apparently conditions were like late Spring in Austria, but three weeks before there were great blizzards, and they were starting out of the second floor windows of the hotel."

In the old days the Kandahar and the D.H.O. of Wengen were great rivals.

To-day Peter is serving under Brigadier Cyril White, a founder of the D.H.O.

Peter writes from Malta:

"There is a little colony of skiers here. There is C. J. White, who is now a Brigadier. Archie Dunlop Mackenzie, who arrived recently; you will remember him, he went to the Arctic for a year, where he was supremely happy, and was miserable when he came back to civilisation. There is a subaltern called Colin Nightingale. We are arranging to have an S.C.G.B. dinner. . . . Antoinette" (Mrs. Peter Lunn) "has only slept down in the shelter one night and that was at the end of a bad day. She is determined not to get shelter-minded. We had spent the afternoon with Rosemary White and had several near misses. We walked back with a friend to find her house had been badly damaged, during the afternoon, and I had to help her salvage her belongings. Then at night we heard the horrid noise of a plane diving overhead and a bomb landed unpleasantly close. In the evening I brought home a bottle of rum. With its aid life returned to normal.

"I had the day off to-day. Toinette and I took some sandwiches into the country; we lunched on the side of a hill, looking down into a small valley. Malta looks at its best at this time of year; there is a lot of greenery and the clover was just coming out. An occasional Red Admiral fluttered past us. Below us was the deep blue of the Mediterranean Sea, stretching away towards Sicily. On a clear day, one can see Sicily with the naked eye and quite plainly through a telescope. But to-day there was a slight mist on the sea. The air raid warning was sounded, and Toinette and I walked down to a little cow hut, to see if we could get inside it; fortunately the door was open. We watched the first part of the raid from the roof, and saw the Junkers diving down and releasing their bombs on to the town.

"As the firing was overhead and we knew the splinters would soon be coming down, we climbed down and stood in the doorway of the hut. I watched another plane coming in over our heads. Suddenly I saw the sun glint on his four bombs; he had just released them. Three of them fell away but one whistled past us into the valley. I had never seen a bomb fall past me as close as that, but it did no damage at all, though we heard fragments of it land quite close to us after it had burst. I shall never forget seeing that bomb whistle past, though of course we have seen bombs falling on innumerable occasions. Once I saw a plane dive-bomb an A.A. position which was about two hundred yards away. Fortunately the bombs did not explode and they bounced again into the air. They were Maltese gunners and they never stopped firing; they're a wonderful people.

"Poor Rosemary White" (the wife of C.J.W., one of the founders of the D.H.O.), "has been bombed out of her town house. She was there when it happened. Fortunately in the shelter underneath the house. They didn't get a direct hit, but the ceilings came in and all that kind of thing."

Mürren, of course, was not the only school for Beetles. Wengen, the Parsenn, Villars and Grindelwald were the nursery of young skiers who developed on the snows qualities which were to be tested in an infinitely more exacting school. Jimmy Gardner, for instance, who raced so often for the D.H.O.—juniors and seniors—piloted a fighter plane in the Battle of Britain and, as a Lieutenant Commander attached to the Fleet Air Arm, in the air battles over the Mediterranean. He was awarded the D.S.C.

Though it became increasingly difficult for British racers to hold their own against the best professionals of snow-rich countries, our University skiers continued to win surprising victories in competition against the University skiers of other countries, and this in spite of the fact that they were competing against tremendous odds, both in respect of numbers and of training opportunities.

In the Winter Olympics, held at Bardonecchia, Mackintosh, Maclaren, Bushell and Clyde took the first four places in the Slalom only to be disqualified as a team because the organisers had not yet mastered the rules.

Bill Clyde was the most consistently successful of the University skiers. He won the Slalom at the World International Ski Meet in 1933 and in 1934, and the Combined event in 1935, the year in which the British University team won both the Downhill and Slalom at University World Championship. In 1936 James Palmer-Tomkinson maintained this great record by winning the Downhill race at the University Championship.

Meanwhile Norway had awoken to the importance of Downhill racing and procured two Olympic winners in these events at Garmisch. A British University team visited Norway in 1937. As far back as 1933 Colin Wyatt, an ex-captain of Cambridge, had jumped with distinction at Holmenkollen and won the first International Slalom in Norway, but in 1933 Norwegian downhill racers were not in the class of the best Alpine runners. In 1937, however, the classic Galdhöpiggen race was won at an *average* speed of 49 miles per hour. Of the sixty competitors the first 30 finished within half a minute of each other. Jimmy Palmer-Tomkinson was fourth, only 5 seconds behind the winner. He tied for the Slalom next day. The British team were beaten in the first Anglo-Norwegian team race, but on their return visit next year they won against a somewhat weaker combination, J. G. Appleyard and Donald Garrow finishing first and second in the Downhill, and Appleyard and H. M. Muir (killed in Libya) finishing first and second in the Combined. The ladies' Ski Club entered a team for the Galdhöpiggen race, Philippa Harrison being second in the Downhill and Combined, and Bunty Walker second in the Slalom.

In the last of the pre-War winters the British Universities wound up the Silver Age with a succession of victories. They beat the Swiss Universities and the Italian Universities, securing the first five places in the downhill race against Italy (P. Waddell, A. P. Dodd, D. Garrow, M. Muir and A. Fawcus).

The first five! What a triumph against a country in which the University skiers outnumbered ours by at least twenty to one. Finally Robert Readhead won the Duke of Kent's Cup and Marion Steedman the Ladies' Alpine Kandahar.

A letter from James Palmer-Tomkinson, dated June 16th, 1942, lies before me as I write :—

" It is curious that my life before the war is completely gone and forgotten with no regrets, with the exception of Switzerland, which is as vivid as ever, and the memory of one or two outstandingly good days hunting, and some pleasant days climbing in the Lake District which I link up in my mind with Switzerland. Perhaps it is through having a Swiss wife, but I don't think so. All the pleasantest moments of my life have been spent there and most of my best friends, many of them Swiss, have been found there.

" Doris still gets the Swiss Ski Year Book, which is always full of photographs and names of people one knew, which makes one rather sad because one somehow still expects to see one or two English names appearing. I can't help feeling in a complacent sort of way that we added to the fun of ski-racing. I still believe an Englishman is capable of getting somewhere at the top of a big ski-race using the good old method of taking a five-to-one chance holding a really fast line, or falling and finishing half-way down the list.

" I used to get great amusement baiting the Schwarzenbachs on the subject as they were always content to go for a mediocre place and get it, but I can't believe they got a quarter as much fun out of it.

" You probably heard that my brother was reported missing during an operational flight coming back from France, and nothing has been heard of him since, or ever will be I am afraid. We never had much hope from the start so haven't had much anxiety wondering whether he was safe or not. It was a very sad blow to me and my family even though we had expected it to happen some time or other.

"He was, I'm told, an outstandingly good pilot and loved it and had an extremely happy life from start to finish. He is a loss to English ski-ing if it exists after the war, as he had the makings of a really first-class performer as a racer, and combined with that a really genuine love of the high mountains and the people and country of Switzerland, which is refreshingly rare these days of funiculars and jazz bands. In fact, in his whole life he combined a love of speed and excitement with a delight for pottering about on a river bank fishing or watching birds. . . .

"On balance I suppose war is always bad, but in many ways I believe it has saved this country, which was, I believe, in great danger of becoming as rotten as France, with little initiative and no thought beyond a maximum of comfort, security and synthetic amusement. Perhaps that is the ideal towards which civilisation is working, but I can't believe it is right.

"You have only to compare the mountain people, whose life is never easy or safe, with the townsman and there can be no doubt which is the more worth preserving."

CHAPTER XIII

Racing for Fun

SOME day in the far distant future, skiers interested in the origins of the sport may consult the earlier numbers of the British Ski Year Book, if these have not long since disintegrated into dust. It is even possible that historians of more important matters than ski-ing may search our records for slight clues to the social history of this age. Sport reflects politics. I learned far more about Europe at International Championships and Congresses than from the writings of professional prophets.

As a chronicler of the leading downhill ski races, I tried not only to provide contemporary readers with a technical survey, but also to record those details which the sports writers in past ages so seldom reported. Thus, to quote one example, we know that all Olympic judges came from Elis, and we know exactly what would happen in the modern world if all the judges at an Olympic skating competition, were recruited locally, but we do not know what happened when a competitor from Elis won on a foul, since this is the sort of detail for which you may search the Olympic records in vain. Again, we know that Phaylus jumped so far that he landed beyond the pit and broke his leg, but we do not know what his mother and friends said about the organising committee. One day scientists may tap the ether waves of the past, and enable us to listen in to the comments of a Greek crowd watching the Olympic Games. "Jumped 22 feet, and broke his leg. . . . No sand beyond the 20-foot mark . . . that's what will happen if these lousy Eleans have a monopoly of organising the games. . . . They say Alcibiades should have been disqualified for fouling. . . ."

The modern Olympics have nothing but the name in common with the classic Olympics, and the Arlberg-Kandahars of the world which will emerge from this war will be very different from the A.-K's in the golden age of downhill ski-racing. Let me then try, before it be too late, to recapture some faint lingering flavour of the days that are gone.

The archetype of International meetings, decided on the combined result of a downhill and slalom race, is the Anglo-Swiss University Meeting, first of its kind. Walter Amstutz, a brilliant mountaineer and skier, was brought up at Mürren, and had the wit to see that these new-fangled British races were not completely daft. He enjoyed slalom racing, and in his undergraduate days at Berne helped to found the S.A.S. (Schweizerische Akademische Ski Club) the principal objectives of which were to promote downhill ski-racing and to organise an annual match against the British University Ski Club. Walter had the satisfaction not only of winning as an individual but also of leading his team to victory in the first Anglo-Swiss. This result was reversed in the following year thanks in the main to Leonard Dobbs who won the downhill race, and Christopher Mackintosh who won the combined and the slalom.

The Anglo-Swiss was by far the pleasantest of the classic ski meetings. It was important enough to provoke keen rivalry and not important enough to attract the attention of people who exploit sport as a criterion of national prestige. It was unspoiled by all that tiresome pomp and parade, which is such a tedious feature of Olympic Games, and which was beginning to spoil the FIS Meetings. And it ended not with a formal banquet but with an uproarious party. The party following the first meeting will live in the memory of all who were present. Of all good parties that I have known, this was outstandingly the best. I recall it with quite peculiar gratitude because I am indebted to the events of that evening for deliverance from a device imposed upon me by an over-cautious surgeon. He had warned me that all sorts of dreadful things would happen to me if I did not wear a vast steel splint, neatly designed to take my weight off my feet and transfer it to my tail. In the course of the evening an argument developed between Tony Knebworth and Christopher Mackintosh on the subject of the old Scottish sport of tossing the caber. No caber being available to settle the point in dispute I courteously offered my steel contraption, which Christopher tossed with great skill through a plate glass window. After a night in the snow it did not seem to fit as accurately as it should, and I soon discarded it. None of the dreadful things predicted by the surgeon has happened, and though I often ski on my tail, I no longer walk on it.

The Anglo-Swiss was one of the few sporting events which improved international relations. It revolutionised the relations between the British and the Swiss. In the old days the British had met the Swiss as guides or as ski-teachers or as genial and popular hotel proprietors but they had seldom met them on terms of equality. We were popular as clients in hotels and as employers of guides, but our habit of regarding Switzerland as nothing more than the "Playground of Europe" was resented by the Swiss.

The Anglo-Swiss broke down the barriers and brought young British and Swiss students into close and cordial relations. The Swiss adored Mackintosh and Tony Knebworth, and Walter Amstutz and Werner Salvisberg and many other Swiss were extremely popular with the British. The British superiority complex could not long survive in an atmosphere of frequent defeat, for though there was a moment when we were actually leading in the series, the Swiss soon re-established their lead and won more matches than we did.

Our first allies in our campaign for downhill racing were the Swiss students; our second the Arlberg club. In 1928 I paid my first visit to St. Anton, and set a slalom for schoolboys on the nursery slopes, the first slalom to be set in the Arlberg. Hannes Schneider, the King of St. Anton and the founder of the Arlberg school, was the most famous skier of the day, and I knew that his support of the slalom would be invaluable. It was a foregone conclusion that downhill racing would be recognised sooner or later, but the Norwegians were bitterly opposed to the slalom, which they despised as a nursery-slope competition suitable only for ladies.

Schneider gladly accepted my suggestion that the Kandahar should organise in the Arlberg a Meeting to be known as the Arlberg-Kandahar, and should present a cup to be decided on the combined result of a downhill and slalom race.

The first meeting in 1928 was a sensational success, a clear demonstration of the popularity of the slalom. The A-K assumed, from the first, the character of an unofficial World Championship meeting, and continued to be regarded as the blue ribbon of downhill racing, long after the FIS had instituted an official World Championship.

Hannes and I were more concerned to maintain the traditional *Stimmung* of the A-K than the quality of the entry, for the A-K owed its popularity to its unique atmosphere. Otto and Toni and Bill and Willy raced each other for the fun of racing rather than to demonstrate the virtues of a particular nation, club or political system. A famous manufacturer of whiskey once offered us a large and expensive trophy to be awarded on the result of a team race to be held in conjunction with the A-K. We declined the trophy, for team racing would have ruined the event. An individual competitor in the

A-K who races badly lets down nobody but himself and can enjoy the traditional party following the A-K without remorse, but a skier who has let down a national team may suffer pangs of remorse for weeks. Hannes was a Paladin of ski-ing. He was a man of outstanding integrity of character, a great Austrian patriot, a devout Catholic and, as such, marked out for destruction by the Nazis. But in those days nobody foresaw the day when Hannes would be thrown into prison, to be replaced at the head of the school which he made world-famous by one of Hitler's nominees.

The A-K had two great traditions, genial and uncantankerous rivalry and perfect weather. Bad weather was normal at the FIS Meeting (The World Championship) but unknown at the A-K. FIS, we said, stands for *Fahrt in Sturm*, A-K for *Auf-klärung*. Our rule of faith was severely tested in 1937 in what was destined to be the last Arlberg-Kandahar. On the Sunday of the race I awoke to find snow falling. It was still snowing a few minutes before the race was due to start. " The A-K luck has broken at last," said Jimmy Riddell. " I'm not so sure," said I. A sudden explosion, the signal for the start, echoed among the hills. As the sound died away, the clouds were torn aside, and the sun burst through. The breach widened and the mists vanished. " You've worked a miracle," said Jimmy. Never had the A-K opened more dramatically. This sudden *Auf-klärung* was symbolic. It was as if the fates had granted us a respite, a few hours of traditional Kandahar sunshine before the storm broke, not only over Mürren but also over Europe.

I did not see Hannes again until the FIS Meeting at Engelberg in 1938. The FIS tradition of bad weather and evil snow conditions had been violated, for the snow was excellent and the sky cloudless. " If the FIS is fine," said Hannes, " we shall probably have storms during the A-K." He little knew how right he was. A few days before the advertised date of the Arlberg-Kandahar the Germans marched into Austria and threw Schneider into a concentration camp. I called a meeting of the Kandahar members present at St. Anton and we unanimously resolved to cancel the race. I need not recapitulate in detail the events that followed, for I have told the story in *Come What May*. Hannes was released, thanks to the intervention of powerful people, and was allowed to leave for the U.S.A., where he is now in charge of the ski school at North Conway.

The Kandahar decided to change the name of the race to "Alpine-Kandahar," and to hold it alternately at Mürren and Chamonix. I explained our attitude in the next issue of the British Ski Year Book, and the publicity given to the Nazi treatment of Schneider was a factor in the sharp decline of British tourist traffic to the Arlberg in the following winter. The Nazis were perturbed for many reasons. They regretted the decrease in the flow of British sterling into Austria, which helped to finance their purchase of raw materials for war. In spite of their triumphs in the Olympic Games, they retained their reverence for Britain as the arbiter of sporting codes, and were deeply mortified by the decision of a British club that they were not the sort of people with whom English sportsmen cared to associate. The Nazis, like all upstarts, are snobs.

The Nazis believed that if they could persuade the Kandahar to reverse its decision, the flow of British pounds into Austria would be accelerated, and the stigma on their reputation in the world of ski-ing would be removed. Highly-placed Nazis accordingly wrote me some very winning letters in the course of the summer, and Salcher, the new head of the Arlberg Ski School, asked me if I would meet him before or after the World Championship in Poland. I replied that I was travelling to Vienna on such and such a day and that if he cared to board the train at St. Anton, he could travel with me to Innsbruck.

Salcher was wearing the most famous of all ski-ing badges, the A-K badge awarded to those who finish first, second or third in the A-K.

He began by asking me whether I really intended to destroy the greatest of all downhill races. He was disappointed. He had always thought of me as a great sportsman who never mixed politics and sport. "Yes," I said, "they tried that line on me last year at St. Anton, and I asked them whether Schneider was in prison because he skied badly. We are to be bound by our code, which you Nazis hold yourselves free to break. You want to have your cake and eat ours."

I explained to Salcher that I was snobbish enough to dislike mixing with people who received their orders from a Government who organised pogroms and murder. One had to draw the line somewhere, even in these democratic days. And I drew the line at association in sport with the representatives of the Nazis.

The restaurant car in which we met was crowded, and I was

careful to say what I had to say as slowly and as loudly as possible. I spoke in German :

" I brought the A-K to St. Anton, because we loved the old atmosphere. You see, *we* still ski for fun, to prove that one pair of legs is better than another, not that one kind of nose is better than another. We liked the old St. Anton and that is why we came there. We detest the new St. Anton and so we stay away." I was gratified to observe that the travellers at neighbouring tables were listening to me with that careful attention which is so flattering to a public speaker. " Finally, I regard war as inevitable, if not this year, next year. And I don't propose to encourage the flow of British sterling into Austria to be returned in the form of German bombs."

" Ah," said Salcher, " you should take a lesson from Mr. Chamberlain. He works for peace."

When he left at Innsbruck I looked out of the window, and waved a cheerful farewell to his disconsolate figure.

" Tell them," I said, " that I shall not return to St. Anton with Mr. Chamberlain's umbrella even if it rains."

I am told by those who should know that I was lucky not to be arrested. At the time it did not occur to me that I was taking the slightest risk, for I did not think that they would arrest a prominent member of the FIS Committee on his way to the world championship in Poland. Whether my confidence in my immunity was well based I cannot tell, but I am glad that I said what I said. Few Englishmen, in the months following Munich, had the chance to hit the Nazis where it hurt them to be hit, and I recall with pleasure the fact that I exploited my unusual opportunities to the full. On my return to Mürren I wrote Herr Salcher a letter, in which among other things I said :

" You tell me that you are anxious that ski-ing at St. Anton should not be political. But words cannot alter facts. As your own Goethe has said,

> . . . Eben wo Begriffe fehlen
> Da stellt ein Wort zur rechten Zeit sich ein.

The old atmosphere of the A-K, unpolitical and light-hearted, can be preserved if the race alternates between Switzerland and France. All that would remain would be the name, if we held it at St. Anton. The Arlberg-Kandahar, like the great German Universities and the

Salzburg festival, would join the melancholy list of lifeless ghosts,

> Sie waren lang gestorben,
> Und wussten es selber kaum.

I hope I may still quote without offence the greatest of German lyric poets, the Jew Heinrich Heine. . . .

"You were good enough to pay me compliments as the creator of the world's greatest downhill race and you reproached me for imperilling its future. But even if the A-K were to come to an end, I should not for one moment regret the decision of our Club. All evil, a great thinker once remarked, comes from mistaking means for ends. Sport is not an end in itself but a means to an end, and that end is the promotion of friendship, tolerance and that spirit which your Christian forbears called chivalry, and which the Greeks called *aidos*. 'Aidos,' writes Mr. Gardner, 'is the direct opposite of *hubris*. It is the feeling of respect for what is due to the gods, to one's fellow men, to oneself, a feeling that begets a like feeling towards oneself in others. It is the spirit of reverence, of modesty, of courtesy. Above all, it is the sense of honour, and as such inspires the athlete and the soldier, and distinguishes them from the bully and the oppressor.'

"It is because ski-ing in Germany is controlled by a Government which encourages the bully and the oppressor, a Government which has no *aidos*, and far too much *hubris*, that I, for one, would have only agreed to return to St. Anton under present conditions to help an old friend, Hannes Schneider.

"One's decision in such matters is determined by one's scale of values. I do not attach any particular importance to the fact that I founded a successful race. If that race were to disappear I should feel less proud to have created it than to have sacrificed it on the altar of ideals which belong to the heritage of European civilisation. You are, in effect, inviting me to sacrifice my principles to my vanity, and I can only reply in the words of one who led an earlier German revolution, 'Hier stehe ich und kann nicht anders.' . . .

"Hannes is in exile, Niemöller in prison, and Streicher at liberty. Why then should we return to St. Anton? But nothing lasts for ever, not even *Der Stürmer*, and one day I shall come back to the country I love, and Hannes and I will once again set an A-K slalom in St. Anton. Till then,

"Au revoir,

"ARNOLD LUNN."

The success of the Arlberg-Kandahar expedited the recognition of downhill racing by the *Féderation Internationale de Ski*, popularly known as the FIS.

I did not realise that the official imprimatur which I was so anxious to secure would transform downhill racing from a friendly sport into a grim criterion of national prestige, but I have no regrets. It is the struggle that matters, not the prize, and whatever may have been the ultimate consequences of our campaign, the campaign itself was not only great fun but instructive. My experiences as the protagonist of downhill racing reinforced my conviction that rational argument is not to be despised, but that reason never triumphs unless reinforced by less reputable allies. Had not the Alpine skiers been directly interested in supporting our proposals, the opposition of those who stood to lose by the recognition of downhill racing would have been difficult to overcome.

In the days before downhill racing was recognised by the FIS, the only official criterion of ski-ing skill was provided by competitions in which the Scandinavian nations had a monopoly of success, langlauf (cross-country) and jumping. It was not surprising that the Norwegians should have been reluctant to concede equal status to the new-fangled races in which the Alpine skiers specialised. That a long-distance race in the course of which some two minutes out of sixty are spent in sliding downhill is an inadequate test of downhill ski-ing is self-evident, but self-interest is often more potent than self-evident truth, and it was some years before we succeeded in establishing the fact that the best way to test downhill racing is to race downhill.

The downhill sections of classic courses such as Holmenkollen are extremely easy judged by Alpine standards. Moreover the langlauf is a track race, and the technique of sliding down a beaten track is very different from the technique of continuous turning on steep slopes in very deep snow.

The skiers whom I saw on my first visit to Norway in 1909, could run away from any Alpine skier so long as they were ski-ing on the level or uphill, but as downhill skiers they were not impressive. They were magnificent ski-hikers, covering immense distances in the day ; but they did not seek out, as Alpine skiers sought out, steep ground. On the contrary, they evaded the kind of terrain which is the special delight of the Alpine runner. I remember Count C. G. D. Hamilton, of Sweden, on my return to Finse in

1930, drawing my attention to the ski tracks on the surrounding slopes. "Observe," he said, "the steep slopes are untouched. There are no tracks of stunt straight runs or of continuous downhill turning. The tracks run straight down the gradual slopes and straight *across* the steep slopes."

The standard of downhill running has, of course, been completely revolutionised in Norway since 1930, but I am writing of a period before the influence of Alpine ski-ing had spread to the north.

A good jumper possesses all the qualities necessary for success in downhill racing, as Sigmund and Birger Ruud subsequently proved. But before downhill racing had been introduced into Norway, crack Norwegian skiers were always bewildered, when they first attempted to ski on steep Alpine slopes, particularly where the conditions called for continuous turning in deep snow. It was our unkind habit at Mürren to take Norwegian visitors for a run through a steep wood which served to convince them that even those who were "born on ski" had something to learn from Alpine skiers.

It was not surprising that Norwegians should resent the efforts of the English to introduce radical changes in a sport which they had practised thousands of years; and it is to their credit that Norwegians who visited the Alps were ready enough to admit that Alpine skiers had a contribution to make to the sport. Captain Christian Krefting, for instance, who visited Mürren in 1930, contributed to *Aftenposten*, of Oslo, a generous tribute to British skiers. In 1911 Captain Krefting had won the Norwegain Ski Championship open to cadets of the Military Academy, and he was a first-class skier judged by Norwegian standards. "It was an alluring thought," he wrote, "to come to Switzerland as a Norwegian and show these newcomers to our sport what ski-ing really was. . . . We laugh at the English ski-ing, and say that the English only take trains uphill and come down, that they spend the whole day climbing up and coming down the nursery slopes behind the hotels, and practise a lot of peculiar twists and turns, and we think they understand nothing at all of what ski-ing really is. This was how I also looked at things when I arrived out there in blissful ignorance." He then points out that the English use their nursery slopes for mastering the telemark, christiania, etc., "otherwise they have to lie down every moment, and to lie down is a thing that every skier tries to avoid." "The name 'downhill racing,' " he continued, " gives an average Norwegian a very faulty conception of what happens. This is natural as we conceive hills as hills and not as practically vertical drops. I stood on the different points where the races started and felt quite giddy looking down. To get down in our usual Norwegian way was quite out of the question—that would be tempting Providence too much."

He describes the Roberts of Kandahar Race, and adds :—" This race was an imposing sight—to watch these plucky young Englishmen coming down these steep hills with an incredible speed . . . it kindled in me an ambition to be able to master these hills as well as these men did. The polite smile was changed to one, first of surprise and then of admiration. I had long ago given up the idea of being able to impress by my Norwegian knowledge of ski-ing."

I predicted even in those days that the Norwegians would produce champion downhill racers once they had grasped the fact that their old supremacy in ski-ing could not be maintained by concentrating on " classic competitions." And I always knew that a good performer in the " classic competitions " would soon adjust himself to Alpine ground. Tor Klaveness, for instance, on his first visit to the Alps in 1920, not only led the Oxford team to victory against Cambridge, but also won the Roberts of Kandahar Race. My prophecy of Norwegian success was fulfilled in 1936 when Birger Ruud won the Olympic downhill race, and another Norwegian, Laila Schou-Nilsen, the women's race.

In 1928 the FIS held its Congress at St. Moritz during the winter Olympic Games. At this Congress I formally proposed that the FIS should adopt the British rules for downhill and slalom racing.

My fellow delegate, Alec Keiller, was for years the inspiring leader of British langlaufers and ski-jumpers. His task was far more difficult than mine for it was by no means easy to entice young Englishmen on to the jumping-hill or on to langlauf courses, once " the downhill only " fashion swept the Alps. None the less the Oxford and Cambridge undergraduates we continued to coach in the technique of the " classic competition " achieved some remarkable successes at international University Ski Meetings.

Alec Keiller is one of the most versatile men I have ever known. He has achieved fame as an archæologist ; he is a great authority on witchcraft and criminology and also a great linguist.

Alec supported my proposals with his head and the Norwegian opposition with his heart. He had never skied in Norway, and was both surprised and irritated by a public statement of mine to the effect that the Norwegians did not share our prejudice against braking with the stick. But he was shaken when he and I watched the great "ski-king," Gröttumsbraaten, of Norway, braking with his stick down short slopes which every Swiss and Austrian competitor ran straight in a free stickless style. But the final blow came in the course of a sub-committee meeting appointed by the Congress to discuss our proposals. "I object," said the Norwegian delegate, "to the British rule forbidding 'braking with the stick.'" "You've won," groaned Alec, and buried his head in his hands.

The Congress agreed that the British rule should be provisionally adopted for experimental purpose, and that the question of official recognition should come up for review at the next Congress to be held in Oslo in 1930.

In 1929 the Polish Ski Association was entrusted with the organisation of the FIS meeting for the year, a meeting which was, in effect, the World Ski Championship, long before it was officially recognised as such. The FIS meeting of 1929 was historic, as the first FIS meeting at which a downhill race was included in the programme. Downhill racing was still on trial, and this event was regarded as experimental and unofficial.

No country excepting Great Britain and Poland selected downhill racers as such for this event. The Swiss, for instance, entered their langlaufers and jumpers who happened to be present at the meeting. There were sixty competitors in all.

Bill Bracken, the British Captain, just missed victory by three seconds, finishing second to Czech, of Poland. All the British team finished in the first half including Harold Mitchell, who put up a particularly fine performance, for he broke his ski a long way above the finish, and ran down to the finish, more than a thousand feet, on one ski. G. Nixon was 6th, W. J. Riddell 8th, F. P. Maitland 10th, E. W. A. Richardson 12th, C. Pitman 15th, and H. Mitchell 24th.

The sensation of the meeting was the magnificent performance of the two British ladies, Miss Elliott (14th) and Miss Sale-Barker (15th). They beat forty-five men. Their courage excited universal admiration. They shot down one particularly villainous glade strewn with stumps, over ice-crust snow. A few days later, when they went into a restaurant at Warsaw, all those present stood up and applauded.

In 1930 I attended the Congress at Oslo. The FIS meeting at Oslo was arranged to coincide with the most famous of all Ski meetings, Holmenkollen. Holmenkollen is unique. We have nothing quite like it in England. We have national sports, but we have no sport which can claim to be *the* national sport of England, as ski-ing is the national sport of Norway. Oslo is the ski-ing capital of the world, and to the thousands who pour out of Oslo to watch the jumping on Holmenkollen, Holmenkollen Day is the greatest day in the year.

To find the parallel to Holmenkollen you must go back to the Olympic Games at the height of their glory. Pindar somewhere remarks that a man who spent his time trying to discover a contest more glorious than the Olympic Games would be equally ready to waste his leisure searching for a star that shone more brightly than the sun. A true Norwegian would say much the same about Holmenkollen.

I looked at that great crowd and my spirits sank. I felt like a pinchbeck Luther up against something more formidable than Papal Bulls. And I knew that if I was a Norwegian I should feel nothing but contempt for this pert heretic from a country where snow falls in fitful showers on to muddy roads, a country which had never yet been represented in the lists of Holmenkollen. It was bad enough at St. Moritz where I had first broached the reform of the racing rules. No Englishman was competing in the Olympic Games at St. Moritz, a fact of which I had more than once been reminded. And the depression I then felt returned tenfold as I watched Norseman after Norseman leap from the Schanze, confident and erect, and dive in easy effortless untroubled flight through the wind down to the snow slopes far below.

Yes, if I had been a Norwegian I should have felt much as that fine old Tory Plutarch felt when his most sacred convictions were challenged by a young Modernist anxious to reinterpret the hallowed mythology of the old religion. "For our ancient and ancestral faith should suffice. It is the foundation of all piety, and if its established and traditional maxims be disturbed, if your sophistry invades every altar, nothing will be left immune from criticism." ἀρκεῖ γὰρ ἡ πάτριος καὶ παλαιὰ πίστις should be inscribed on the banner that waves over Holmenkollen.

The recognition of downhill racing was inevitable ; but the fate of slalom was in doubt until the end. Colonel Holmquist, who presided over the Congress, a happy blend of firmness and tact, is a Swede, and as such he was not biased in favour of the classic competitions. But he was determined to prevent a schism in the FIS between the Scandinavian and the Alpine skiers. Captain, now Colonel, N. R. Oestgaard is a Norwegian. He was and is an Adjutant of the Crown Prince. When we first met at St. Moritz he seemed to me reserved and not cordial. He clearly resented the impudence of the Englishman who believed that he could add something of value to Norway's traditional sport.

" What would you say ? " he remarked, " if I were to suggest altering your cricket rules ? " " I should be delighted," I replied, " for if you succeeded we might have fewer draws."

A faint ghost of a smile flitted across Captain Oestgaard's dignified features. I did not then suspect his strong sense of humour which I discovered in later years. But I learnt afterwards that he quoted my reply to Walter Amstutz.

Oestgaard is a man of great intellectual integrity, and one of the few men whom I have met who is open to conviction even where his national pride is engaged. At this Congress, for instance, he resolved to vote for the British proposals though his own Association was far from convinced.

Captain L. G. D. Hamilton, a Swede, and the honorary secretary of the FIS, was the first whole-hearted missionary of our cause in the North. He had the enterprise to visit Mürren shortly after the Congress. " Mürren," he wrote, " interested me more than any aspect of ski-ing I have seen in recent years. The incredible skill I admired at Mürren awakened a great interest in downhill racing."

The Swedes, indeed, were the first of the Northern nations to develop downhill racing, and to admit that they had something to learn from Alpine runners. My own book, *The Complete Ski-runner*, was translated into Swedish, a signal compliment of which I am proud.

Of the central European nations the Swiss and the Austrians supported our proposals, as did also my own old friend, Aldo Bonacossa.

When our proposals came before the Congress, a delegate rose in his place and began to criticise slalom rules in some detail. I dreaded a long discussion on these rules, the result of which might have postponed the whole matter to the next Congress. As he spoke I fiddled nervously with the Union Jack in front of me. The flags of the various nations were placed before the seats of the delegates. Suddenly the Union Jack tumbled down. *Absit omen*, I murmured.

The delegate finished, and the President gave a glance in my direction. I was determined not to speak unless it was absolutely essential so to do. The President, as I hoped, turned to the delegate and said : " Perhaps you will put your views before a special downhill racing committee." The President then looked down the table and asked whether anybody else wished to speak. It was a tense moment. Nobody stirred. Up went his Chairman's hammer, and still he hesitated.

" Angenommen," said the President. Down went his hammer and up went the Union Jack.

I had worked hard for that " Angenommen ! "

CHAPTER XIV

FIS Panorama

THE FIS will be revived after the war. But no world championships of the future will mean to the racers of the future what the first FIS meetings meant in the Eocene age of downhill racing to pioneers of the sport. And it is with the atmosphere rather than with details of times and courses that I shall write in this chapter.

The first of the FIS downhill ski-racing meetings, which were always in effect, and which were later recognised officially as World Championships, opened at Mürren on February 19th, 1931.

The Norwegian sceptics were still unconvinced that these new races served any purpose other than to provide Englishmen who lacked the necessary training to compete in langlauf races with a less exacting test of virile qualities. Continental skiers assumed that we had demanded the recognition of downhill racing because we were convinced that we had some hope of winning world championships in this branch of the sport.

I was therefore anxious not only that the organisation of the races should be beyond reproach, but also that the British team should put up a good performance. I was very grateful for the co-operation of Col. E. T. R. Long, an old rowing blue, who undertook the somewhat trying task of inducing holiday skiers to take their training seriously.

This meeting was ruined by appalling weather conditions without precedent, according to official reports, in the experience of that generation. At the St. Bernard Hospice the snow reached the record height of 30 feet. Railway communications were interrupted throughout Switzerland. Zermatt and Andermatt were completely cut off, and the Press continued to report fatal avalanche accidents.

The only championship event to be completed was the Ladies' Slalom, which was held on February 19th. The downhill race was divided into two parts—the aggregate time for both parts counted towards the result—but only the first part could be completed. Many of the competitors had had to leave before the Men's Slalom could be held, which was therefore not reckoned as an official part of the championship.

A race down the famous " Inferno " course had been included as an unofficial extra, and we succeeded in racing over the final section of the course, one of the steepest racing courses in Switzerland. But, unfortunately, this race from Grütsch to Lauterbrunnen did not form part of the official championship programme. The race was won by Guzi Lantschner, of Austria, who beat Christopher Mackintosh by just over two seconds. Both raced magnificently.

My son, Peter, who had won the Roberts of Kandahar earlier in the winter, had been included in the British team. He was sixteen years of age, and would not have been eligible for a FIS Langlauf race. The Swedish President and Norwegian Vice-President of the FIS argued that the eighteen-year age limit should also apply to downhill racing. Some years later a Norwegian girl, aged sixteen, won the Ladies' Downhill Race at the Olympic Games ; and I had the pleasure of congratulating Captain Oestgaard on his failure to impose an age limit which would have deprived Norway of a sensational victory at the 1936 Olympic.

The British Ladies' Team fulfilled all expectations. Miss Esmé Mackinnon won the Ladies' Slalom, the uncompleted straight race, and the unofficial race from Grütsch to Lauterbrunnen. In the Slalom Miss Kessler was 3rd, Miss Gossage 4th, Miss Crewdson 5th.

In the Downhill Race we again took four out of the first five places—Miss Mackinnon and Miss Carroll finished first and second respectively, Miss Kessler 4th, and Miss Gossage 5th.

The men were less successful. The Downhill Race was held in a blinding snowstorm. Mackintosh, Bracken, Waghorn, and Riddell failed to cope with the driving snow and finished low down. Tony Knebworth kept his head and finished 7th.

My wife and I were standing with Captain Oestgaard and Count Hamilton at the top of " Shrub Slope," and were naturally anxious lest Peter should justify their criticism of his inclusion in the team. The competitor who had drawn the number just before Peter sailed past. We looked at our watches. The seconds passed. And then suddenly we saw a small figure blinking through the storm, holding steadily to the line which he had planned. He finished 13th out of 26 competitors.

Walter Prager won the race, and the Swiss took the first four places. The Swiss took the first three places in this order : Walter Prager, Fritz Steuri, and Ernst Feuz.

The unofficial race from Grütsch to Lauterbrunnen produced a controversy perhaps without precedent in the history of ski-ing.

Inge Lantschner from Austria arrived at Mürren with a great reputation and was expected to win the Championship. She was bitterly disappointed by her failure to beat Esmé Mackinnon in the Slalom and in Downhill Race, and was determined to have her revenge in the unofficial race over the lower section of the Inferno course. She raced well, but Esmé Mackinnon raced better.

The finishing posts had been placed just outside Lauterbrunnen Station ; and as Miss Mackinnon appeared a funeral procession emerged from the station and marched slowly in front of the finishing posts. A British spectator gave an agonised cry of "Bahnfrei," *i.e.*, "Clear the course." Now a downhill racer can charge gaily through spectators, and scatter casual onlookers from crowned heads to the village idiot, but there are some things, such as funeral processions, to which even a downhill racer must concede right of way.

Esmé Mackinnon's time was taken by the timekeeper at the point at which she stopped, and from that point to the finishing post after the funeral procession had passed, and the aggregate time was returned as official in accordance with the decision of the Italian referee, and there, of course, the matter should have ended ; and, perhaps, would have ended had not Inge belonged to a famous ski family, most of the members of which had become ardent supporters of the Nazi cause, which was to lead in the fullness of time to the enslavement of their native country. To the Nazi all that matters is victory by fair means or foul. Inge was determined to win if possible by ski-ing faster than Miss Mackinnon ; but if she could not win on her merits she was quite prepared to accept the co-operation of a funeral procession.

The Austrian representative on the Race Committee was instructed to demand that the minute and a half which the funeral procession had taken to pass between Miss Mackinnon and the finishing posts should be added to Miss Mackinnon's time. The Race Committee, on which every competing nation was represented, rejected with contempt this unsporting demand ; but the Lantschner family continued to complain for years after the event that I had cheated their sister out of victory.

The World Championship was held at Cortina in 1932, at Innsbruck in 1933, and at St. Moritz in 1934, where it was admirably organised by Walter Amstutz.

Meanwhile the odds against the British team were rising steadily. Every Alpine valley was potentially capable of producing far more first-class racers than we could hope to find among that small minority of Englishmen who were in a position to give the necessary time to developing into first-class racers. Yet in 1934 C. S. Hudson finished 5th in the Slalom ; and in the combined result there were two Englishmen in the first ten—Bill Clyde 7th, and Peter Lunn 8th, and the British were the third team in a championship for which thirteen nations entered competitors.

Meanwhile Hitler had assumed power and the Nazi ideology was beginning to infect international sport. Baron Le Fort, who had raced for Germany in the first FIS meeting, had now been appointed the Nazi ski leader. He spoke with a new reassurance at committee meetings. " The best days of the FIS are over," a Swiss colleague of mine remarked. " There is a military touch about the German competitors. They are no longer skiers, but ski soldiers."

Le Fort was an entertaining adventurer. He had his career to make, but he himself was in no way a dupe of the Nazi racket. He had Latin blood in his veins, and the Latin is temperamentally a sceptic.

I am sure Baron Le Fort was not personally responsible for the instructions issued to the German team competing in the 1935 World Championship at Mürren. They were forbidden to accept individual hospitality. The team had to be invited as a whole or not at all. International sport, so sentimentalists assure us, helps to build up international friendship. But the Nazis seem to have believed either that such friendship was undesirable, or, alternately, that friendship could be promoted by isolating their teams from other competitors.

It was at this same 1935 FIS that a Nazi broadcast a running commentary on the Slalom from the course. The Slalom was run in a storm, and the Nazi gave a moving description of the gusts with which Christel Kranz, of Germany, had to contend, but when Fräülein Ruegg, of Switzerland, who won the Slalom, was battling against a veritable blizzard, no hint of difficulties emerged in his lack-lustre remarks on a brilliant performance. He contented himself with consoling the Germans for the defeat of their champion by an offensive comment on Fräulein Rüegg's personal appearance. The Nazi cad had arrived.

The 1935 FIS was, however, comparatively uninfected by the Nazi microbe. It was the last FIS in the great tradition, as indeed, I suspected at the time, for I made a special effort in the British Ski Year Book to recapture the atmosphere of the meeting and to preserve for such of our ski-ing posterity as are interested, an intimate and synthetic study, from many angles, of a great athletic event as characteristic in its way of the Europe which we shall never see again, as the Olympic Games of the glory that was Greece.

In retrospect the FIS divides itself into three distinct phases.

The first period began when all those who aspired to a place in the British team arrived at Mürren, or whatever might be the venue selected for training.

A racer of the FIS class has to take severe punishment during the training period. Racing speeds often exceed sixty miles an hour, on ground which is frequently bumpy. The racer must master the art of falling as softly as possible at express speeds, for falls are frequent. Fatal accidents are extremely rare. No member of the Kandahar was killed racing or practising for a race, but it was only a minority of those who raced year after year who escaped unscathed. I reckoned to lose about one-third of my team during the training period, and in the 1935 FIS half my available racers, four out of eight, injured themselves before the FIS, one failed to finish in the Downhill Race, and another member of the team limped home with a sprained ankle, so that only 25 per cent. of the team and reserves had escaped injury by the time the FIS was completed. Trial races for the selection of the team provided an additional strain on nerves and temper. Young racers are like temperamental thoroughbreds, and every allowance had to be made for a temptation to kick. Fortunately the British were more light-hearted in their attitude to the FIS than most of our rivals, and were comparatively immune from " FIS fever." We still skied for fun. It is quite possible to ski for fun, and yet to take ski-ing seriously, to be serious about technique and training, but light-hearted about results. Some such philosophy is the secret of pleasurable sport, and it was because British skiers remained to the end ski-ing hedonists and never degenerated into ski-ing puritans that every effort was made by continental clubs to secure a British entry for all the leading international events.

The second phase of the FIS opened about ten days before the opening race. Slowly the championship centre began to fill up.

During the last days before the FIS the atmosphere is often pregnant with rumours. Will racers be allowed to *schuss* such and such a slope, or will safety controls be inserted to insure against too great speeds and broken bones? The course is to be changed, say some. More controls are to be added, say others.

The most sensational running is usually seen not during the race itself but during the final practice runs. A racer, while practising, can pause and rest before attempting some spectacular straight run, and the stunt which may come off on a practice run will often fail when mind and body are exhausted by a gruelling race.

During the practice days you may see groups of competitors clustering together on key points of the course, studying the tactics of their competitors, and watching with gloom their more brilliant runs.

I shall never forget those last few days before the '31 FIS, when the sun still shone from the undimmed splendour of an Alpine sky. The teams were practising down the Schiltgrat. . . . Suddenly the murmur of voices drops, and the hiss of sharply divided snow warns us that yet another racer has hurled himself through the gap by Parson's Shoulder. Ah! Here he comes in a trailing cloud of diamond dust, where the snow intercepts the sun; and now watch him as he dives in a line of unrelenting straightness. I can still see the austere beauty of those parallel lines, straight and unswerving from "Broody Bump" to the outrun far below.

In '35 the skiers from the Alpine lands followed with anxious curiosity the practice runs of the great Norwegian, Sigmund Ruud. Anton Seelos, the Austrian, had every hope of winning the slalom. Ruud, a champion jumper, had no hope of the slalom, but might easily establish a winning lead in the straight race. We all remembered his sensational performance in the '31 Arlberg-Kandahar, when he had flashed down the upper slopes of the Schiltgrat in a succession of *schusses* varied by two fantastic leaps. Real ski-ing for Sigmund only began when he left the ground. Even the gambols of Willy Steuri, that strange blend of ski-ing genius and ski-ing clown, seemed sedate by comparison. No contrast could be greater than that between the classic perfection of Seelos' style and Ruud's exuberant baroque. Witness the following incident. I had placed the penultimate control on a road just below a steep and icy slope. A steep hairpin turn through the controls was necessary to carry the skier on to the right line for the final slope. Some competitors took the slope above the road too fast, and shot through the control too quickly to turn to the left, and lost many seconds regaining the proper line of descent. Others, more cautious, stemmed slowly down the steep slope, and approached the road at snail's pace. Ruud's solution was to exploit a small bump on the slope above the road, straighten out and jump. He landed thirty vertical feet below on the road itself, with the result that he all but came to a standstill and was able just to trickle through the control with his ski nicely pointed towards the finishing post. He had found the ideal solution, the maximum speed of approach to the road, and the maximum check to enable him to steer his ski through the narrow control. Study the expressions on the faces of competitors as their rivals practise a course. Their reaction to good ski-ing is anxiety, to brilliant ski-ing despair, but the racers who were waiting on the road while Ruud passed were startled by the sheer loveliness of this impromptu leap into round after round of spontaneous applause.

The course selected for the downhill race was an invention of Godi Michel's, an ingenious combination of two famous courses, Schilthorn and Schiltgrat. It started well above "Kandahar Gully" on the Schilthorn and joined the Schiltgrat course in "Martha's Meadow," finishing about a thousand feet below "Kandahar Finish," and about five hundred feet above Gimmelwald.

I am trying to describe the FIS from many angles, a synthetic narrative, if you will, and I therefore asked Peter to put down some of his impressions on paper. I quote from his report:

". . . I have never known competitors so enthusiastic about a course. The Swiss and Austrians and Germans with whom I spoke declared that it was the finest downhill racing course they had ever seen. Steep and exacting, and a magnificent test not only of straight running but also of control. The Norwegians alone dissented from this verdict. Ruud joined me just as I was starting up towards 'FIS Funnel.' The course was much too steep, he declared, and the Norwegians were not accustomed to steep open slopes. They would suffer from vertigo. What would we think if English jumpers at Holmenkollen were pushed over a hundred-metre jump? Ruud went on in this strain for some minutes, and I felt so sorry for him that, noticing that he had no skins, I offered to lend him a spare pair which I was carrying. I forgot for the moment that it is a point of honour with the Norwegians not to use skins. Indeed, skins and funiculars are always linked together in the minds of the true Norse as symbols of ski-ing degeneracy. Rund gave me a look which made me feel like the subject of a Bateman cartoon, 'The man who offered to lend skins to a Norwegian.' 'I've waxed appropriately,' he said, and snorted uphill. I felt very cheap as one stern Norwegian after another shot uphill on bare ski while I toiled after them on skins."

Ruud carried his protest to the Committee, and drew my special attention to the fact that the FIS Congress had passed a resolution urging that the dangers of straight racing should be reduced. I told him that I was a member of the Committee specially charged to carry these resolutions into effect, and I reminded him that the danger of a course depended not on its steepness but on the way in which the controls were set. I thought of those prehistoric days when the Norwegians were wont contemptuously to dismiss downhill races as suitable only for " women and untrained men." And I could not help being pleased that the course down which ladies from the plains of England and Holland were quite cheerfully practising should be condemned as too dangerous for Ruud. Many people who knew that Ruud had jumped his ninety metres, and who remembered his spectacular audacity in the Arlberg-Kandahar Race, were both amused and puzzled by his protest ; but there is nothing really inconsistent between enjoying ninety-metre jumps and disliking ski-ing on very steep open slopes. The Norwegian is accustomed to the friendly sight of trees, and he feels far happier poised in mid air after a giant jump than in contact with a steep slope where his eye can travel without a check to the valley some hundreds of feet far below.

The provisional control in FIS Funnel had been placed a little too high, and left free an alternative line which avoided the Funnel, and which rejoined the top of the FIS slalom slope *viâ* a steep cliff. The next day the Norwegians were seen stamping down the snow just above and just below this cliff with the clear intention of jumping it in the course of the race, a vertical drop of some thirty metres. Of all rumours which have helped to raise the temperature of FIS Meetings, none has ever achieved such a sensational success as the Great Norwegian Mystery Jump. The intense rivalry between the

Northerners, determined to regain their old predominance in ski-ing, and the Alpine runners no less determined to prove that they were the Gröttumsbraatens and Haugs of Central Europe, transformed the FIS from an affair of fourteen nations into a battle between the Scandinavian and the Alpine skiers. Some of the racers thought that Ruud was having a little joke with us, an elaborate leg pull, and others gloomily asserted that Ruud would jump over the Lauterbrunnen Cliff itself, if necessary, and get away with it. Some had no intention of trying to follow Ruud's line, and others swore that if Ruud jumped they would jump too. The latter were very gloomy, for a racer who jumped short would have been impaled on some ugly-looking posts dug into the ground just below the cliff.

Fortunately the preliminary notice had made it clear that the controls were provisional, and would be moved in accordance with a new theory of course-setting. I was therefore entitled to remove these controls on my own responsibility, but I decided that it was wiser to summon the Race Committee, and the Race Committee unanimously approved an alteration. A race is not a jumping competition. Moreover, on a jumping-hill a competitor who has been injured can be removed, but long before an injured racer had been removed from the bottom of Ruud's cliff, another racer might have landed on his prone body. I conveyed the unanimous decision of the Race Committee to Sigmund Ruud. He was very friendly, but a little disappointed. He agreed, however, that it would hardly be reasonable to remind us (on Monday) that the FIS wished the risks of racing to be reduced, and to complain (on Wednesday) because we took steps to prevent impromptu leaps over the cliffs. Ruud must, however, be congratulated on inventing a new cure for vertigo. Giddiness, it appears, is due solely to contact with the snow. If you feel the height, leave the ground.

Storm and blizzard had beaten us in 1931 and we were determined to carry through the 1935 FIS successfully. The competitors were competing against each other, the organisers against the weather.

Had it not been for the memories of our disappointment in 1931, I should certainly have postponed the Ladies' Race ; but the derisive screaming of the storm which greeted me when I emerged from the summit of the Allmendhubel Station decided me. Driving snow

Opposite: *BERNINA PASS.* *By kind permission of Albert Steiner.*

obscured the slopes where I had planted the control posts. But my faith was rewarded. The storm lifted in time for the race, which Christel Kranz won. Poor Jeanette Kessler, the British hope, after racing brilliantly, broke a leg just above the finish. Evie Pinching, fourth in the Downhill, and in Combined, put up the best performance for Britain.

On the morning of the last event, the Downhill race for men, a weak sun was shining from a sky dappled but not obscured by clouds. The glass registered 602, a new low record for Mürren. I could only hope that the blizzard which was tearing the snow in long streamers from the summit ridges, would not drop until the race was finished, for once the wind dropped everything would be obscured by a smother of blinding snow. I took up my position a little above the finish.

From time to time a window opened in the roof of scudding mist, and disclosed a fleeting glimpse of weak and watery blue. So long as the scurrying clouds did not relax their tempo, the storm would probably hold off, but my heart sank whenever I detected a suggestion of lag in their movements. I looked at my watch. 11.30 . . . only another hour to go. Would the weather hold out? The Downhill race was not the only race that was decided that day.

I have a bias in favour of races starting precisely at the advertised time, and I was never more anxious that our reputation for punctuality should be maintained than I was on this occasion. At 12.30 precisely Michel, who was at the start, telephoned down to Max Amstutz—" Glatthard, Switzerland, has started."

Voices dropped. . . . A faint echo of a *Heil*! from unseen spectators warns us that Glatthard is approaching. He passes. Then comes Allais of France, who skies superbly, but not quite well enough to beat the ultimate winner, Zingerle of Austria.

Rumours of disaster float down the course. Somebody had broken a leg. Peter? . . . No, not Peter, but an old ski-ing friend of Peter's, Nöbl of Austria, who, as I learnt later, in spite of having broken a leg, coached Peter down the funnel with encouragement and advice, an example of that true sportsmanship which even international sport cannot destroy.

12.50 p.m. . . . Peter is due to start in ten minutes, and the sky is clouding over. Kleisl, who drew the number just before Peter, swings past. At such moment one's hearing develops unusual

Opposite: *PUNTA RASICA*. *By kind permission of A. Pedrett.*

acuteness, and the low music of the valley river, subdued but not silenced by the frost, blends with the syncopated clatter of Kleisl's ski and the rasp of his steel edges. The seconds drag and a distant cheer tells me that the worst minute in the FIS, so far as I am concerned, is at an end. Peter tackles the steep traverse to the road with good judgment and finishes tenth, sixteen seconds behind the winner—a British record as yet unbroken so far as the official FIS Downhill Race is concerned. He had beaten four of the Swiss team of six, all the French save Allais, all the Germans save Kraisy, and all the Norwegians save Birger Ruud.

Jimmy Riddell was slower than Peter, but raced well and was the best British on the combined (12th). But there was still Jimmy Gardner to come. He was making his first appearance in the FIS, and had done very well in the slalom, finishing 12th, the best Britisher, and I was hoping that he would do well in the combined. Bruce Maclaren, who sprained his ankle in practice, and who ought not to have been racing, had managed to finish 31st, a fine performance, and Jimmy was the only member of the team unaccounted for. I walked anxiously up the course.

And now at last there is news of Jimmy. He had damaged his back by a heavy fall, but the injury was not serious. My worries for the 1935 FIS were at an end.

Seelos of Austria won the combined championship, though he had only finished 9th in the Downhill, one place ahead of Peter. Under the rules which were adopted at the next congress and which reduced the value of the Slalom, Allais would have won. Christel Kranz of Germany won the Ladies' Combined.

A few days after the meeting, I tried to describe the FIS from the angle of an imaginary competitor whom I called Bill Roundell. I showed the result to Peter and asked him what he thought of it. "Not much," said Peter, "at least I don't feel like that when I'm racing. . . . When one's practising, of course, one gets a big thrill if one's ski-ing well, and goes through agony if one's frightened, but somehow in a race all these sorts of feelings are completely swamped by one dominating absorbing urge, the urge to get to a particular point, the finishing post, as quickly as possible."

"Is there nothing in a race you enjoy?" I asked.

"No, nothing. I am sick with fright before it begins, actually sick sometimes, and there is no room left for pleasure in the concentrated anxiety of the race itself."

"But I suppose you enjoy ski-ing," I persisted anxiously. "You're not going to tell me that you don't like practising for races."

"No, I don't enjoy practising," he said, thoughtfully. "For instance, there is a big *schuss* which I have taken straight four or five times; twice the snow was deep and easy, and I got no kick out of it at all, and on the other occasions I was just sick with fear."

"Surely you enjoy just ordinary touring," I persisted.

"Not much. As you yourself once said in one of your books, 'Ski-ing isn't really fun, because one is either ski-ing too slow and ashamed or too fast and frightened.'"

I report this conversation as accurately as I can remember it. It depressed me. I remember what ski-ing was to me when I was twenty. I remember six days which I spent among the Oberland glaciers when I was Peter's age, and I can still see the stars shining from the cold austerity of a January night, and the moonlit snows racing up to meet us as we skied down the Finsteraarhorn Glacier before the dawn.

We had none of the glory of racing, but at least we did enjoy ski-ing.

A young Norwegian, who was at a dinner party at St. Moritz just after I had persuaded the FIS Congress provisionally to recognise downhill racing, suddenly exclaimed, "Do you know the man in all the world who has done most harm to ski-ing? I will tell you—Arnold Lunn."

I am inclined to think he was right.

I asked Peter to write down his idea of what the FIS meant to "Bill Roundell." And this is what he wrote:

"Bill Roundell went to bed at 10 p.m. the night before the FIS, but it was two in the morning before he fell asleep, to dream that he was one of a long line of competitors, waiting for the start of the race; neither he nor anybody else appeared to consider it unusual that they were having a *Geschmozzel*.

"From far away he heard the starter's voice, '*Bereit . . . Fertig . . . Los.*'

"He shot off, and skied as he had never skied before; he could see nobody ahead of him, and he turned round to find out by how much he was leading.

" All the other competitors were still on top of the hill ; it had been a false start, and they were about to try again.

" Desperately he tried to climb back so as not to be too late, but he could obtain no purchase with his ski. He slipped further and further backwards, down and down.

" Then the white mountains rose up and covered him.

. . . . . .

" The next morning, Bill, after studying the weather and the thermometer, waxed his ski ; then he dressed and went down to breakfast.

" He ate very little and when he had finished, he discovered that he had got up much too early, and that he had nothing to do for an hour. He tried to read the papers in the lounge ; three times he went to look at the weather, and twice he asked the concierge if there were any letters for him.

" After a further attempt to read the papers, he decided that he would wait, until it was time to start up the course, in the café on the top of the Allmendhubel.

" When he got there he found that a great many other competitors had decided to do the same ; they sat together drinking coffee, which they did not really want. All of them were either unnecessarily hearty or very silent.

" At last it was time to start up the course, and they drifted out to put on their skins.

" ' Why haven't you got any sun-glasses ? ' one of the Austrians asked Bill.

" ' I don't need any,' he replied.

" ' Don't be an ass ; any one can get snow-blindness in this light. Look here, as I have a hat as well, I don't really need mine. You had better take them.'

" Bill protested, but when he saw that by so doing he only irritated his friend, he accepted them.

" They went on up the course ; Bill felt weak and sick, and a mis-quotation from Newbolt drummed monotonously in his brain :

> A sword swept,
> And over the mountains one by one
> The voices faded and were gone.

" As Bill had drawn a late number he was able to watch some of the other competitors down the first part of the course.

" Otto Furrer took a very steep line and staggered.

" 'That settles it,' Bill thought, 'I shall do two turns on that slope.'

" He watched Nöbl run as straight as possible between the second and third controls ; he saw him shoot into the air over a bump and lose *Vorlage*. Then he dropped out of sight into the gully.

" Bill watched in vain for him to reappear on the opposite slope. After a moment's inactivity he saw little black figures dart simultaneously towards the same spot.

" One minute before he was to start Bill drank some brandy ; an assistant official, who was a friend of Bill's, beat his legs with the palms of his hands, in order to make the blood flow more freely.

" 'For Christ's sake leave me alone,' Bill muttered, and then felt sorry when he saw the expression on his friend's face.

" Once Bill had started, his concentration on the landmarks with which he had made himself familiar during practice, and the perpetual struggle to keep his balance, banished all emotion. He felt no fear now, so completely had the struggle to reach the finishing posts dominated his mind.

" Towards the end of the race he passed a group of spectators, who cheered heartily ; it did much to revive his flagging energy on the last fields.

" As soon as he had passed through the finishing posts he sank to the ground ; he looked round to find what time he had taken.

" He saw Tom coming towards him ; he was congratulating him on his run. Bill had done well, and an ecstatic feeling of relief flooded over him ; his face worked strangely.

" 'I wonder why I always feel like bursting into tears at the end of a race ? ' he said.

" 'I always do,' Tom replied.

" Together they watched the remaining competitors through the finishing posts ; then they shouldered their ski and climbed back to Mürren."

The FIS was over. We could relax. The blizzard had broken just as the last race had passed the post. The organisers had won our battle against the weather. Godi Michel and Max, upon whose shoulders so much of the organisation had fallen, were gossiping in the bar. Phyllis Holt-Needham, who had handled overstrained competitors and officials with an admirable mixture of firmness and tact, and the faintest flavour of irony as a corrective of FIS fever, sipped a champagne cocktail, and then returned to Room 4 to wrestle with the prizes. And meanwhile I locked myself into the bathroom, the only place in which the Chairman of the Race Committee is reasonably sure from invasion, in order to have time to think out something which will sound funny in four languages. I consoled myself with the thought that racers relaxing after a FIS are not unduly critical.

The British are often criticised as feudal and reactionary. Be that as it may the only FIS parties at which nobody was allowed to wear evening dress, and at which the only decorations permitted were ski-ing badges, were those which were organised by the feudal English.

Two years later when the FIS was organised in democratic France the distinguished politicians of the Front Populaire appeared at the banquet resplendent in evening dress, and be-ribboned with decorations.

World Championships and Arlberg-Kandahars at Mürren ended with a party and not a banquet. And these parties had an international reputation. "Le plus inoubliable," wrote a Frenchman who was present at the 1935 FIS, "le plus beau fut le banquet du soir au Palace. Monde fou. Salle à craquer."

The Mürren FIS of 1935 was the last FIS of the golden age. Hitler had discovered the FIS, and the plague of nationalism was destined to infect the ski-ing brotherhood. But in 1935 the FIS was still a family, distinguished by an atmosphere, which a great French skier described as "une affectueuse camaraderie unique dans tous les sports."

In 1936 the World Championship was held at Innsbruck.

A sudden spell of *Foehn* and thaw had been followed by a north wind and sharp frost which had transformed the melted snow into sheet ice. I have never seen worse conditions, and undoubtedly the FIS Committee, of which I was a member, ought to have cancelled the race, and transferred the World Championship to St. Anton.

The most dangerous section of the course, "the Devil's Glade," provided the racer with a choice of a reasonably safe but slow line over bumps, or a fast, dangerous line down a narrow ribbon of smooth snow bordered by a long, ugly line of villainous tree stumps protruding about 18 inches above the snow.

The racer who was ambitious to do well, had to shave the tree stumps knowing that the slightest mistake might involve a fatal accident. Four members of the French team came to grief in the Devil's Glade. Most of the racers thought the risk too high, and preferred to lose time on the bumps rather than to risk a possibly fatal accident by following the stump-bordered ribbon of smooth snow. I waited below the glade knowing that Peter would elect the dangerous alternative.

Willy Steuri drew No. 1. He lurched rather than skied down the course, blood streaming down his face. Peter had drawn No. 3. I looked at my stop-watch when Steuri appeared . . . . 70 seconds . . . . 80 seconds . . . . and still no sign of No. 2. Competitors were starting at minute intervals . . . 100 seconds . . . . and then came Peter. He had gained 20 seconds on Steuri. He had taken the ribbon straight and held it.

Many of the racers came to grief on the icy traverse near the finish. Their steel edges failed to grip, and they slipped sideways at a speed faster than the speed of most straight *schusses*. Sigmund Ruud somersaulted five times down a slope studded with stones and tree trunks and staggered to his feet with both ski broken off at the bindings, his face bleeding, but comparatively unhurt.

Seventeen of the fifty-four competitors were too seriously injured to finish and left the course on stretchers.

Ian Chalmers, who was watching the race near the finish, wrote to me as follows :—

"I happened to see all the three big meetings, Garmisch, Innsbruck, and St. Anton, but the one thing which will always stand out in my memory was Peter's running on that death-trap of a course at Innsbruck.

"He came down just after Steuri had been carried off the course, running as if he was in a hurry to get down to Half-way House, and so noticeable was his control and easy style that several of the Press representatives went into raptures about it ; such expressions as 'tadellos' and 'sehr nett,' were to be heard all round. . . ."

Incidentally this race made ski-ing history in more ways than one, for there were three serious casualties among the spectators.

Meanwhile the wretched ladies were waiting to start. The

casualties were reported by telephone and announced by the starter in a voice of ever deepening melancholy.

The course was shortened for the ladies ; but even so it proved a nerve-racking race not only for the ladies, but for the spectators. Only one competitor, the winner, stopped beyond the finishing post without a severe toss, and those who fell continued to slip helplessly down the ice, sometimes feet first, sometimes head first.

Gallant volunteers leapt on to the ice and tried to field the ladies before they scored the boundary on the tree stumps.

But there was one competitor, Evie Pinching, who swept through the finishing post erect, ski well together, and finished with a superb christiania. To the intense surprise of everybody including Evie herself, she discovered that she had won the race.

Next day Evie finished second in the Slalom, and was first on the combined result, the winner of the World Championship for Ladies, a magnificent performance of which we were all very proud.

Rominger (Switzerland) won the Downhill Race and the Combined Race. Peter was 10th on the Combined Result ; and Dick Durance, of the United States, was 12th.

In 1937 the World Championship was held at Chamonix. The French organisers were charming and witty people for whom ski-ing was still a sport, and not the criterion of national prestige. But the Olympic virus, which will be diagnosed in the chapter which follows, had infected international ski-ing. The 1937 FIS was less informal and far less fun than the 1935 FIS.

" What fun," I wrote, " the FIS was in the Golden Age before politicians had discovered downhill racing ! In the Mürren FIS of 1931 the teams gathered informally for the Draw. There were no National Anthems before, during or after the races. In accordance with Swiss tradition the Union Jack was hung upside down and there were no protests from the British. To-day the FIS opens with a ceremonial procession, for which the teams are mobilised like troops going into battle. Bands play, flags flutter. The teams are marshalled into a hall and introduced in alphabetical order. The captains introduce the teams, and as each name is called the skier rises smartly to attention, and every team is welcomed by the corresponding National Anthem. The Germans, the soul of courtesy, give the Nazi salute while *God Save the King* is being played, and the British stand about looking uncomfortable because they don't know exactly what to do when Germans shoot out their arms. It is gauche to make no gesture in reply when the German National Anthem is being played. A sub-committee on ski-ing ceremonial should be formed without delay. I suggest as an appropriate gesture a slight lifting of the right hand with deprecatory movement to indicate, "Thanks awfully, old chap, but you needn't keep your arm stuck out any longer on my account." Also we need a badge, a British badge, to balance the swastika. What about a neat little umbrella?

"If I were a FIS dictator I should forbid National Anthems and I should forbid national flags, and I should insist that no politician should be allowed to speak or even appear at a FIS banquet unless he could prove that he had jumped thirty metres or passed a simple test in downhill racing."

Had this test been imposed at Chamonix we should have been spared the excruciating tedium of the banquet with which the FIS concluded.

Major Oestgaard and the President of the French Ski-ing Association were almost the only skiers at the top table, which was crowded out by eminent representatives of the Front Populaire.

These gentlemen made speeches on everything but ski-ing. They expressed their indebtedness to the distinguished patrons of the world championship, to the Senators, and to the Deputies who had interested themselves in Chamonix; to the Prefect of Savoy, and the President of the Commune, to the Chairman of the P.L.M. Railway, to the Directors of the Charabanc services and to the Manager of the Brévent Cable Railway. The only people who were not thanked were the racers who provided the fun, and Ovalmaltine who provided the finishing posts.

Somewhere about 11.30 one speaker so far forgot himself as to refer to the competitors, and was startled by the ironic and prolonged cheer with which this unseemly digression was greeted by the exasperated skiers.

Allais, of France, won the Downhill and Slalom Races and the World Championship, Christl Kranz, of Germany, won the corresponding events in the women's races. J. P. Wakefield, 27th, was best for Britain. In the Slalom Peter, 16th, was the best of the British team.

In the Ladies' Races the untiring enthusiasm of Mrs. Wolfe,

mother of the American racers, was at last rewarded—Clarita Heath, of the U.S.A., finishing 4th.

For Britain Helen Palmer-Tomkinson, 7th, was the best in the Straight Race, and Rettles de Cosson, 7th, in the Slalom.

A few weeks later Peter entered for his last International race, the Arlberg-Kandahar, in which he finished 14th out of 54. In his long racing career he had only once failed to finish, at Chamonix when he broke a ski. He is the only international racer who has raced in all seven of the World Championships, and he also raced in the Olympic Games. He had a remarkably consistent record, for he had never failed to finish in the first half of the field save on the one occasion when he broke a ski. Out of the 23 results recorded in these events, Downhill, Slalom and Combined,* he finished seven times in the first ten. In the British team he was best on nine occasions, and second best on ten occasions. He knew exactly what he could do, and always kept his head—whether racing in a snowstorm as in the 1931 FIS, or in the death-trap of Innsbruck as in 1936.

I missed him in 1938, not only as a parent, but also as a non-racing captain. Every member of the British team failed, and for the first time in the history of the FIS we did not have a single competitor high up among the "Kanonen."

Allais and Christl Kranz successfully defended their respective titles, and for the first time the American ladies beat the British ladies. That fine racer, Miss Marian McKean (U.S.A.) finished 6th in the Downhill Race.

It was appropriate that for the last FIS before the outbreak of war we should return to Zakopane, for it was at Zakopane that Downhill Racing had been included for the first time in the FIS programme.

As Chairman of the Downhill-Racing Committee, I had the difficult task of keeping the German representative in his place, and of preventing the Germans acting as if they had already conquered Poland. All pretence that international sport should promote international friendship had been abandoned. The atmosphere of Zakopane was discreetly indicated in the title of the article describing

*The slalom in 1931 was unofficial and no combined result was published.

the world championship in the British Ski Year Book, " *The Battle of Zakopane, by our Military Correspondent.*"

I have described those momentous days in *Come What May.* The Germans carried all before them, thanks to the Austrians and Sudeten Czechs, who were now included in the Third Reich.

The Ladies' Team did better than at Engelberg. Helen Blane, the Captain, finished 7th in the Ladies' Team, beating the Swiss and the Poles. For Britain Jimmy Palmer-Tomkinson, 15th in the Downhill Race, put up the best performance. Both teams did badly in the Slalom.

The German skiers who competed at Zakopane returned to Poland a few months later. While competing at Zakopane they had acquired useful knowledge which was of great value to them when they exchanged ski-ing dress for the uniform of the Brigade to which they were attached during the capture of Zakopane. It is foolish to belittle international sport merely because it fails to promote international friendship.

CHAPTER XV

Rehearsal for War

THERE are few things in life which I recall with greater pride than the fact that in the ill-omened year of Munich I helped to defeat the Axis forces at the FIS Congress of Helsinski, and removed the Arlberg-Kandahar Cup from St. Anton two weeks later.

The gods often punish us by granting our requests. For many years I campaigned to secure FIS recognition and the Olympic imprimatur for my baby, the slalom race. And I had no sooner succeeded in introducing the slalom into the Winter Games than I found myself involved in a successful attempt to sever all relations between the FIS and the Olympic Committee.

The story of this controversy has more than a passing interest, for it throws light on the Nazi attitude to sport and also on the Nazi conviction that Britain and France would come to terms either just before or just after Poland had been overrun.

The origin of the controversy was a dispute about the amateur definition ; the principal issue at Helsinki was the attempt of the Axis to dominate the FIS.

The FIS lays down certain minimum requirements which are binding on all Associations who are bound, for instance, to deprive a skier who races for money of his amateur status. The FIS leaves the national Associations free to stiffen up these minimum requirements. The Norwegians, British and Americans regard a ski-teacher as a professional, whereas most of the Central European countries consider that a ski-teacher is a professional teacher but not a professional racer.

The Olympic Committee accept as amateurs all who are entered as such by their respective Associations, subject to certain minimum requirements. Athletes who accept money prizes, or broken-time payment (that is, compensation for loss of salary during the training period) and ex-professionals who have regained their amateur status are, *in theory*, ineligible for Olympic competitions.

In fact, the Olympic Committee are capricious in their attitude to their own rules. It is a custom in yachting circles to give money prizes, but yachtsmen compete in the Olympic Games. Ex-professionals who have regained their amateur status have been admitted to the Olympic Games. Italy had entered football teams composed of " amateurs " who receive a regular salary—the Italian Press publishes the transfer fees of these " amateur " footballers—and Italy is not unique in this respect. The " amateur " status of most continental football teams is so dubious that our own British Amateur Football Association refused to enter a team for the Olympics.

The Olympic Committee must have known that the veto on broken-time payments is seldom observed. The German team began their training on the glaciers in August, and received the equivalent of about ten shillings a day for pocket money. And everybody knew that Christl Kranz, the famous German skier, was the Sport leader for her region and drew a salary from the Government for her work in connection with ski-ing.

These German " ski troops," as we called them, trained at Government expense from midsummer onwards, had far more opportunity to perfect their racing than ski-teachers who spent most of their time on the practice slope or on slow runs with mediocre pupils.

The Olympic Committee knew that ski-teachers had competed in the 1924, 1928 and 1932 Winter Olympics, that a Norwegian proposal to increase the minimum FIS requirements, professionalising all ski-teachers, had been defeated at the FIS Congress of 1932, and that the FIS had agreed to compete in the Olympics subject to the competition being organised in accordance with FIS rules. Yet the Olympic Committee raised no protest against our amateur rules until we were irrevocably committed to take part in the Games. Six months before the Games opened they informed us that they could not accept ski-teachers.

Had they stated that they were sincerely anxious to restrict the Games to a genuine amateur, and that they hoped that we would take steps to exclude, not only ski-teachers, but also all those who received broken-time payment, I am inclined to believe that we should have contented ourselves with a formal protest against the discourtesy of raising this thorny issue at the last moment. But throughout this controversy we felt that the Olympic concern for the purity of the Games was highly selective, and tended to exclude from the Games the best Swiss skiers while admitting to the Games the Nazi " ski troops."

The Olympic Committee seemed to us to be more concerned with appearances than with realities. They were anxious to preserve the façade of amateurism which gave tone to the Games, and were resigned to the evasion of their own rules provided that this evasion was not too blatant. A Nazi might be in receipt of broken-time payment without the public being any the wiser, but everybody knew that Otto Furrer or Willy Steuri were ski-teachers. The ski-teacher had to be excluded because he was an honest professional. The Nazi ski troops could be admitted because they had the decency to disguise their professionalism.

The Swiss, Austrians and French were in favour of boycotting the Olympic Games and organising in their place a World Championship at Innsbruck. They sounded me as to whether they could count on British support.

I was, of course, proud of the fact that my son was captaining the Olympic team and I knew that our crack racers, of both sexes, were ambitious to represent their country in the Olympic Games. I had my own reasons for hesitating to support the proposed boycott of the Games, for the slalom was included for the first time and I had been asked to referee the slalom, which was in some sense my creation. But in spite of this close alliance between parental and personal vanity, I recommended that we should support the proposed boycott. Peter discussed the question with Jeanette Kessler, the captain of the Ladies' Olympic team, and reported that the racers were agreed to support a boycott of the Games unless the veto on the ski-teachers was withdrawn. Our teams were composed exclusively of amateurs according to the Olympic and FIS definition. None of our skiers were affected by the veto on ski-teachers. I should be interested to hear of any precedent for the action taken by our team. It is all too common for teams to protest against the conditions which reduce their chances of victory, but I do not know of any case of a team threatening to boycott an important Meeting to secure the reversal of a decision which *favoured* their chances. I was proud of their readiness to sacrifice the honour of representing their country in the Olympic Games, and also of their anxiety to secure the inclusion of their most formidable rivals.

The proposed boycott was abandoned after the French had withdrawn from the anti-Nazi front. The French Government had voted a large sum of money for the expenses of their French team, and insisted that the team should enter. It was therefore decided that we should enter teams both for the Olympic Games and also for the World Championship, which was to be held a week later at Innsbruck.

I had other reasons for believing that whether we entered teams or not, we should not ignore the religious and racial persecution in Germany. I drafted a letter, which the Archbishop of York signed with a few unimportant modifications, and which invited the Olympic Committee to obtain from Hitler the promise of a general amnesty for the victims of Nazi persecution. The subsequent fate of that letter and the story of the Winter Olympic Games are the subject of a chapter in *Come What May*.

The Archbishop's letter failed, and all that remained was the negative protest of declining to accept invitations to official banquets, addressed to me as a member of the committee, or to walk in the procession with which the Games opened. Neither my son or I had any wish to salute Hitler, and we accordingly kept out of the procession.

Though Christl Kranz and Franz Pfnür, of Germany, won the Downhill-Slalom combination, the Norwegians brought off a double in the Downhill Race, Birger Ruud and Laila Schou-Nilsen winning their respective races. The British captains Peter (12th out of 60) and Jeanette Kessler (7th out of 39) were best for Britain. Dick Durrance, for many years the outstanding American racer, finished 10th.

I did not enjoy the Games. I disliked the pomp and parade, for sport ceases to be fun when people take it too seriously. And, where sport is concerned, I am something of a Quaker, with a strong bias against ritual. Again I resented the exploitation of the "glory that was Greece" on behalf of the racket that was Nazi Germany. The link with Greece began and ended with the exploitation of the name "Olympics." "We are not on earth," wrote Dr. Goebbels in 1934, "for the purpose of cramming our skulls with knowledge: that is quite unimportant. Bringing up tough guys that is what the business of the high schools should be." The tough guys who organised the Nazi Olympics had certainly not crammed their skulls with unnecessary knowledge about Greece. Had they realised that the Romans had conquered Greece, they might have avoided the crowning ineptitude of inscribing an Olympic medal with a Latin motto. A phrase from the Periclean speech, φιλοκαλοῦμεν μετ' εὐτελείας (we cultivate beauty with economy) would have provided a motto both Greek and apt for an Olympic gold medal which was not gold, but only gold plated.

There is far more real sportsmanship in Village Cricket than in Test Cricket ; in meetings such as the Anglo-Swiss University Ski Match than in the Olympic Games. There is, of course, nothing new in the folly which seeks to measure national prestige by the barometer of sport. When Alcibiades was attacked by Nikias did he reply that he had entered seven chariots and taken the first three places at Olympia and brought great glory to Athens thereby ? Who cares to-day whether Athens beat Sparta at Olympia ? Who cares how far the discobolus was thrown by the young man who caught Myron's fancy ? That young athlete lives because art endures. " It is a foolish custom," wrote Xenophanes, " to honour strength more than excellent wisdom . . . small joy would there be for a city should a citizen win a victory in the Pentathlon. These things do not make fat the dark corners of the city."

I was revolted by the Nazi Press, by the blare of self-praise for the organisation, by the boastful headlines, by the exploitation of German successes for the greater glory of their disgusting Nazi creed. And so when I was asked, at the end of the slalom which I refereed, to broadcast my comments, I could not bring myself to pay the compliments which were expected, but instead I addressed the microphone and the invisible audience in a speech which had at least one virtue, brevity. " Germans, there are still some people who ski for fun."

During the World Championship at Chamonix, Major Oestgaard said to me, " It's such a relief not to have people coming up to one every five minutes asking one to admire the wonderful organisation. And even if the organisation here isn't quite as good as at Garmisch, the atmosphere is infinitely pleasanter."

When I compared the Garmisch Games with the World Championship at Mürren, I was not impressed. The Germans had perfect weather for the Olympic Games ; whereas we were struggling against storm and blizzard. The Nazi organisers had a labour battalion placed at their disposal, whereas we ran our Championship with the old guard of the Kandahar and our Swiss friends, Godi and Max. But our races started to time just as the Garmisch races did, and the competitors, I am told, far preferred Mürren.

At Mürren we believe that competitors are the people who matter, that officials are necessary and spectators unnecessary

Opposite : *WINTER SUNSET.* *By kind permission of Schär-Zogg.*

nuisances. Competitors always had the right-of-way on Mürren funiculars during both the races and the training period.

At Garmisch the competitors were regarded as necessary nuisances, for Olympic Games cannot be organised without Olympic athletes. But the people that really mattered were the distinguished personages who stood beside Hitler while he took the salute at the Games, the Olympic Committee and the eminent visitors who were given places of honour at the various competitions. The athletes were only the bricks to build the temple of fame for the greater glory of the Führer, the Nazi party and the Olympic Committee.

Everything which the Führer *saw* was beyond reproach. The façade organisation was superb, but competitors were given no precedence on funiculars and did not find the atmosphere congenial, or the organisation particularly helpful. On the other hand the medical service was superb and competitors who damaged themselves before or during the Games were deeply impressed by the medical attention which they received.

Peter's comment was that Garmisch suffered from the vice of over-organisation.

The FIS Congress met during the Games and *unanimously* resolved that the FIS should withdraw from the Winter Olympics, unless the Olympic Committee accepted as amateurs all those who were amateurs under FIS rules.

The FIS World Championships were remarkable for their friendly atmosphere, due to many reasons of which not the least important was the fact that they were virtually open championships. We realised that if we excluded ski-teachers we should also have to exclude teams, such as the Nazis, who were receiving broken-time payment. We were not prepared to face the task of organising an Inquisition, whose efforts would be doomed to failure. We realised that a Nazi sport leader must produce winning teams or go, and that ways and means will always be found to subsidise "amateurs" whose services are required to demonstrate the superiority of the Nazi or Fascist ideology. It was childish of the Olympic Committee to expect us to ignore these facts. The only effective choice at the Olympic Games is to throw them open to all professionals, or to admit disguised professionals.

The Olympic Committee was fully entitled to define the terms of admission to their Games, and the FIS Congress was no less entitled to reject those terms. And with this unanimous rejection

Opposite: *THE TREASURES OF THE SNOW*. *By kind permission of A. Pedrett.*

(for which Norway, Britain, the U.S.A. and Canada voted) all of whom regard ski-teachers as professionals, the controversy should have ended. And would have ended had not our resolution been regarded as a mortal affront by two very sensitive people, Herr Hitler and Count Baillet-Latour, President of the Olympic Committee.

The Count was justly proud of his position as President of the most exclusive club in the world, for the Olympic Committee is not recruited by the vulgar process of election from below. The members of the Committee are not nominated by national committees, but co-opted by their fellow Olympians. Distinguished persons such as retired Ambassadors or eminent aristocrats, are invited by the Committee to join the august circle of those who constitute a College of Cardinals presided over by a Pope of sport whose *ex cathedra* utterances are binding on the faithful.

The President clearly believed that he possessed some special charisma which enabled him to pontificate about sports which he had never practised, by sole virtue of his high office. No other theory can explain his readiness to contribute some foolish and sadly misinformed remarks about ski-ing to Roland Palmedo's delightful symposium, *Ski-ing, the International Sport*.

The genial disdain with which the FIS rejected the high honour of Olympic recognition irritated the Count and infuriated Herr Hitler. For the Nazis had been very successful in the Games, and were beginning to exploit their connection with the Games for the glory of their creed. The tactics of infiltration, which they have employed in preparation for war, were also adopted on the Olympic Committee. The Olympic Committee should never have allowed the Germans to found in Berlin the International Olympic Institute or to publish at their own expense the *Olympische Rundschau*, a review dedicated to the "promotion of the Olympic ideas and to the peaceable union of all peoples." The Nazis had yet another reason for resenting the FIS decision. The Japanese had been invited to organise the Olympic Games of 1940 and were anxious that ski-ing should be included in the programme. They appealed to the Nazis to secure a reversal of the FIS decision at the FIS Congress to be held in Helsinki in 1938.

The German Foreign Office therefore got busy. The satellites of the Axis were ordered to instruct their representatives at the Congress to support the Axis policy. The Olympic Committee pay lip service to the maxim that sport must not be allowed to interfere with politics, but they raised no objection when the Axis applied persistent political pressure to secure the reversal of the unanimous decision of an autonomous sporting body.

I travelled to Helsinki with my old friend, Count Aldo Bonacossa. In reply to my statement that what we objected to was not the exclusion of ski-teachers but the inclusion of disguised professionals in a meeting from which honest professionals were excluded, he smiled sweetly and said, " The Olympic Committee is composed of diplomats who know that it is impossible to be rigid about principles in this wicked world. That the competitors in the Olympics are amateurs is a convention which everybody understands, and which nobody takes very seriously. To admit ski-teachers would violate the convention. You should be more tolerant. When I stay in an English country-house I know that the man who unpacks for me will hide all my clothes, so I go up to dress a quarter of an hour earlier than I should in Italy in order to have time to unearth the clothes which he has hidden. I adjust myself to English conventions in England and you should adjust yourself to Olympic conventions when you go to the Olympic Games. It is no use, my dear Arni, trying to be a Hercules and clean out the Olympic stable."

At the Garmisch Congress, the issue had been the status of those whom we defined as amateurs. At the Helsinki Congress it was the status of the FIS which was at stake. Was the FIS an autonomous body, or a branch of the German Foreign Office? At Garmisch the German delegate had reminded us that we could not reverse our unanimous decision at a subsequent Congress without a fatal loss of prestige. "A subsequent capitulation would damage irretrievably our reputation." At Helsinki, two years later, this same German delegate proposed the reversal of our decision at Garmisch. Fortunately the FIS Congress remembered his warning that such a capitulation would be fatal to our reputation, and the Hitler-Baillet-Latour Axis was defeated.

I travelled back with Bonacossa from Helsinki.

" I shall be glad to go to the Downhill Racing Championship at Engelberg," he said, " because it will be so nice to meet some real amateurs again. You see, Arni, you have converted me by your eloquence and I am prepared to believe that ski-teachers are the only real amateurs in the world of ski-ing.

" Did you see the list of delegates to the FIS which the Finns published? They gave our names and professions, and it seems that *we* are all professionals. Oestgaard is a professional soldier, Moser a professional lawyer. After my name they put 'Count.' When one has worked hard and taken two very difficult examinations for doctorate of engineering at Munich, it is a little sad to be described as professional Count. After your name, Arni, there was no profession; perhaps they were too polite to describe you as professional 'Enfant Terrible.' I wonder how they would have described Count Baillet-Latour?"

" Professional Zeus?" I suggested.

In 1939 the Olympic Committee decided to bury at Olympia the heart of their founder, Baron Pierre de Coubertin.

Coubertin founded the modern Olympic Games. He thought that the nations of the world would draw closer together in the friendly contests of sport. In this work he was influenced by Thomas Arnold of Rugby, but his inspiration was the Games of Ancient Greece. And it was his dying wish that his heart should be buried at Olympia, the site of the ancient Games.

My father, who was lunching in Athens with the Greek Minister of Education, told him that Peter had captained the British Ski Team in the Olympic Games. Peter, who was at the luncheon party, described what followed in an article entitled " The Pilgrimage of an Infidel."

" In that case," said the Minister, " he must of course come with us to Olympia."

" I tried desperately," wrote Peter, " to catch my grandfather's eye, to explain somehow across the luncheon plates that the Olympic Committee regarded my father as the arch-heretic. 'The Olympic Committee will murder me,' I thought, 'and will then murder the Minister for bringing me.'

" 'That will be delightful,' I heard my grandfather say."

Peter travelled on the royal train with the Olympic Committee.

" I realised with a pang of shame," he wrote, " that my father would have given his right eye to be cooped in a train for four hours with the Olympic Committee, and that I was making no use of my advantageous position. . . .

" Considering that the members of the Committee knew that my father was behind the FIS motion, which had meant the withdrawal of ski-ing from the Games, they were all amazingly friendly to me. . . .

" The Minister of Education drove me back to my hotel. I was indeed grateful to him for the hospitality and great kindness with which he had treated me. It had been a most enjoyable and pleasant experience, but in view of the recent controversy, I still felt that I had been unfair to him and obtained the invitation on false pretences. Rather shamefacedly I mumbled something about my father being the arch-heretic in Olympic circles. His Excellency smiled. 'As indeed Count Baillet-Latour explained to me,' he said."

The Japanese having failed to liquidate the " Chinese incident," the Summer Games were transferred to Finland, and the Swiss were invited to organise the Winter Olympics, minus the ski-ing events. But " professional Zeus " was still unreconciled to his double defeat. Long after the Swiss had begun to prepare for the Winter Games they were approached with the request that they should include the ski-ing events as " demonstrations." According to the Olympic rules, a sport which is not represented by an International Federation may be included in the Games as a " demonstration." Now ski-ing, of course, *is* represented by an International Federation, and ski-ing events are therefore ineligible for inclusion as " demonstrations." But Zeus is not bound by his own laws, and the Swiss were therefore invited to introduce ski-ing by a back door. To have accepted this demand would have been an act of treachery to the FIS, and the Swiss accordingly informed the Olympic Committee that they were not prepared to include ski-ing events disguised as "demonstrations." Though the offer of the Winter Games to Switzerland had not been made conditional on the inclusion of ski-ing, and though this suggestion was only made after the Swiss had already spent great sums of money in preparing for the Games, the Committee, with an Olympian contempt for the code which is binding on mere mortals, removed the Winter Olympic Games from Switzerland and transferred them to Germany. Never in the history of the

Games had one country been asked to organise the Games two Olympics in succession, but then, of course, neither Baillet-Latour nor the Nazis are bound by ordinary precedents.

" Professional Zeus " is a bonny fighter. He was determined even at the eleventh hour to reverse the FIS Congress decision, and the Axis satellites were therefore instructed to demand the summoning of an Extraordinary Geneva Meeting of the Congress. Up to the very outbreak of war the Nazis were devoting a vast amount of time and energy to securing the necessary two-thirds majority for a Special Congress, and to an attempt to persuade the various National Associations to send competitors to take part in the " ski demonstrations " at the Garmisch Winter Olympics. It was clear that the Nazis were counting on a Munich at the expense of Poland either just before the outbreak of war and just after the overrunning of Poland, for they acted on the assumption that the Games would be held. The Nazis regarded Oestgaard and me with particular venom, as indeed emerges from the last circular which they issued just before the outbreak of war. The Norwegians and the British had everything to gain by the exclusion of ski-teachers, since their potential Olympic runners were all amateurs, and both the Norwegians and the British classify ski-teachers as professionals. Indeed Oestgaard had proposed at the 1932 Congress that ski-teachers should, in future, be ineligible to compete in any FIS event. He had been defeated and had loyally accepted the decision of the FIS. He was therefore all the more determined that our amateur rule should be changed, if at all, by the FIS acting on its own responsibility without pressure from Dictators, whether of Germany or of sport.

It was this Anglo-Norwegian alliance which defeated the Axis at Helsinki. They expected the Swiss and French and other nations, who regarded ski-teachers as amateurs, to vote against the Axis proposals, but they found it difficult to forgive Oestgaard and me.

The FIS Committee recommended a complete boycott of the bogus " ski demonstrations " at the Garmisch Games. The Axis resorted to bribery. They offered to provide, not only free accommodation but also travelling expenses from their native countries to Garmisch, not only for the Olympic teams, but also for sixty skiers from each competing country. A tempting bait, particularly to the American skiers, for whom a free trip to European ski-ing grounds was a very attractive bribe. But there is every reason to suppose that the Americans would have remained loyal to the FIS. The final circular issued by the Nazis should find its way into any representative anthology of English prose. Here is a characteristic extract:

"The organising committee of the V. Olympic Winter-Games 1940 is preparing an impressive manifestation in honour of popular and world-spread ski-ing, called 'Tag des Skilaufes.' This solemn festivity will take place on Saturday, 10th of February. . . . The main event of the day will be the downhill ski-ing of about ten thousand skiers from all parts of the world in from" ("in front" is how we should put this in English) "of the International Olympic Committee and the guests of honour, who will be standing on the opposite slope. This manifestation is meant to be a parallel to the play 'Olympic Youth' at the Olympic Games in Berlin 1936. . . . The skiers of each nation should form a groupe (*sic*) to themselves while ski-ing down the Kransberg . . . before joining the others for a general song.'

This manifesto, I wrote, stresses the dignity and importance of the "solemn festivity," but solemnity soon degenerates into pomposity when people are solemn about the wrong things. As I read these letters my mind travels back to the first Anglo-Swiss races. There was no windy rhetoric at the dinner which followed about YOUTH, or International solidarity as fostered by International sport. But there was friendliness and fun which is perhaps more valuable than strained rivalry and "solemnity." And there was lots of "general song." I remember Mackintosh gave us a whole repertoire of Swiss songs, such as "Auf dem Bankli" of which only the words that I have quoted are quotable. And Werner Salvisberg sang a moving ditty to the effect that his mother was an Appezeller, and Tony Knebworth, who could not sing, insisted on singing "She was a maiden poor and lowly."

In those days ski-ing was not a "solemn festivity." It was fun.

CHAPTER XVI

Thanks to Bimbo

MANY years ago, on August 9th, 1915, to be precise, I left the Concordia Hut with my friend Boris, and with Boris's unpleasant friend Bimbo. I was anxious to prove that my leg, the open wound on which had excited mild derision in the breasts of the good folk entrusted with the job of vetting would-be warriors, was more efficient than they seemed to suppose. I was in Switzerland on business, and before returning decided to do a little summer ski-ing.

The Gletscherhorn was our objective. I had often admired this graceful peak, which holds its own in that proud company of noble summits with which every visitor to Mürren should be, and comparatively few visitors to Mürren are, familiar.

We left our ski on the slopes below the Lauitor. We were lazy and out of training and should have carried them higher, but this was in the early days of summer ski-ing and we had not yet learned to drag our ski on a string.

We trudged upwards and halted frequently. I reminded Boris that the great Napoleon invented the marching rule of ten minutes' halt and a snack of food every hour. Boris said, "What's good enough for Napoleon is good enough for us," and so we " kept a Corsican," at steadily diminishing intervals.

We had a long rest on the Lauitor, and it was on the Lauitor that Boris introduced me to Bimbo. Boris is a much-travelled man. After leaving Oxford he wandered about Africa and returned with a magnificent collection of African idols, ranging in height from Googa, the gem of the collection, who stands six feet, to little Bimbo, a pocket deity some nine inches in height. " Let me see," said Boris, as he produced Bimbo from his sack, " you haven't met Bimbo. Let me introduce you. Mr. Lunn. His Holiness Bimbo."

I looked at Bimbo and did not like him. His figure was repulsive. A long tube of a body stopped short suddenly and was suspended above two squat legs. Bimbo's black little face wore an expression of unintelligent obscenity. Blandly stupid and yet evil.

" I don't like Bimbo," I said.

" Hush," said Boris, " he's very sensitive."

" He's an ugly little brute," I added.

" I wish you'd be careful," said Boris, anxiously, " he's apt to be vindictive."

Boris is a Russian and he was employed in one of our Services. At the beginning of the War my brother mentioned the fact that the little flat at the head of our offices was empty. Would Boris like to park himself there? Boris accepted the suggestion. The flat was large enough to house his pantheon of heathen deities; just the solution he was looking for, since his landlady strongly objected to their presence in his digs.

My brother did not think of mentioning his kind offer to my father who had independently offered the flat to a charming Belgian baroness, a War refugee.

The baroness arrived at lunch time, dumped her luggage and left to spend the afternoon and evening with a friend. Boris arrived at tea time, and spent an interesting hour arranging his idols round the room. The baroness returned in the evening, opened the door, turned on the light and found herself face to face with twenty-five black idols. She uttered one long, terrified scream; but she was a courageous woman and, for all she knew, this might be my father's idea of a friendly welcome. She undressed, crossed herself, commended herself to her patron saint, and tried to fall asleep. Half an hour later Boris, who had been to a good party, a very good party indeed, stumbled up the stairs crooning the quaint old love-songs of Zanzibar. He opened the door, aimed for the bed and hit the Belgian baroness. Some things are difficult to explain, and some are impossible. Boris decided to return to the party. It had been, as I say, a very good party indeed. The baroness decided to return to Belgium. "There may be a war on in my country," she said, "but it will be very restful after your flat."

From the Lauitor we ought to have climbed straight up to a little notch in the south ridge of our peak, but the direct line to this gap involved traversing a steep snow slope above a bergschrund, and since the slope was both steep and exposed to the sun, I feared that the snow might slip. We accordingly decided to force a direct route to the summit and may, for all I know or care, have invented a new route. A steep slope of snow, which in places was only a thin veneer overlying ice, led to the rocks. We were forced on to the rocks since the slopes beside them were composed of ice. These rocks consisted of steep buttresses and ridges protruding out of an ice slope. We stuck to the rocks as closely as possible to avoid the step-cutting which was unavoidable the moment we left them. We led alternately.

One short section remains in my mind as one of the trickiest passages that I have ever encountered. It was necessary to traverse round a protruding buttress of rock in order to reach the gully on the other side. The rock ended abruptly about the level of my knees (I was leading at the time) and below was ice. I cut one step and decided to trust to hands and crampons for the rest. My axe I jammed into a crack in the rocks. The rock was smooth. I could just get three fingers of my right hand on to a little ledge. There was a better handhold to the left if I could reach it. Somehow or other I managed to squirm round and to swing myself across, with the help of my crampons, into the gully on the other side. But unfortunately the rope caught the axe, which I had left behind me for Boris to bring along, and it fell. That left us with only one axe.

" What did I tell you," said Boris, " this comes of being rude to Bimbo."

We reached the arête at 5 p.m. Laziness, long halts on the lower slopes, lack of training and the iced condition of the rocks all helped to delay us.

I shall not easily forget the moment when we struck the ridge. A blow with our last remaining axe, and the cornice crumbled. I thrust my head through the gap and looked across great spaces of light to the Matterhorn and Mont Blanc. In one revealing moment we had exchanged a cramped foreground of snow, rock and ice for the width of far horizons and of snows softened in golden haze. There are few things more beautiful than these evening views of distant hills seen across sixty miles of liquid air.

We were now on the ridge, one of the prettiest ridges I have ever seen. In my boyhood I should have indignantly repudiated the suggestion that any mountain could be ugly, but the day has passed when a mountain, merely because it is a mountain, appeals to me. There are valleys in the Alps which depress me by their ugliness and there are ranges which bore me with their monotony. One's love of hills does not grow dim with time, but it does become more discriminating.

I can still shut my eyes and see the last graceful snow crest leading to the rocky needle of our peak. The ridge was crested with a cornice, every line of which had the delicacy of foam frozen in the moment of breaking. It seemed a defilement to shatter the cornice with one's axe. The slope on each side was extremely steep and, for the most part, we proceeded by cutting and kicking steps, below the ridge itself with one arm steadied over the crest of the arête.

We reached the summit at six. It was difficult to tear ourselves away from our quiet perch set high above a warring world. Europe was at our feet. Europe at war. But it was the dull thud of the evening guns from Alsace that sounded unreal, the fractious clamour of insects vainly endeavouring to fret the ancient quietude of the hills. It was impossible to believe that the long battle line was etched into the distant Vosges, that soft ground swell in a sea of purple shadows, impossible to remember that Austria still held Italy at bay somewhere behind that dim far line which was the Dolomites. A few white clouds might almost have been shrapnel, almost but not quite, for, as the Earth prepared herself for sleep, the war which had transformed Europe into a slaughterhouse seemed to belong to an order of reality that had no kinship with these dream hills and visionary plains.

On our return we did not, of course, retrace our difficult ascent. We went straight down the ridge to the little gap where we ought to have struck the ridge on the ascent. At this point we hesitated. To return by the Lauitor meant a dismal plug through soft snow followed by a short and tiresome reascent. Below us, a steep slope led down to the glacier between the Ebnefluh and the Gletscherhorn, and down this slope we decided to descend. Before long we struck the inevitable bergschrund. It is always difficult to locate from above the best spot at which to cross a schrund. A small avalanche had fallen down the slope and, as the breadth of the avalanche had not been appreciably lessened in its passage of the schrund, it seemed a fair deduction that at the point where the avalanche had crossed the schrund, the unseen crevasse below could not be very broad and was probably choked up. So I aimed for this point and was relieved to find that my guess was correct.

But though the crevasse below was narrow, there was no way of evading a ten-foot jump on to a steep snow slope below.

" Well, you'll have to lower me," I said, complacently, " and then you can jump."

" Let's toss up who jumps," said Boris.

" Nonsense," said I, " chaps with game legs are never allowed to jump. My doctor would be horrified by the suggestion. And besides, it's against the best Alpine tradition."

I was accordingly lowered in comfort, and took up my stance just below.

" A good forward and downward jump is all that is needed," said I.

"That's all very well," said Boris, "but the slope below is very steep."

"Don't worry about that," I replied, with easy sangfroid. "I'll drive my axe into the snow and belay the rope round it. Come on. Go at it with a rush."

Boris went at it with a rush, landed heavily, plunged forward, and shot down the slope. The rope tightened suddenly round the axe head and pulled him up without the faintest jar—to me.

"Well, what are you complaining about," I asked. "I've done my part right nobly. I said I'd check your fall, and I have checked it."

Once across the schrund it seemed as if all our troubles were over. We ate and drank what remained of our provisions and plodded on. "We shall soon be home now," said Boris. "And then for the world's best supper," said I. But we were not to sup that night.

On reaching the foot of the couloir we ought to have turned and crossed the glacier in front of us, a glacier divided by a black snout of rock, nameless on the map but christened by us, for reasons that will shortly be clear, the "B.B.B." No, this is not a compliment to the Beetschen binding, for two of the B's stand for "Black Bluff" and the first "B" stands for "blessed" or some such word.

On the left of B.B.B. the glacier, as we soon discovered, takes a sudden plunge and curves down for five hundred feet or more at an average angle of thirty degrees. We had not descended very far before we found ourselves involved in a tiresome icefall. Meanwhile it was beginning to get dark. We were forced first to the right, and then to the left to dodge crevasses. We crossed to a peculiarly evil-looking crevasse by a snowbridge as frail as post-war virtue. We dared not cross this on foot, but lay down and swam slowly across distributing our weight as widely as possible. I caught a sudden glimpse into the dark depths of the crevasse from the very middle of the bridge and did not like it. It was now dark and there was no moon. But we were making good progress, and only one vast enormous schrund remained. We tried to get round this, first on the left and then on the right. On the left our progress was checked by a wall of ice, on the right by the schrund itself. At this point the schrund seemed fairly small, and it was just conceivable that we could cut down into the bottom and work out towards the rocks on our right along the bottom of the schrund itself. Boris held the rope while I tentatively cut a few steps. But escape on the right was barred by a complicated system of smaller crevasses.

"Nothing doing," I said.

"I knew we should never get off this beastly mountain," said Boris. "I told you not to be rude to Bimbo. He's got his feelings like anybody else."

"We've got no food left and nothing to drink," said I.

"Oh, well, the night is not too cold anyway," said Boris.

We threw ourselves on the snow. Our first sensation was one of relief. For the last hour our eyes had been searching the foreground, a foreground which receded as the shadows advanced, for a clue. We were mentally and physically exhausted by the fatigue of unravelling the labyrinth of crevasses. Moreover we had been climbing for sixteen hours and we were both badly out of training. It was rest that we needed, mental and physical rest. Food and warmth seemed matters of secondary consideration. We turned out our rucksacks without unearthing the traditional prune and decayed cheese, but to my intense relief we had at least one pipe between us, and plenty of tobacco. We looked at our watches. It was half-past nine.

"Only six hours and the night will be over," said Boris.

We had one pipe between us, and this pipe we smoked in turns. We divided up the hours into ten-minute periods. For ten minutes we sat and smoked. For ten minutes we stood up, and worked at excavating our hole in the snow, partly because the exercise kept us warm, partly because the deeper the hole the greater the protection from the cold night air. Fortunately what little wind there was, the mere ghost of a breeze, was blowing down the slope, so that the slope itself with the little rampart which we built was sufficient protection. We should have been far worse off had we faced the wind. Our snow cave sooned assumed respectable dimensions. It was soon large enough to hold us comfortably and deep enough to be almost head high when we were sitting down. We laid our axe across the bottom and sat on it to keep our tails dry. The rucksacks served as cushions for our backs.

Towards midnight Boris's feet lost sensation, but we soon restored them to life by taking his boots off and rubbing his feet in snow.

The time passed fairly quickly. It was not unbearably cold, and the pipe was a great comfort. The small red glow served to remind us that warmth had not completely vanished. There was something vaguely consoling in the thin ghostlike wisps of smoke trailing upwards towards the stars. Sometimes we talked and sometimes we broke into song. Boris and I are old Harrovians, and so we naturally sang the fine old Harrow footer songs, which at least helped to remind us that there are worse things than spending the night on a glacier—a good old-fashioned " House game " on Harrow clay, for instance.

And then, of course, there was Bimbo.

Boris had removed Bimbo from his pocket and placed him tenderly on the snow. And throughout the night he kept up a running conversation with Bimbo.

" I'm afraid this is not the sort of climate you've been accustomed to," said Boris, " rather different from the African jungle, I'm afraid. And I really must apologise for my friend Arnold. He means well, but he's apt to be a little abrupt with strangers."

Early in the night we saw lights wandering about near the Concordia. I distrusted my eyes for I know that when one is exhausted it is only too easy to see things that exist only in one's imagination. Later we learned that a military patrol had, as it happened, marched up late that night to the Concordia. The last thing we desired was a friendly search party ; first, because search parties are expensive ; secondly, because they are humiliating. No guideless climber enjoys being rescued by guides.

Fortunately the cold was not unbearable, for acute discomfort would have blinded us to the beauty of the night.

By day the mountains shrink from the pitiless inquisition of the sun. Their underlying unity is lost in a myriad details of rocky rib and ice slope and snowy crest. At night they recapture their souls. They impress you with a sense of massive strength, of strength which conceals reserves of personality. The misty crests, the gleam of ice pinnacles are the focus of unseen influences. The vast shadowed mountainscape seems curiously alive. And the stars ! No man can begin to understand the glory of the firmament if he is content with a few casual skyward glances on a fine night, glances which suggest the illusion of unmoving stars permanently pricked into a velvet background. Only those who have watched the stars hour by hour can begin to understand the beauty of the heavens, a beauty which is dynamic in its suggestion of controlled and rhythmic motion.

Knowledge born of experience is alive. Academic knowledge acquired at second hand is dead. We all know that the stars move, but to *feel* the incomparable majesty of the nightly procession you must endure a sleepless vigil with your eyes on the sky, eyes that search for evidence of those star movements which record the slow passage of the long, cold, exhausting hours.

I remember watching Venus sail out behind the Grünhorn. We followed her slow climb into the roof of heaven, and her slow decline as she challenged the first fitful hint of dawn. One by one the constellations which had looked down upon the first hours of our vigil wheeled slowly through the sky and dropped below the rim of shadowed hills.

I am glad we took the wrong turning—thanks to Bimbo—round the B.B.B., for that night above the Aletsch Glacier has enriched the heritage of remembered beauty with a glory that resists the erosion of time.

Time did not begin to drag until long past midnight, but towards one in the morning fatigue began to tell. At three we both fell asleep simultaneously and slept for several minutes. This was clearly alarming. Bimbo could not be trusted. It was therefore agreed that, for the rest of the night, one of us should sleep while the other kept awake with the aid of tobacco. Ten minutes' sleep, ten minutes on guard and ten minutes of simultaneous stamping to keep warm. This was the cycle which we arranged, and we kept to our routine fairly consistently.

Oh, the joy of those short naps ! Oh, the rage when a sharp dig recalled one, cramped and stiff, to one's turn on guard !

And throughout the night, Bimbo squatted beside us in the snow. In the intervals of fitful dozes I was dimly conscious of a small indignant black shape against a white background.

At four o'clock the eastern sky began to pale, and the hour that followed was the worst. When the sun finally rose, it seemed to take a malicious pleasure in avoiding the slope on which we were waiting with such passionate impatience for its life-giving rays. Instead the sun wasted its warmth on the icy armour of the irresponsive Aletschhorn. The sky behind the Finsteraarhorn was clear and limpid. Little cirrus flocks of cloud crisped into flame, but no healing rays were allowed to reach our shelter. We sat and watched the slow march of the sunlight. We were cold and miserable. The long night had done its work, and we chattered with cold. We had no food, the food which means warmth, and no drink. And we were very, very tired.

And then suddenly the crest of a distant peak flamed up, a single crystal point of dazzling light. The point expanded into a line of fire, the line broadened into a semi-circle, and at last the full orb of the sun leaped the mountain barrier, and flooded us with warmth and light and colour.

We stretched out our hands as though to bathe them in the healing rays. And our hearts went out in one long pæan of lyrical thanksgiving. No sun-worshipper in bygone days ever prostrated himself with greater reverence before the lord and giver of life.

Pleni sunt coeli et terra gloria tua. Benedictus qui venit in nomine Domini.

Half an hour passed before we were fit to move. But our troubles were not yet at an end.

Our first task was to circumvent the great bergschrund. We decided to try and reach the rocks of the B.B.B. and we succeeded eventually by an ingenious little route which threaded between séracs and which made full use of a choked-up channel between icy walls, a channel which might have ended in a crevasse. But even when we had reached the B.B.B. we were not sure of success. Boris thought that we could find an easier route on to the glacier by bearing round to the right. He left me to explore while I sat down and thought about the Absolute. He reappeared in forty minutes, having descended to just above the glacier only to find that an enormous schrund barred further progress in that direction. He was almost inarticulate with rage. Out came Bimbo. "A fat lot of use you are. Go back to Africa, you filthy little impostor."

We scrambled down the B.B.B. and finally discovered a sharp narrow ridge of ice and snow between two crevasses, which led to easier ground beyond. Down this saddleback we had to go. At this point Boris dropped our last remaining axe. "That's what comes of being rude to Bimbo," he remarked in a chastened mood. The axe rattled into the schrund. I nearly wept with vexation. But our crampons saved us. I took off one crampon and with its help hacked the necessary steps into the saddleback.

It was a tricky piece of work. Boris was taking no risks. "I'm sorry I lost my temper, Bimbo," I heard him say, "I'm really very attached to you, Bimbo, and I promise you a first-class sacrifice if you guide us safely out of this mess."

Which Bimbo did, so perhaps it pays to be polite to the least prepossessing of deities.

CHALET BERNA, GRINDELWALD,
June, 1922.

CHAPTER XVII

Between the Aare and the Reuss

I

SUN and frost and powder snow, an Alpine pass leading through noble scenery, a leisurely descent at an easy touring pace down a valley one has long wished to explore. Such is my conception of the perfect ski-ing day. In that far-distant epoch when I had never heard of a slalom, I did not appreciate the tranquil joys of leisurely ski-touring as I do to-day, for those joys are doubly delightful against a background of racing, racing *per se* or racing *per alium*. Even racing *per alium*, vicarious racing, can be extremely exhausting if one is following with lively interest the fortunes of a particular individual or of a particular team.

In February, 1930, the Kandahar sent over a strong team of ladies to compete in the Swiss Ladies' Championship Race which was one item in the programme of the Swiss Championship Meeting at Engelberg. The team spent the first day in going over the course, escorted by Herr Adolf Odermatt and Major Stoker.

We lunched at the little inn at Trübsee, an inn which is connected with Engelberg by a cable railway. There is a little chapel attached to the inn and an offertory box in the dining room. Surreptitiously I placed half a franc in this box and commended our team to the protection of the patron saint. Subsequent enquiry elicited the fact that every other member of the team had paid a quiet visit to the offertory box. Miss Sale-Barker, however, on being pressed, admitted that a modest five centimes represented her notion of an adequate premium for supernatural insurance. I was taking no risks, and I added a franc to cover any deficits.

The Swiss Ladies' Championship was won by Miss Doreen Elliott. Miss Sale-Barker came in sixth, a very fair return for five centimes.

The result surprised us all, for when I arrived at the bottom of the course I found five very depressed young women, who were convinced that they had been badly beaten, and who overwhelmed me with a catalogue of remorseful blunders. " Where are you going to ? " they asked me, as I moved off. " Back to the Trübsee," I replied, " to rob the offertory box."

On the day after the race our party crossed the Joch Pass (7,265 ft.) to Meiringen. Herr Odermatt kindly accompanied us as far as the Engstlenalp. Herr Odermatt, who has rendered great services at Engelberg to the S.C.G.B., is a great sportsman and a magnificent skier who on one occasion just missed the Swiss Championship. Both he and Frau Odermatt are keenly interested in the development of ski-ing among the Swiss ladies. It was, indeed, largely due to Herr Odermatt's initiative that a ladies' race was included in the Swiss Championship programme.

As we stepped out of the Seilbahn at the Trübsee and buckled on our ski, we felt that we had paid in advance for the happiness of the hills. A short climb, some fifteen hundred feet, leads from the Trübsee to the Joch Pass where we met the wind, a wind strong enough to create the illusion and to awaken memories of serious mountaineering, and cold enough to make the sheltered hollow below the pass seem an elysium of snug content.

When I crossed the Joch Pass in summer many years ago, there was a vast mound called Pfaffenhaufen or " Parson's Heap " which owes its name to the following legend. In the seventeenth century the Abbot of the Benedictine monastery in Engelberg was a man of great physical strength, a *bon viveur* who appreciated a pretty girl and a glass of wine and enjoyed a mild gamble at cards. One day the Abbot wagered a friend that he would carry a load of 200 kilos up the Joch Pass, across which there was a busy traffic between the monastery and Meiringen. Just below the pass the Abbot drank from a cold stream, and died immediately as the result of heart failure. The monks deemed his sudden death to be a clear proof of God's anger and they buried him where he died, piling a huge mound above his remains. And thenceforward the peasants as they passed his grave threw a stone on to the mound in order to ward off the evil spirit of the Abbot. And to this genial habit the mound owed its huge size. In 1925 the grave was excavated and the skeleton of a man, who had clearly possessed great strength, was unearthed. It only remains to add that there are no records in the archives of the monastery to confirm this entertaining story.

Beautiful open slopes of western snow led down from the pass to the Engstlensee, but they had been tampered with by the wind. Of all ski-ing surfaces powder snow varied by crust is the most dangerous. The writer, actuated by the highest of motives, set a good example by putting in three cautious curves. He was, therefore, much pained to observe the lady members of the party flashing past in a long, glorious, but most immoral " Schuss " to the plain below.

In summer, the Engstlensee must be a dream of beauty, and even in winter it was most impressive. We halted at the Engstlenalp (6,033 ft.) and drank open wine in front of the deserted hotel. The valley walls framed in one of the most perfect of Alpine pictures, the triple-crested Wetterhorn. These Oberland peaks have a personality and a character that is all their own. The mountains of other ranges often suggest mass production in their wearisome repetition of ridge and spire and pyramid, but the Jungfrau, the Eiger and the Wetterhorn were made by hand. " God made them and broke the mould."

From the Engstlenalp, long northern slopes of powder snow varied by wood-running lead down to the Genthal. The wood was amusing and steep wood tracks provided convincing proof of the fact that the modern ski-runner has still to master the technique of stick-riding. The last long slopes of powder gave out, and were followed by three kilometres along the flat. Eventually we took off our ski in a forest just above the road from Innertkirchen to the Susten Pass. We had enjoyed about 3,500 feet of good running.

We walked down a mule path and called a halt among the pines, which stooped and recovered in the alternate gusts and lulls of the Foehn wind for which Meiringen is famous. The ski-runner has some excuse for hating this wind which ruins his snow and spoils his temper, but if you have ever lived through the five months of winter of an upper Alpine valley, you will look upon the Foehn with kindlier eyes. The Foehn is the herald of spring. In a few short days it can strip the snow from southern slopes and restore to the numbed and frozen earth the grateful solace of the sun. The Foehn is full of solvent energy. Vast masses of wet, heavy snow thunder down the ravines, and where they have passed the first of the flowers soon pierce through the awakening earth. Beauty follows fast on the steps of this boisterous wind. " Out of the strong comes forth sweetness."

Our last perfect halt was on the road to the Susten Pass. We sat on a pile of newly-cut logs. Below, the river torrent was singing a tentative tune, not of course, the full-throated chorus of May, but the opening bars of spring's great fugue. The stream had settled its account with the frost, and was freed from its winter prison. Thanks to the Foehn and to the exceptionally mild winter, the spring had staked its claim on a little plot of sanguine grass, grass green as only grass is green to eyes that have tired of the snow.

I have seen more majestic mountain views by far, but the picture which etched itself into memory during those few lazy moments will outlive many Alpine recollections—the foreground speckled with green and bathed in sun, the middle-distance a dark shadowed ravine mantled in dour pines, and the white crests of the upper ridges, from which the wind was tearing off the snow in long streamers of diamond dust, lit by the rays of the declining sun.

I said that this was a perfect day, and on a perfect day one is never really tired. Just as we were beginning to feel that we had had enough, we heard the cheerful honk of a motor piloted by Hugh Eaton, who had come over from Engelberg to meet us. Unless one arranges to be met by car or carriage, one has a dreary trudge of about two hours from the point where one joins the Susten road to Meiringen.

We had tea at the Bär Hotel, and then motored back to Lauterbrunnen. The sun setting in a golden bank beyond the waters of Brienz and the moonlight cradled in the Jungfrau snows are the crowning memories of a perfect day.

II

The patient flag-keepers had been standing in the full glare of the March sun for four long hours, storing up a fine confused complexion for the future. Armed with a megaphone, my duty was to warn the timekeepers when the course was clear, a duty to which the patient Mr. Pittman had to recall my attention more than once. For my thoughts were wandering. This, the Arlberg-Kandahar, was the last great race of the Mürren season, and the *Wanderlust* was beginning to disturb me with a vision of distant hills, hills innocent of slalom flags and competitors.

Bracken ran down superbly and the slalom was his. Of the six first prizes we gave at this meeting, it seemed as if the Kandahar would win four. Peter ran well and finished ninth in the slalom. Then came the ladies. Audrey Sale-Barker swept past, an easy winner of the Ladies' Arlberg-Kandahar. I sighed with relief. All my anxieties were over for the season ; I could begin to ski for pleasure.

For it had been an anxious season, as all those who have helped to organise a great international championship will appreciate. Captain Oestgaard told me that for weeks before the FIS Meeting at Oslo he never got to sleep before midnight and invariably woke at five in the morning. I can well believe it, and I cannot conceive that the FIS Meeting at Oslo could have been a greater strain than our meeting at Mürren.

At least Captain Oestgaard had the satisfaction of knowing that the Norwegians would sweep the board and that jumping or langlauf would not be prejudiced if they did not do as well as was expected.

At Mürren downhill racing, or at least the slalom, was on trial. Bad organisation might put back the clock for years ; a bad performance by the British team would have provoked mocking comments on the pioneers of downhill racing. An added source of anxiety, so far as I was concerned, was the fact that the British team included my son. There was enough reason here to worry without that grim battle against unprecedented climatic conditions. Yes, I had had more than enough of racing by the time the last competitor ran through the finishing posts of the Arlberg-Kandahar.

III

We, that is, Eric Lewns, Peter and I, left Mürren the day after the Arlberg-Kandahar, March 17th, 1931. We left on ski, and ran down from Grütsch to Lauterbrunnen on perfect spring snow. That night we slept at the Scheidegg and ran down to Grindelwald next day with Vivian Caulfeild. Ski-ing with Vivian Caulfeild is the next best thing to solitary ski-ing, indeed in some ways it is even better, a compliment that will make V. C. blush.

I enjoy ski-ing alone for two reasons. In the first place the mountains keep their most intimate secrets for the solitary climber. When all other memories grow dim I shall still remember, as if they were yesterday, the moments which I have spent on the few big peaks, such as the Wetterhorn, which I have climbed without companions.

In the second place solitary ski-ing is attractive because one can go one's own pace. The ideal ski-ing companion is hard to find. Most people are either too fast, which is shame-making, or too slow, which is tiresome. Ski-ing from its nature, is competitive, whatever the tourers may say. Among the tourers who declaim most violently against racing, there are many who are the victims of unbridled

Ehrgeiz. They will not admit that they are anxious to get downhill faster than their fellows, but in effect they transform every run into an unofficial race. I am strongly in favour of racing—in races ; I dislike intensely racing on tour.

Worst of all are the humbugs who start the run with some such pious exhortation as this : " Now you chaps, let's enjoy ourselves and run downhill at a comfortable cruising speed ; " and then proceed promptly to leap down the slopes as if they were competing in the Roberts of Kandahar. Their object is to convey the impression that this, their fastest possible speed, merely represents their notion of a slow cruise, but it is time this humbug was exploded. When one is past forty one must begin to guard against that last infirmity of ageing minds, the ambition to prove that one is still as young as one feels. The vanity of age is more ridiculous than the vanity of youth. It is seemly that a young man should be a thruster on tour, but the spectacle of a veteran hurling himself downhill and arriving in a state of extreme exhaustion is very painful. In ski-ing matters, whatever Cicero may say to the contrary, there is much to be said for that *laudatoque proverbio quod monet mature fieri senem, si diu velis senex esse.*

There is none of that competitive nonsense about V. C. and the present writer. We hold one record of which we are both rather proud—the longest time from the Little Scheidegg via the Männlichen to Grund, four hours to be precise. V. C. is an expert at avoiding routine slopes. Nothing pleases him more than to escape from tracks and to dive into trees and glens hoping for the best. He is not duly perturbed when he strikes the worst. Besides one always learns something. In the course of our historic Männlichen descent I evolved a new theory for crossing a fallen tree. We were trying to climb out of a ravine into which V. C. had dived with more courage than discretion, and the steep slope which we were traversing was interrupted by a vast tree which had been blown down so that it lay right down the slope. Nothing is more tiresome than to ski across a slippery tree trunk at an angle of thirty degrees or so. V. C. tried to scramble across, slipped and fell down the tree which he embraced with loving affection. " Lay your head on the trunk :" thus spoke the decisive voice of a man of action. V. C., who was by now thoroughly frightened, obeyed. " Don't move your head," I muttered and proceeded to cross the tree by sliding my ski across Vivian's head, which provided admirable purchase. "Have you got steel edges?" asked V. C. anxiously. My reply that fibre would suffice to get a good grip on his skull brought small comfort.

It is tremendous fun ski-ing with V. C. now that I have mastered the art of arguing about technique while we are ski-ing downhill. Anybody can talk going uphill—I am sure I can—but to maintain the right distance for conversation while running downhill is almost as difficult as roped racing.

Dante has summed in three inimitable lines the character of a perfect ski duet

> Nè il dir l'andar, nè l'andar lui più lento
> facea, ma ragionando andavam forte
> sì come nave pinta da buon vento

which may be rendered "Neither did our chat retard our pace, nor our speed spoil our discussion, but talking hard we went bravely on, like a ship driven by a fair wind."

V. C. has always some entirely new idea about ski-ing; I have never skied with him without returning the richer for some brilliant analysis of a ski-ing turn, or some pregnant hint on ski-ing technique. I make this confession with regret, for I, too, am a writer of ski-ing books and, if I could get away with it, I should like the reader to believe that whatever is of value in Caulfeild's next book has been picked up in the course of these Scheidegg runs.

We parted at Grindelwald, V. C. returning to the Little Scheidegg while we started up towards the Great Scheidegg. Our plans were vague, as they should be on the ideal ski-ing holiday, one recipe for which is to carry all one's luggage on one's back and post the rest of it to Basle, where it may be picked up on one's way back to England. If you follow this recipe yours will be a peace of mind unknown to those who have to be in a given valley by a given date in order to establish contact with clean shirts. The Swiss air is pure and a blue shirt does not show the dirt, and if you are a faddist you can carry two blue shirts instead of one.

We climbed slowly up the Great Scheidegg while the March sun beat down upon our backs. Half way up we halted under the cover of a hay chalet where I promptly fell asleep. One effect of the FIS Meeting was an intense drowsiness and flatness which persisted for a fortnight after I had returned to England.

As the result of this torpor, we were late in reaching the Great Scheidegg. In mid-March one should time one's descent just before the sun leaves the slopes, for whereas snow which is just beginning to freeze is delightful, spring snow which has formed crust for the first inch or two is very trying, and particularly trying if one is wearing steel edges, as we soon discovered.

Snowcraft at present is far from being an exact science. One is always being confronted with anomalies. On this expedition we struck pure spring snow on north slopes just above the 4,500 feet line ; some little distance down, below the point where spring crust had replaced powder snow even on northern slopes, I came across a slope of pure "leaf powder," great flakes of crystalline powder snow looking like small leaves. This particular formation is seldom found excepting, as in this case, near a river bed, and is probably due to the cold mists which rise from the river. We passed Rosenlaui and entered that "delightful vale strewn with hamlets," which excited the enthusiasm of Archdeacon Coxe, when he passed that way in 1776. "After ascending about three hours," wrote the Archdeacon, "we refreshed ourselves and our horses in a delightful vale strewn with hamlets ; a sloping hill adorned with variegated verdure on one side ; vast impending rocks lifting their heads into the clouds on the other ; a beautiful pyramidical mountain (the Wetterhorn) covered with snow rising before us."

Coxe had a keen appreciation of mountain scenery, which was more usual even in the eighteenth century than is sometimes supposed. There are many appreciative references to mountains in John Wesley's Diary, which was compiled long before the dawn of the romantic revival.

It is a curious fact, a fact on which no one seems to have commented, that the love of mountains finds earlier expression in painting than in literature. There are few views more beautiful than the distant view of Monte Rosa from the Lombard Plain, more particularly at sunrise or sunset ; but until Tennyson "climbed the roof at break of day" and saw the dawn on Monte Rosa from the roof of Milan Cathedral you will find no reference in literature to a view with which every Italian must have been familiar.

But where the poets were silent the painters were at work. I once wrote a book on Venice which called for a careful study of the Venetian painters. Now in clear weather the Alps can be seen from the Lido and this mountain background was perfectly familiar to all the Venetian School. The landscapes of Titian, Giovanni Bellini, Giorgione and Lotto are often pregnant with loving and accurate observations of the hills, as you can prove for yourself if you visit the National Gallery. There is a real feeling for the poetry of the mountains in the snowy hills seen through the open window in Lotto's portrait of the Protonotary Giuliano. The Bellini *Madonna* in the same gallery has an attractive background of snow mountains and the mountains of storm are painted with power and imagination in Titian's *Madonna with St. Catherine*. It is surely a fair assumption that painters, other than those who make a deliberate cult of ugliness, seldom spend much time on natural objects which repel them. The shapeless lumps which do duty for mountains in so many medieval paintings represent very fairly the disgust with which mountains inspired the painters in question. But you cannot study the paintings which I have mentioned without being convinced that the Venetian painters at least loved the mountain background to their seagirt Republic.

We were pleasantly tired when we turned into the Bär Hotel at Meiringen, the hotel which has been for me the starting point and finishing point of some of the best days that I have ever spent among the hills.

We left Meiringen next morning at about eight o'clock for Mägisalp, a little alp which lies above Meiringen on the other side of the valley to Rosenlaui. It would have saved time to have taken the train to Brünig and thence to have followed the level road towards Hohfluh, but we chose the more direct route in spite of the fact that it involved more climbing. Two nice young men from Meiringen, one of whom, Immer,* had competed in the Arlberg-Kandahar, carried our ski for the three hours' climb to Reuti.

About two hours above Meiringen we halted in a little glade with a perfect view. Framed in between the pines we could see the Wetterhorn, the truncated and snowy pyramid of the Mönch and the sharp wedge of the Eiger.

Peter asked whether the laws of composition which produce a good picture are the same as those which produce a satisfying view, but the reader will be relieved to hear that I have no intention of quoting my lengthy reply. Let him study, if he has not already done so, Sir Charles Holmes's admirable *Notes on the Science of Picture Making*, and then ask himself how far his own favourite mountain views conform to Sir Charles's standards of rhythm, unity, vitality, infinity and repose. One thing at least is certain. Any-

* The other "nice young man" was Glatthard, who won the Arlberg-Kandahar in 1935.

body who takes the trouble to read Ruskin among the older critics and Sir Charles Holmes among modern critics, and to study painting with their aid, will be rewarded by noticing many effects which he would otherwise overlook. Let him, for instance, read and re-read Ruskin's marvellous chapter on the truth of tone, and then walk into the National Gallery and compare Poussin's *Phocion* with Turner's *Crossing of the Brook.* The fact that Ruskin is grossly partial to Turner and most unfair to Poussin is irrelevant. Ruskin's value is that he forces you to look at trees and clouds and mountains with more discerning attention, if only for the fun of proving him wrong.

I feel about art criticism very much as I feel about geology. Any geological theory is good which forces you to look at mountains more closely. Are glaciers on the whole conservative or destructive? Were the Alpine lake basins scooped out by glaciers? It does not matter in the least which of these two views you decide to champion provided that you are sufficiently interested to examine every glacier and every valley in the hope of finding evidence which corroborates your theory. Similarly, any art critic who is sufficiently stimulating to drive you into the National Gallery will probably help you to find not only in art, but also in Nature, a far wider range in colour and tone than the uneducated eye can see.

Calm your impatience, dear reader, it took us three hours to get to Mägisalp, and here are you expecting to get there in as many paragraphs.

IV

The Mägisalp Hut is situated at a height of 1,891 metres (6,214 feet) above the sea and is 4,226 feet above Meiringen.

From the hut one can return to Meiringen by the route by which we climbed, but a far more entertaining run is to return via Balisalp. A small lateral ridge, which runs parallel with the main ridge, enables the ski-runner to do most of this run on northern snow. It is easy to lengthen the run by climbing up under the Frutt Pass.

This is the route which we followed and we were delighted both with the ski-ing and with the views. From Balisalp there is some pleasant wood-running and then the ground opens out. The rest of the run down to Hohfluh is on south slopes and would normally be crusted in winter. Hohfluh is a little village halfway in the road from the Brünig Pass to Reuti.

As the result of heavy snowfalls there was snow on southern slopes right down to Meiringen itself; we kept on our ski from Hohfluh to the valley. It is very unusual to find snow on south slopes two thousand feet above the sea as late as March 18th.

The ski-ing was very good indeed until we struck a path about five hundred feet above the Meiringen Valley. As we skied down this path the sky was cloudless, but there was a curious drag in the snow which could only mean one thing, Foehn. The blazing spring sun may melt the snow to a great depth, but it never produces this peculiar drag. The path was fairly steep and apart from the Foehn we should have slid down it at a high speed. I was much intrigued by this forerunner of the Foehn. There was no sign of cloud in the sky: in fact the Foehn did not develop for another four-and-twenty hours, and I have never yet known snow begin to drag before some definite evidence of Foehn is in the sky.

We paused for a few moments when we reached the valley. The spring was very late, too late for my taste, for I would gladly have sacrificed a few hundred feet of ski-ing for those first tender washes of vivid green which one has a right to expect in mid-March on southern slopes. As I took off my ski, I remembered how "Booly" Evans and I had wandered to this very spot on the day of rest which followed a never-to-be-forgotten ski tour in May. From a cluster of marsh marigolds, on a plot of damp marshy grass, a butterfly, the Greek symbol of immortality, rose slowly and fluttered away to the neighbouring wood.

V

We caught the afternoon train over the Brünig and left it at Hergiswil for the steamer which took us across to Stansstad.

We reached Engelberg in time for an excellent dinner at the Bellevue Terminus. Next day we did the Joch Pass with Herr Adolf Odermatt and young Maclaren, a promising young racer who ran in the Arlberg-Kandahar, and who was alleged to be learning German at Engelberg. He enlarged on the educational advantages of Engelberg with such eloquence that Peter suggested that, instead of proceeding to Müllheim-in-Baden as arranged, he should remain at Engelberg and explore the intricacies of the German tongue with the friendly co-operation of Maclaren and the assistance of Herr Adolf Odermatt.

I intended to spend two days at Engelberg and try some of the runs which I only knew by hearsay but, alas, the Foehn which had made itself felt at Meiringen blew up in full force when we reached the summit of the Joch Pass, and ruined the otherwise excellent run down from the Trübsee.

We woke the next morning to find wet, Foehn clouds on the hills. The party accordingly broke up. Lewns went back to the Scheidegg and Peter and I went on to Basle. We had registered our luggage to Basle, where Peter was to be met by his Müllheim hosts. As we approached Basle I felt slightly apprehensive as to the impression which we should produce on our German friends, more particularly as Peter's sole remaining handkerchief had been used, among other things, to rub wax into his ski. I left him at Basle under strict instructions not to blow his nose till he had unpacked.

CHALET BERNA, GRINDELWALD,
June 1st, 1931.

CHAPTER XVIII

Edward Whymper

I

EDWARD WHYMPER, whose life is the theme of Mr. Frank Smythe's interesting biography, was born on April 27th, 1840, a fact which Mr. Smythe leaves the reader to discover by private research. Fortunately, Whymper records his birthday in the journal from which Mr. Smythe quotes long extracts in his book.*

The Whympers were of Dutch origin and the family came over to England with William of Orange. The word "Whymper" is a corruption of the Dutch word "Wimper," which means eye-brow. Edward's grandfather was a brewer; his father, Josiah, a wood engraver and a painter. At the age of fourteen Edward was taken away from school and apprenticed to his father's business. A year later, Edward began a diary, long extracts from which are reproduced by Mr. Smythe.

The diary is a valuable social document with a sure appeal to all who are interested in the Victorian age. It is the work of a clever boy, with considerable gifts for expression. Had Edward been a youthful genius the diary would have been less representative of the period, and therefore less valuable as a social document.

There are many passages in Whymper's diary which remind us of the class-consciousness of the mid-Victorian Age. The barrier between the classes, and above all the strong line of division between rich and poor, was far more pronounced in the eighteen-forties than in the Middle Ages. In this respect the nineteen-thirties compare favourably with the age into which Whymper was born. Here is a characteristic extract :—

"*June 27th*, 1855.—*Lord Robert Grosvenor last week mentioned in the House of Lords that the aristocracy were setting the commoners a better example than they had before in such matters as driving in the Parks on Sunday; which speech drew forth some handbills recommending an assembly in Hyde Park to see the aforesaid good example. A number of low fellows accordingly met and saluted the nobility with cries of 'Don't employ y'r servants on Sunday,' etc., and they actually went so far as to compel the Duke and Duchess of Beaufort and several other noblemen and ladies to get out and walk, the police not interfering. This is a free country indeed*

* *Edward Whymper*, by FRANK SMYTHE. Hodder & Stoughton.

when such things as these are allowed, and quickly passed over without much notice being taken of them."

"*July* 8*th.—The mob, finding nothing to be done there, went down Piccadilly and in Belgrave Square breaking windows. This shows what kind of people they were. As Mr. Peel said in the House, 'They were mere* canaille,' *and I quite agree with his suggestion that a few six-pounders fired into them would do a deal of good.*"

No English boy of fifteen could conceivably write like that to-day. Or, again, like this :—

"*February* 19*th.—Sir J. Walmsley has attempted to introduce a bill (for desecrating the Sabbath really) but for Sunday recreation as he calls it. He would have the British Museum, National Gallery, and the Crystal Palace open on the Sunday, in order to improve the national mind (he says). It was justly said at the meeting to-night that for Englishmen who always regard liberty as one of the greatest blessings, to wish to deprive the largest body of people (the religious) in the country of their privileges would be an act of the highest injustice and oppression.*"

Thus the Sabbatarians in the name of liberty refused to be deprived "of their privileges," which included the right to deny the minority the liberty to look at pictures or listen to concerts on Sunday. Sabbatarianism was the subject on which the youthful Whymper felt most strongly.

"*May* 15*th.—The bands playing on Sundays in the parks have been stopped by Lord Palmerston. . . . For my own part I do not consider that playing music (especially sacred, which they did) is so criminal (in a religious light) as getting drunk or going excursions in the country on a Sunday.*"

On June 15th Whymper records an improper suggestion made to his firm by a Mr. Macpherson, who wanted a block finished quickly : "As the block is for a religious publication, there would be no sin in working on the Sunday."

"*It is very strange that such an argument could be used from an educated person living in the* 19*th century. It would better suit the* 12*th or the* 13*th.*"

The Plymouth brethren appealed to the streak of dour puritanism in Whymper's character.

"*February* 20*th*, 1859.—*I like Mr. Gosse* exceedingly. Besides being a clever and learned man (and the conversation of such must always be pleasing to me), he is an excellent Christian, brim full of his Bible, and very apt with his texts. He is a Plymouth brother, which is the same as saying he is no sect, and his opinions and views on religion coincide almost*

* Edmund Gosse's father, immortalised in *Father and Son.*

perfectly with my own. The stay of such a man in one's house is, I think, almost sure to do one good."

Mr. Smythe must, I think, have forgotten this passage when he exclaimed, " Was ever so cold-blooded and cynical a diary compiled by a youth ? "

Whymper, who was nineteen years old when he wrote the extract quoted above, so far from being cynical, was naïve in his unsophisticated attitude to religious and social orthodoxy. At the age of nineteen he writes as follows :—

" *February 8th.—We shall, I think, be nicely busy this year, for we keep on having little jobs come in, as well as big ones. Thanks be to our Father in Heaven from whom all blessings flow, and may we strive to deserve them, so far as we mav be said to deserve anything.*"

And again :—

" *Abril 19th.—Sir W. Clay, I believe, intends putting up for Lambeth. I hope he may succeed in keeping the ignorant radical Fred Doulton out.*"

The youthful Whymper faithfully reflects the social standards oı the Victorian Lower Middle Classes. His father's position in the social hierarchy is not easy to determine. Edward Whymper, as we shall see, had some difficulty with his aspirates. His father was elected a member of the Royal Society of Painters in Water-colours. His pupils included Frederick Walker, A.R.A., and Keene, the well-known contributor to *Punch.* And he might perhaps have moved in a higher social *milieu* and sent his sons to better schools had his business been more consistently prosperous and had his family been less large. Joseph Whymper had eleven children, of whom Frederick wrote two books, which sold well, *Travels in Alaska* and *The Romance of the Sea* ; and of the surviving sons Mr. Frank Whymper, Mr. Samuel Whymper and Mr. Charles Whymper, R.I., have travelled extensively, the last named being well known as an artist.

Edward Whymper was not what the Victorians would have described as a gentleman. Instead of rebelling, as he might have done, against a social system which relegated him to a low rank, he seems to have accepted society as he found it. He was equally conscious of the barrier between himself and the upper classes, and the barrier between himself and the class immediately below his own.

" *December 13th.—Mr. C. Clark, N.A., preached both times. Hoh ! The aitches. It is perfectly 'orrible to 'ear 'eaven, 'ope, 'eart, etc. For they are legion. Without this, to say the least, Clark may be a very clever young man; but with it, I think no man should attempt to speak in public.*"

It is as well that Whymper did not practise what he preached, for he was an excellent lecturer but " troubled by a tendency to drop his aitches." " This worried him," writes Mr. Smythe, " and round about 1905 to 1908 he got his nephew, Mr. Robert Whymper, to attend many of his lectures and call attention to every omission by snapping his fingers."

" What are the principal impressions to be gathered from perusal of this diary ? " writes Mr. Smythe. " The first is undoubtedly the appalling monotony of the life led by young Whymper. It is a sad document, this diary. It might have been written by a prisoner in a cell who, realizing the uselessness of railing against captivity and confinement, set himself to record the little events of life, the daily round."

Mr. Smythe reads his own antipathies into Whymper's journal. Mr. Smythe's idea of Hell is to catch the 9 a.m. train every morning and leave his office at 5.30 p.m. every evening, but it would be difficult to prove that genius could never flourish within the framework of an ordered life, and it is fantastic to suggest that the discipline of a regular job is necessarily fatal to a youthful genius. Whymper had escaped from the office at about the age that Mr. Smythe left school, and it would be just as easy to prove that Mr. Smythe's life has been permanently blighted by the fact that he had to keep regular hours at Berkhamsted as to maintain the thesis that Mr. Smythe attempts to develop in this biography.

" The ' No news ' in his diary is not merely the record of a fact but the cry of a soul which finds itself imprisoned it knows not how or why."

This is a good example of the lengths to which Mr. Smythe is driven in his search for a romantic explanation of an unromantic journal. If every boy who filled up a diary with such entries were a genius, the world would be full of geniuses.

There is no evidence whatever in the journal to suggest that the youthful Whymper felt himself cribbed and confined by a uncongenial task. Still less that he was unhappy. He enjoyed watching and playing cricket. " I formed the nucleus of the North Lambeth Cricket Club, which I hope may last for years." He shows a healthy interest in murders, war, prize fights, sudden death (" A porter was completely cut up on the North Kent line at Blackheath station by a train which stole upon him without his perceiving it. Very showery "), and, above all, in his job. So far from resenting " the fearful monotony in his father's office," he displays a keen interest in the commercial progress of the firm and a great pride in his own craftsmanship. He enjoys his job and is determined to succeed. " This block I have been engaged on for a long time past, not so much as a specimen of my talent for effect, but for minuteness and correctness of detail. I hope this may be the means of bringing my name before the public as a correct architectural draughtsman, which if I once get I will do my best to keep."

There is no evidence whatever for the mystic *manqué* in Whymper's diary either as a boy or man ; and because everything that Whymper wrote contradicts Mr. Smythe's theory, he is compelled, in desperation, to suggest that what Whymper wrote is largely irrelevant to what Whymper felt. Mr. Smythe is not deceived by all this pretence of enjoying cricket, all this pose of being interested in his profession. " It seems almost as though Whymper was afraid to face up to his own thoughts and ambitions." Mr. Smythe would cease to be puzzled by the consistent realism of Whymper's diary if he would " face up " to the fact that Whymper's " thoughts and ambitions " were his own, and not Mr. Smythe's.

Perplexed by Whymper's obvious interest in his chosen profession, Mr. Smythe is driven to suggest filial devotion as a clue. " Was this because he was unswervingly loyal to his father ? " But the real clue is provided by Mr. Smythe's entertaining description of Whymper's business activities in later life. Whymper re-edited annually his own excellent guides to Zermatt and Mont Blanc and toured Switzerland to collect advertisements for these guides, and the sums due from his agents for the sales.

" No hotel or inn," writes Mr. Smythe, " was too small to take a copy or two on ' sale or return,' or to buy a piece of ' space ' to advertise itself. . . . Whymper had an exceptionally keen sense of money values and was quick to sense sharp practice, evasion or dilatoriness in others." Whymper toured Switzerland collecting his dues. On some occasions hotel keepers who owed him money for advertisements or copies sold faded away on his arrival, and Whymper records how he once searched an hotel from top to bottom to discover the evasive proprietor. When all else failed he had recourse to the law. " It is impossible," writes Mr. Smythe,

" not to admire the grim determination behind the sales of the Zermatt and Chamonix guides."

Calvinism, as Mr. R. H. Tawney has shown, is a fertile soil for the development of the business virtues, and Whymper's background of Dutch Calvinism left its impress on his character. This unromantic hero of the Matterhorn romance was as at home in a business deal as on the Alpine ridges. The same grim determination which carried him to the crest of the Matterhorn inspired his exploration of basements in search of defaulting creditors, but it is surprising that Mr. Smythe should have ignored the clue which he himself provides in his entertaining word picture of Whymper collecting his dues.

II

Mr. Smythe implies that if Whymper was not romantically wretched in his office job, he ought to have been. But it was the fact that Whymper loved his work, and had mastered his chosen craft, which gave him his splendid chance. His work attracted the attention of William Longman, the publisher, who was in need of illustrations for a book on the Alps and who commissioned Edward Whymper for this purpose.

Whymper was twenty years of age when he left England for the Alps. He crossed the Channel on July 23rd, 1860, visited Kandersteg, crossed the Gemmi to Leuk, explored the Saas valley and sketched the view from the Fee Alp, one of the few Alpine views which excited his enthusiastic appreciation. From Saas Fee he went to Zermatt.

Mr. Smythe makes an excellent point when he contrasts Whymper's first impressions of the Matterhorn, as recorded in his diary, with the sentiments which he put on record for the public :—

" Saw, of course, the Matterhorn repeatedly ; what precious stuff Ruskin has written about this, as well as about many other things. When one has a fair view of the mountain as I had, it may be compared to a sugar loaf set up on a table ; the sugar loaf should have its head knocked on one side. Grand it is, but beautiful I think it is not."

And this is what he wrote, when he was writing for the public. The quotation is from *Scrambles amongst the Alps* :—

" Ages hence generations unborn will gaze upon its awful precipices and wonder at its unique form. However exalted may be their ideas, and however exaggerated their expectations, none will come to return disappointed ! "

Whymper was a superb salesman. He sold the Matterhorn to the British public, and—like other salesmen—his private opinion of the commodity which he marketed did not always coincide with his publicity pronouncements. Few mountaineers had less appreciation of mountain beauty, or a greater appreciation of mountain adventure.

He returned to the Oberland, went up the Lauterbrunnen valley and disliked the Staubbach even more than he had expected to. " I had previously expected to be disappointed, but felt quite sold, and would not stop to look at it."

Whymper returned to the Alps in 1861, made the first British ascent of the Pelvoux and, emboldened by this success, attempted the Matterhorn from Italy.

His seven unsuccessful attempts on the Matterhorn (1861-1865) were all directed against the Italian side of the mountain. His persistent neglect of what is now the normal route from Zermatt is difficult to explain. The three brothers, Alfred, Charles and Sandbach Parker, had attacked the Matterhorn by this route, a year before Whymper made his first attempt on the mountain, and *without guides* had reached a height of 12,000 feet on the eastern face. They were driven back by storm, but reported that the eastern face appeared practicable for many hundred feet above the point from which they had retreated.

Seen from the Riffel the East face appears precipitous, and " several years passed away " before Whymper freed himself from this illusion. But it is only in dry summers that the face seems precipitous from the Riffel (for the first snowfall discloses the terraces on this great natural staircase), and when viewed in profile the East face is disclosed as a monstrous imposture, for the average angle up to the " Shoulder " does not exceed forty degrees. Neither Whymper, nor the great guides Bennen, Almer and Croz, detected the obvious weakness of the obvious route to the summit. " Carrel," writes Guido Rey, " did not believe the ascent from the north to be possible."* Whymper therefore erred in good company.

Writing after the event, Whymper states that he had convinced

* *The Matterhorn*. By Guido Rey. Translated by J. E. C. Eaton, p. 137. This book contains the story of the early attempts written from the Italian angle. Mr. Smythe might well have made more use of Rey's book, particularly in the chapters on the conquest of the Matterhorn.

himself that the East face offered the best chance of success, but that he failed to convince Croz and Almer with whom he attacked the Matterhorn three weeks before it was finally conquered. They selected the silliest of all conceivable routes, a gully on the Italian face, which is the natural chute for falling stones, leading to a point on the Furggen ridge, from which they would have had to cross a face, under incessant bombardment. Whymper's explanation is that Almer and Croz flatly refused to attempt the East face, and apparently preferred any alternative route, however dangerous and however difficult, to the obvious route which was staring them in the face. Whymper's explanation is confirmed by his diary, quoted by Mr. Smythe (p. 163), but neither he nor any subsequent writer has produced a plausible explanation for one of the strangest aberrations in Alpine history. Whymper was one of the greatest amateurs of the day ; Croz and Almer among the greatest guides. Their joint attempt on the Matterhorn is a classic example of the fallibility of experts, for the most inexperienced of novices could hardly have picked a worse route.

Many of Whymper's attempts on the Matterhorn were made with the great Italian guide, J. A. Carrel. Carrel, an ardent patriot who had fought in the Italian wars of liberation, was determined to make the first ascent from Italy by the Italian ridge, and—if possible—to lead an Italian party to the summit. Carrel, like Whymper, had something of the undisciplined nature of the mountain he loved. Like Whymper, he was a born leader, and, like Whymper, he did not readily consent to play second fiddle. It is not surprising that Whymper and Carrel did not form a successful partnership.

Early in July, 1865, Whymper arrived at Breuil hoping to engage Carrel for yet another attempt on the Matterhorn, but Carrel had previously been engaged by two Italians (Giordano and Sella), who shared Carrel's desire that the conquest of the Matterhorn should be an Italian triumph. Carrel told Whymper that he had been " engaged by a party of distinction," and it was only after Carrel had left for the Matterhorn that Whymper realised that he had been " bamboozled and humbugged."

Whymper decided to cross the Théodule to Zermatt and engage the first competent guide he could find for an attack on the mountain from Switzerland. It was at this point that Lord Francis Douglas, brother of the Marquess of Queensberry, arrived from Zermatt.

Douglas was fresh from his conquest of the Gabelhorn, the first ascent from Zinal. He confided to Whymper that old Peter Taugwalder had prospected the East face of the Matterhorn and was confident that the mountain could be climbed by that route. Douglas had decided to attempt the ascent and was readily persuaded to join forces with Whymper.

On the following day they crossed the Théodule to Zermatt, where they learned that the Rev. Charles Hudson had just arrived in company with Michel Croz, with whom he was proposing to attempt the Matterhorn.

Hudson was the greatest amateur of the day, a pioneer of guideless climbing who had led a guideless party up Mont Blanc by a new route. He had not wasted years in exploring the more difficult routes to the summit. He went straight for the easiest route, and had no difficulty in persuading Michel Croz to accompany him. The late Captain Farrar, in a scholarly article, contrasts the ease with which Hudson imposed his views on Croz with Croz' reluctance to try this route when it was suggested by Whymper.

" Surely the first question," wrote Captain Farrar, " which springs to one's mind is to account for the sudden change in the attitude of Croz. As late as June 21st we find him deliberately pass by the E. face and attempt instead the Furggen couloir with the object of gaining the E. face high up. Nineteen days later he arrives at Zermatt with Hudson to attempt, as a matter in the ordinary course of his guide's business, the ascent by this very E. face. We can reasonably account for this change by the impress of the study, the experience, and the knowledge of his new employer." (*Alpine Journal*, xxxii. p. 27.)

Whymper and Douglas persuaded Hudson that it would be undesirable for two parties to be on the mountain at the same time. They agreed to join forces, and to include in the party a young man of nineteen, Douglas Hadow, who " had done Mont Blanc in less time than most men." Hadow, though a strong walker, was an inexperienced climber, and was destined to prove the weak link in the chain.

III

They left Zermatt on July 13th, 1865, and reached the summit next day. The East face up to the " Shoulder," less than a thousand feet below the summit, was so easy that they did not even bother to rope. From the "Shoulder" they turned over on to the North face, and here the climbing was difficult, but far easier than the final section of the Italian route.

In the course of the descent, a little distance below the summit, Hadow fell. Or, at least, Whymper assumed that it was Hadow who had first slipped, though, as Mr. Smythe shrewdly insists, this was perhaps an assumption. "It was impossible for Whymper to suppose that Croz *could* slip, yet Emile Rey, the greatest guide of his generation, slipped on easy ground and was killed." The rope broke between old Taugwalder and Francis Douglas. Hudson, Hadow, Douglas and Croz fell; Whymper and the two Taugwalders survived to tell the tale.

Old Taugwalder laboured for many years under the suspicion that he had cut the rope. He left his native valley for America, returning only to die. This suspicion, as Whymper points out, was absurd. It would have been impossible to cut the rope in the second that elapsed before it tightened, and pointless to cut it after it tightened, for if a slip on rocks can be checked, all danger is over.

It was ungenerous of Whymper to point out that "an old and weak rope" had been selected by Taugwalder as the link between him and Douglas, for I do not think that Whymper really believed this selection to have been deliberate.

C. Egger, a pioneer of ski-mountaineering and the author of some scholarly articles on the history of ski-ing, contributes to the monthly publication of the Swiss Alpine Club (*Die Alpen*, July, 1940) a balanced and convincing article on the Taugwalders (*Les Taugwalders du Cervin*). I agree with Herr Egger that the answers which old Taugwalder gave at the Inquiry are clear and logical ("sont même d'une clarté et d'une logique remarquables"). Herr Egger is left with the impression "that Whymper, consciously or unconsciously, wished to deflect attention from himself to his guides, in order to diminish his own responsibility for the accident. For Whymper tied himself on to Taugwalder, after the delay caused by depositing the names on the summit; he ought therefore to have perceived that it was the weakest rope which united Taugwalder to Douglas, all the more so, as he had himself provided the ropes."

It is clear that Whymper did not like Taugwalder, and it is highly probable that Taugwalder did not like Whymper. Few people did.

In his published account of the accident, Whymper accuses the Taugwalders of cowardice, insensitiveness and an attempt to exploit the accident to obtain higher remuneration. In a memorandum made to the secretary of the Alpine Club, found among Whymper's papers and published by Mr. Smythe ıor the first time, he makes the further suggestion that the Taugwalders would not have been ill-pleased had Whymper been killed " as an opening to a future notoriety of a very lucrative nature, and that they were prepared to avail themselves of any opportunity that might offer during the descent of bringing about that loss."

Mr. Smythe, whose analysis of the accident is of great value, is altogether too kind in his comments on this monstrous suggestion. It is clear that he does not for one moment believe that there was the least foundation for Whymper's gross libel. He dismisses the accusation as unproved and improbable, but he has no word of condemnation for the criminal irresponsibility with which Whymper committed to paper a charge of attempted murder, which was unsupported by a shred of evidence. Mr. Smythe should not have wasted a sentence in disproving this fantastic absurdity.

" No one," writes Mr. Smythe, " can justly impugn Whymper's veracity in the matter of his conversation with the Taugwalders." Why not? Mr. Smythe, on page 211, draws attention to a striking contradiction between two accounts of a remark which Whymper alleges to have been made by Croz, a remark which, as Mr. Smythe justly says, was " curious," implying as it did a slur on the mountaineering capacity of Croz' employer, Charles Hudson. Mr. Smythe elsewhere contrasts the bald statement in Whymper's diary that the crevasses at the side of the Gorner Glacier " rendered getting on it a work of time to a novice," with the highly coloured account given of the same incident in *Scrambles* : " If the jump should be successful—well ; if not, I fell into that horrible chasm, to be frozen in, or drowned in that gurgling, rushing water. Everything depended on that jump. Again I asked myself, ' Can it be done?' " There is a fashion in these things, and Whymper, who was an excellent showman with a flair for what the public wanted, describes three jumps in *Scrambles*. Mr. Smythe hints a discreet doubt of Jump No. 1. Reynaud, whose involuntary jump is the theme of a spirited engraving—" We saw a toe—it seemed to belong to Moore ; we saw Reynaud, a flying body "—strongly objected to this version of his movements, and Mr. Coolidge's scepticism on the subject of yet another jump provoked an historic incident in the Alpine Club.

One of the most sensational illustrations in the *Scrambles* depicts Almer leaping across a deep notch on the western ridge of the Ecrins. " The rock swayed as he came down upon it, but he clutched a large mass with both arms and brought himself to anchor." The Rev. W. A. B. Coolidge, who trailed a pretty coat and who could do anything with a hatchet excepting bury it, stated in the course of an obituary notice of Christian Almer, published in the *Swiss Alpine Club Journal*, that Almer had told him that he had never made the jump, described and illustrated by Whymper. Whymper circulated a letter to every member of the Alpine Club in which he maintained that in his version of the jump he was supported by Horace Walker, and that Almer's son Ulrich remembered his father having mentioned the jump shortly after the ascent. Coolidge refused to withdraw, and evaded a public discussion at an extraordinary general meeting by resigning his membership of the club.

Mr. Smythe is too partisan in his treatment of this incident, and skates very dexterously over very thin ice.

Moore, in his account of the expedition, never mentions the jump, and Almer is hardly likely to have " soon forgotten the incident," as Mr. Smythe suggests, if the incident was as dramatic as Whymper represented it to be. Such " jumps " are, as it happens, extremely rare in mountaineering. No subsequent party is recorded as having detected this famous gap in the ridge which, had it existed, might well have become as famous as Mummery's Crack on the Grépon. Mountaineers have a great sense of historic traditions and Whymper's spirited representation of this jump would have ensured that the notch itself, had it existed, would have been duly christened " Almer's Jump," or some such name.

We are asked to believe that this deep gap suddenly disappeared as the result of geological erosion. But erosion creates and widens but does not fill gaps, save with chock-stones which leave the gap itself defined but do not obliterate the channels down which they fall.

The only evidence in support of the existence of this gap is the statements made by Walker and Ulrich Almer. But it is easy to reconstruct the probable course of a discussion between the indignant

Whymper and the embarrassed Horace Walker. " Well, my dear Whymper, I'm sure that you are incapable of falsehood . . . my memory is not what it was . . . I vaguely recollect something of the sort, and you could quote me as having implicit faith in your veracity." What could poor Walker do? He was offered the alternative of accusing Whymper of lying or endorsing an account which he knew to be inaccurate.

The Alpine Club subsequently elected Coolidge an honorary member, which Whymper " took as a personal insult by the Committee, intended to convey the idea that he and not Coolidge was at fault over the quarrel." " Personal insult " is, perhaps, rather strong, but the Committee would certainly not have elected Coolidge an honorary member had they not, in effect, accepted his view that the gap in the evidence was more apparent than the gap in the west ridge of the Ecrins.

" If Coolidge was right," Mr. Smythe writes to me, " why did he resign from the A.C. in order to prevent an Inquiry? " Probably because the Inquiry was almost bound to give Whymper the benefit of the doubt. Mr. Smythe adds : " At the same time I traversed the Ecrins last summer—after the book was written—and came to the conclusion that any gap such as Whymper describes was very unlikely on a large scale."

It is unnecessary to take a tragic view of these facts. Whymper was a dramatic writer who depended very largely on his pen for a living, and, like many other writers, he found it difficult to resist embroidering " the mere it was." Compare, if you doubt this, Whymper's account of what Carrel said on returning to Breuil : " It is true. We saw them ourselves—they hurled stones at us! The old traditions *are* true—there are spirits on the top of the Matterhorn " with the sober version of what the Carrels actually said in the letter which Giordano wrote immediately after their return.* Again, it *may* be true that some ignorant priest insisted that the guides should attend Mass, and thus prevented them from joining the other guides who took part in the search for the victims of the Matterhorn accident. It is certainly untrue that they were " threatened with excommunication " (the picturesque touch). " The reader," Mr. Smythe muses, " will be tempted to inquire what the position would have been had there been any hope, even a remote hope, that life was not extinct? Would the claims of religion

* Carrel recognised Whymper by his white trousers. (*The Matterhorn*, by Guido Rey. J. E. C. Eaton's translation, p. 139.)

have overruled the claims of humanity?" I can answer this question. I quoted Whymper's version of this episode in my book, *The Alps*, and was informed by a learned theologian and a priest (*a*) that priests do not possess the power of excommunication; (*b*) that in the history of the Church no Catholic has been excommunicated for not attending Mass; (*c*) that the obligation to attend Mass on Sunday is subject to commonsense and the law of charity; (*d*) that in this particular case the guides ought to have joined the search party; and (*e*) that if a priest advised them to the contrary, the priest in question blundered badly.

Still, the Zermatt priests emerge with less discredit from Whymper's narrative than the Zermatt guides who accompanied him, for it is less damning to be accused of superstitious obscurantism than of attempted murder.

Whymper relegated to a footnote the one tribute which he was prepared to pay to old Taugwalder. "Not only was his act at the critical moment wonderful as a feat of strength, but it was admirable in its performance at the right time."

I owe my life to the fact that one of Taugwalder's grandsons inherited old Taugwalder's strength and presence of mind. I was a boy at the time and my second guide, for no ascertainable reason, slipped and fell on one of the steepest parts of the Matterhorn. Neither Taugwalder, who was leading, nor I were expecting this display of ineptitude, but whereas I was dragged off my holds, Taugwalder contrived to hold both of us as we swung round on the rope.

IV

It is not easy for me to write with detached objectivity either of Whymper the man or of his work, for *Scrambles amongst the Alps* was the first adult book which I spelled out for myself as a child, and I could not, if I would, and would not, if I could, wholly exorcise the spell with which his pen and pencil still hold captive my imagination.

There is the Matterhorn of fact, the pyramid of crystalline rock resting on its pedestal of sedimentary strata. There is the Matterhorn of fancy, woven from the fabric of Whymper's Saga, born from the marriage between the prose in which Whymper tells his tale and the wood engravings with which his book is illustrated

I have climbed the Matterhorn of fact ; I shall never climb the Matterhorn of fancy.

> "And did you once see Shelley plain?
> And did he stop and speak to you?"

I have seen "Whymper plain," but the Whymper to whom I was introduced shortly before he died was not the Whymper of my boyish dreams. *That* Whymper has never died. He is still sliding down the ice slope of the Col du Lion, still sheltering from falling stones on the Matterhorn, still listening to a group of Garibaldi's followers singing the songs of the Risorgimento.

I met Whymper at a meeting of the Alpine Club to which my father and I had been invited to hear a paper on ski-ing by the late E. C. Russell Clarke, one of the founders of the Alpine Ski Club. My father pointed Whymper out to me. To my surprise he was standing alone near the back of the room. Subconsciously I must have expected to see him the centre of a respectful group of admirers. My father introduced me ; Whymper made some banal remarks about ski-ing, and passed on. He looked his age (sixty-eight), but there was a granite quality about his leonine head which time could not erode.

"Whymper used to lecture for me," said my father. "He was quite a success with the Free Church Touring Guild. Of course, he wasn't always at his best, and on one occasion he was very definitely at his worst."

I listened with a growing sense of irritation. Whymper, my Whymper, still moved in a realm to which my father had no access. He was of the company of the immortals. It was as incongruous and as nauseating to think of Whymper lecturing for the Free Church Touring Guild as of Achilles returning to earth to address the Y.M.C.A. on the Siege of Troy. "No, Mr. Achilles, we cannot provide you with a double nectar on the platform. No alcoholic drinks are allowed on the premises."

I have abandoned all effort to reconcile the Whymper of fact and the Whymper of fancy. Mr. Smythe is more persistent. He is not prepared to abandon the Whymper of his dreams without a struggle, and he therefore postulates a youthful Whymper potentially capable of developing into the kind of man spiritually qualified to play lead in the great drama of the Matterhorn. Whymper possessed the faculties which Mr. Smythe would wish him to possess, but these "atrophied." This atrophy, Mr. Smythe assures us, set in very early. It did indeed, for there is no evidence whatever that these qualities ever existed.* There was no atrophy, because there was nothing to atrophy.

Whymper was not wholly lacking in charm, but very few people were allowed to guess the existence of a more human side. Mr. Smythe mentions examples of occasional acts of kindness, but to most people he seemed a granite character untouched by sentiment, unsoftened by tenderness. For only two women, and indeed for only two human beings, did he feel a strong affection, his mother and Miss Charlotte Hanbury, whom he met when he was fifty-nine years of age and who died a year after they first met. His disastrous marriage at the age of sixty-six to a girl of twenty only lasted four years. There was one child by this marriage, a daughter, Ethel, now Mrs. Blandy, who has carried out many fine climbs in the Zermatt district. He made no lasting friendships among either the amateurs or guides with whom he climbed. He regarded his guides, as Mr. Smythe tells us, not as partners in a joint enterprise, but as employees, and he insisted on " unquestioning obedience to all orders," an attitude which led to serious trouble when the guides were men of forceful independence such as Klucker or the Carrels. " Whymper," writes Mr. Smythe, " was a hard task-master to himself and his guides, and the gulf between them was absolute."

Whymper left school at fourteen, but even had he enjoyed what the Victorians in their unself-conscious way described as the " education of a gentleman " it is doubtful whether he would have taken much interest in the humanities. His cast of mind was practical and scientific. Whymper had the sort of mind that is more interested in machines than in men, in matter than in mind. There was no touch of mysticism in his attitude to the mountains. The conquest of the Matterhorn was a mechanical problem, and nothing more. He described with great interest the Cenis tunnel and the action of ice on rocks, but he had virtually no interest in the classical and mediæval background of the Europe in which he travelled. He was surprised to discover that there was a cathedral at Cologne and unaware that " Dom " is the German word for " Cathedral." " I discovered," he writes, " at Cologne that there

* Mr. Smythe, in the course of a letter, mentions certain facts which strongly support his view of " repression " in youth. " Had he married young, the right kind of woman, he might have risen to far greater heights. What went wrong one can only surmise."

was a big church there called the Dom." There is no evidence of wide reading in his books or his journal. None of the classical quotations which adorn his chapter headings are particularly apt, and—being chapter headings—none of them arise naturally out of what has gone before. Had Whymper been as familiar with the classics as these quotations suggest, he could hardly have failed to display some interest in the classical past or to have raised the perplexing problem of the classical attitude to natural scenery in general and mountains in particular. I suspect that Whymper took these chapter headings from a Dictionary of Familiar Quotations or was provided with them by a classical friend. They have a special interest, as they represent Whymper's last concession to the social dogmas of the Victorian age. In that remote period a knowledge of the classics was still supposed to be the hallmark of a entleman.

Whymper, as his diary proves, began by accepting without question the religious and social dogmas of the Victorian middle classes, and there is no evidence that he ever consciously rebelled against the Victorian code, but the quotations from the classics in the *Scrambles* is the last discoverable trace of a conscious attempt to conciliate the social standards of his contemporaries. He never formerly rejected them, but imperceptibly they ceased to influence him. His nephew describes him lunching at Anderton's Hotel in Fleet Street " in a sweater that showed his bare bull-like neck to perfection ; he seldom wore anything under the sweater." He smoked the strongest possible shag, and the carpets, table cloths, upholstered chairs, etc., in his vicinity were frequently burnt full of holes. He invaribly smoked in bed, " and not only were his bed clothes soon riddled with holes but his own chest became scarred by hot ashes too."

Whymper remained to the end amazingly tough. At the age of ixty-two he walked from Edinburgh to London, averaging fifty-five miles a day.

I wish we knew more about Whymper's first contacts with that queer eclectic world of the Victorian Alpine Club. The club was ecruited very largely from the professional classes, from the Universities and public schools, from the clergy and the bar. The lub was a cross-section of the upper middle classes. A candidate's mountaineering claims were considered by the Committee, and his ocial claims by the club at a general meeting. Voting was by ballot and one adverse vote in ten excluded. Since general meetings were seldom attended by as many as a hundred members, any small clique of ten could exclude a candidate from the club. Kennedy, one of the greatest mountaineers of the day, resigned because many candidates, including some whom he had proposed, had been blackballed. Mummery, the greatest climber of his age, was blackballed a few years later, and might never have been elected but for the ingenuity of Mr. Coolidge, who had a private feud of his own with the member mainly responsible for the blackballing of Mummery. "I took charge of his ballot box," Mr. Coolidge confided to me, "and when nobody was looking, I shifted some of the balls from the 'No' to the 'Aye' part of the box." He chirruped a reminiscent chuckle. "Yes, I *cheated* Mummery into the club."

Whymper's first contact with English mountaineers was at Zermatt. He was on his first visit to the Alps. He had no climb to his credit, but this young man of twenty seems to have been serenely unconscious of the social gulf between him and the great men of the A.C. He buffaloed into their society, oblivious of snubs if snubs there were. "The hotel," he writes, "is full of Alpine men, many of them very plucky fellows, and there are the usual number of bores." Hinchcliff, one of the great men of the A.C., "offered to coach me on the Riffelberg, which offer was gratefully accepted." Whymper was grateful, but not in the least astounded by this condescension.

Whymper, at no time, was a clubable man, and there may be some truth in Mr. Coolidge's malicious gloss on a certain incident described in *Scrambles*. "You will remember, my dear Mr. Lunn," said the sage of Grindelwald, "that after climbing the Ecrins, Whymper and Moore spent the night under different rocks. Whymper tells us that he left Moore because he and Croz thought they would try for a roof before finally abandoning all hope of reaching civilisation. The truth is that Moore remained behind because Whymper had got on his nerves. You see, Whymper was pretty uncouth, whereas Moore was a distinguished Civil Servant. He was appointed political and secret secretary to the India Office just before he died. He was a bit of a swell and Whymper grated on him."

It may well be that this gloss on the *Scrambles* throws more light on Coolidge's personality than on Whymper's or Moore's.

The social hierarchy is useful for classifying the undistinguished.

but men like Whymper evade all classification. He was neither a gentleman nor a not-gentleman. He was just Whymper, a genuine eccentric. His compelling personality broke down Victorian barriers. He was elected to the Alpine Club after his *first* mountaineering season, and in due course he was elected Vice-President. It would be unreasonable to criticise the club because they were not quite prepared to put Whymper into the presidential chair. Had they done so, he would probably have lit a pipe at the Alpine Club Dinner before toasting the King, and burnt several large holes in the table cloth.

Whymper had something of the indomitable granite quality of the mountain which he conquered, with the result that we tend, as Mr. Winthrop Young rightly says, to identify him in our memories with the greatness of the Matterhorn. "Through the attitudes of the protagonists (of mountaineering)," writes Mr. Young, "he crashed with a rude personal vehemence that remains hopelessly individual."

Few mountaineers have been more consistently successful than Whymper. Of all the mountains he attacked, there was one, and only one, which Whymper did not ultimately conquer, the Dent d'Hérens. It is less easy to determine how far his successes were due to mountaineering genius of a high order, and how far to great courage, pertinacity, and luck. I remember a conversation on this point with Mr. Coolidge in his library at Grindelwald. Coolidge did not like Whymper, and his little eyes gleamed maliciously and his white beard wagged in sympathy as he did his best to puncture Whymper's reputation. "Whymper," said Coolidge, "was not a mountaineering genius. He never attempted the obvious route up the Matterhorn till he tacked on to Hudson. Now Hudson was the outstanding mountaineer of the day, and if Hudson hadn't been killed, the conquest of the Matterhorn would have been regarded by the Alpine Club as Hudson's victory. I hope I shan't shock you, Mr. Lunn, if I hint that Whymper was lucky that he was the sole survivor of the amateurs in the successful party. I hope you don't think me naughty to suggest that Hudson's death was the basis of Whymper's fame."

The sage of Grindelwald gave a happy cackle, the invariable accompaniment to his more feline remarks.

So much for the *advocatus diaboli*; but there are few mountaineers who would dispute the considered verdict of Leslie Stephen. After reminding the reader that the Matterhorn had retained for many years a dominating influence over the morale of the best guides and amateurs alike, most of whom had no heart for the attempt, he adds : " Mr. Whymper, almost alone, was proof against the influence of the Matterhorn. . . . And for that reason, I at least am ready to give my vote to Mr. Whymper as occupying the same position in the mountaineering world as a Robespierre in the French Revolution."

Whymper's expedition to the Andes " marked a milestone," Mr. Smythe writes to me, " in mountain exploration as distinct from mountain climbing. I was tremendously impressed by the way it was carried out. Whymper's food and equipment was absolutely first class and the whole organisation was many years before its time. There was nothing so efficient until many years later."

There was nothing of the mystic or the romantic in Whymper's attitude to the mountains, at least nothing apparent in his writings, though it may well be true, as Mr. Young claims, that " he wrote under an inspiration which we feel to have been greater than himself and which probably he himself only understood for the short space of his youth."

" To read," Mr. G. W. Young continues, " the life-story of a personality in a human face we have but to look at two portraits reproduced in the *Alpine Journal.* The first is that of a young man, with an uplifted, resolute look and large eyes full of inspiration ; almost a beautiful face, but a face, if we look at it closely, at war with itself : the wilful downward turn of the mouth, an obstinate set of the jaw, are fighting to drag the eyes earthward. Instinctively we wonder which will win. The second is of the Titan in age, with the leonine head, the granite jaw, the penetrating eyes. And we must decide for ourselves which won—the eyes of the prophet or the mouth of the man."

Whymper himself explicitly disclaimed the role of a prophet " I have not made myself," he writes, " either an advocate or an apologist for mountaineering." Certainly there was nothing of the Hebraic prophet in his attitude to mountains. Whymper's attitude both to life in general and to mountains in particular was Hellenic rather than Hebraic. He was Hellenic in his matter-of-fact realism in the importance which he attached to the humdrum business of earning his daily bread, in his freedom from sentiment, and in his distrust of gush. At the age of eighteen he described in his diary the marriage of the Princess Royal. " The Princess," writes

Whymper, " threw herself into the arms of her mother, who, it is said, was very much affected, hugged and kissed, etc., etc. Oh, humbug, bosh and foolery ! "

The Greeks had no love for mountains and appreciated Nature in proportion as Nature was domesticated by man. Whymper had more of a Hellenist in his attitude to mountain scenery than his admirers might be prepared to admit. He was impressed by the *grandeur* of the High Alps, impressed but not captivated. Of the Zermatt valley he writes in his diary : " Everything here is *fine*, but I have not seen any *pretty* views." A Periclean Greek would have disliked the Zermatt valley, but recovered his good humour in the more domesticated scenery of the lakes. " Interlaken," writes Whymper, " is the loveliest place on earth : I see it plainer every day." The contrast between his diary criticism of the Matterhorn (" Grand it is, but beautiful I think it is not "), and his recorded impressions in *Scrambles*, casts some doubt on the sincerity of other passages in his published writings which might be cited as evidence of a deep feeling for mountain scenery. There is only one passage in the *Scrambles* in which I detect the authentic note of mountain awe (if not of mountain worship), the passage in which he describes a sunset as seen from a lonely bivouac on the Italian ridge of the Matterhorn ; but, even in this description, Whymper is concerned more with the sublimity and magnificence than with the beauty of the view.

Whymper was primarily a sportsman concerned to solve a particular mountain problem, and—to a lesser degree—a scientist interested in the problems of glaciology. He had no eye for the more tender effects of mountain places.

" From his chill eyrie on the Matterhorn he had seen ' the sunlight as it steals noiselessly along, and reveals countless unsuspected forms—the delicate ripple-lines which mark the concealed crevasse, and the waves of drifted snow : producing each minute more lights and fresh shadows ; sparkling on the edges and glittering on the ends of the icicles ; shining on the heights and illuminating the depths.' "

Mr. Smythe's use of quotation marks in this passage might lead the unwary reader to suppose that the passage quoted by Mr. Smythe was a description by Whymper of the view from Whymper's " chill eyrie on the Matterhorn." Whymper was too scientific a writer to " see " from the Italian ridge of the Matterhorn the "delicate ripple-lines which mark the concealed crevasses" on the glacier many thousand feet below. The passage quoted by Smythe is interesting as a negative example. This was the sort of writing which you do *not* find in Whymper. Nowhere in the *Scrambles* is there any evidence of loving affection for what may be called the miniature effects of snow and ice, the little things which the authentic mountain lover loves to linger over. Whymper's description of the view from the Matterhorn reads like an auctioneer's catalogue of peaks for sale.

Mr. Smythe is distressed by the fact that Whymper could return to the Alps four years after the Matterhorn disaster, only to wander about the valleys. His nerve had not been affected by the accident, for he subsequently made some fine first ascents in the Andes and Rockies. The fact is that a mountain ceased to interest him once it had been climbed. The true mountain lover can be happy on the heights even if the mountain he himself is climbing holds no secrets for him, even if he himself has climbed it many times before. Not so Whymper. Nothing is more significant than the map at the end of *Scrambles*, recording Whymper's routes in the Zermatt district. When this book was published Whymper had only climbed three mountains previously ascended, Monte Rosa, the Pelvoux of which he believed himself to be making the first ascent, and the Dent Blanche, which he climbed to settle the doubts which had been expressed as to whether the peak had, in fact, been conquered. His list of ascents in the Zermatt district, to which he returned summer after summer, is pitifully small. Matterhorn, Monte Rosa, Dent Blanche, Grand Cornier, Moming Pass, and that is all.* He

* The ascent of the Rimpfischhorn is not mentioned on the above-mentioned map. The following is a complete list of Whymper's expeditions in the Alps as recorded in the Alpine Club Register. I have divided this list into three sections: the first section consists of new ascents; the second section of peaks which had previously been climbed; and the third column of passes which were traversed incidentally in order to reach the base of peaks which Whymper proposed to climb, and which therefore might be classified rather as mountain travel than as mountaineering for the sake of mountaineering. I have omitted passes below the snow line (*e.g.* Col du Bonhomme).

It will be seen that Whymper's new expeditions number 21, and that he climbed only 7 peaks which had previously been ascended, and only 5 about whose previous ascent there was no doubt. His sole glacier expeditions in the Oberland seem to have been a traverse of Petersgrat and an unsuccessful ascent of Ebnefluh.

In addition to Alpine climbs, he visited the Andes in 1879-80 and made the first ascent of Chimborazo, Sincholagua, Antisana and Cotocachi, etc., and also made an abortive expedition to Greenland.

New Ascents:—Grand Tournalin; Col des Aiguilles d'Arve; S. peak of Aiguilles de la Sausse; Brêche de la Meije; Barre des Ecrins; Col de la Pilatte; Col de Triolet; Mont Dolent; Aiguille de Trélatête; Col du Mont Tondu; Aiguille d'Argentière; Moming Pass; Grand Cornier; W. (lower) Grandes Jorasses; Col Dolent; Aiguille Verte; Ruinette Col de Talèfre; Portons Pass; Matterhorn.

was attracted by the Weisshorn but lost all interest in it when Tyndall stole a march on him and made the first ascent.

And yet, in spite of Whymper's unromantic attitude, his *Scrambles* captured the imagination of Alpine romanticists. And this for many reasons. Whymper was clever enough to play up to the romantic school, and it is only when we dissect them that we can distinguish between the passages in which Whymper and, say, Leslie Stephen, describe the scenery of the High Alps. Moreover, there is, perhaps, an element of truth in Mr. Smythe's theory of atrophied faculties. Those eyes of the visionary must have seen rather more in the Alps than Whymper records in that drably realistic Alpine diary. Mr. Young is almost certainly right when he insists that Whymper "wrote under an inspiration which we feel to have been greater than himself."

Again, however disappointing Whymper may be as the interpreter of Alpine mysticism or of Alpine scenery, few mountaineers have been more successful in interpreting the romance of Alpine adventure. His writing is flavoured with a dry humour which is all the more attractive in contrast to the dreadful jocularity which is so common in mountaineering literature. His writing is always effective when sincere, but it is sometimes pretentious and unconvincing. The showman who put the classical quotations at the chapter headings ruins the immortal chapter on the Matterhorn tragedy with a peroration which begins :—

"See yonder height ! 'Tis far away—unbidden comes the word 'Impossible.' 'Not so,' says the mountaineer. 'The way is long, I know ; it's difficult—it may be dangerous. It's possible, I'm sure ; I'll seek the way ; take counsel of my brother mountaineers.' "

But at its best Whymper's writing has a simplicity and directness which again recalls the Greeks. I have sometimes toyed with the fancy that our greatest prose writers may be divided into those whose style has been formed by the Hebraicism of the Old Testament, and those whose style has been formed by the Hellenism of the New Testament.

Ruskin, whose writings Whymper detested, was essentially

Old Ascents : Mont Pelvoux ; Monte Rosa ; Petersgrat ; Dent Blanche ; Théodulehorn, Rimpfischhorn ; Langenfluhjoch ; Col de Collon ; Col de Valpelline ; Mont Blanc ; Col de la Fenêtre.

Passes Traversed : (On the way to peaks)—Breuiljoch, or W. Furggenjoch · Col d'Hérens ; Col d'Oren ; Col de Valcournère ; Théodule.

Hebraic. The *Stones of Venice* opens with a magnificent passage in the style of Isaiah :—

" Since first the dominion of man was asserted upon the ocean, three Thrones of mark beyond all others have been set upon its shores, Tyre, Venice and London. Of the first of these great Powers only the memory remains, of the second the ruin. The third, which inherits their greatness, if it forget their example will pass from prouder eminence to less pitied destruction."

The New Testament is Greek in its simplicity and directness. " And the second time the cock crew. And Peter called to mind the word that Jesus said unto him, before the cock crow twice, thou shalt deny me thrice. And when he thought thereon, he wept."

When Mr. Young assures us that Whymper " is a prophet in an almost Biblical sense," he may be thinking of the great chapters in which Whymper brings the Matterhorn story to its close. There is something Biblical in the simplicity with which the story marches to its destined end, but the style recalls the Hellenism of the New rather than the Hebraicism of the Old Testament. " Long after dusk the cliffs above echoed with our laughter and with the songs of our guides ; for we were happy that night in camp, and feared no evil."

Mr. Smythe, when he is recording his own views or impressions, usually writes extremely well, and he should not have attempted to paraphrase Whymper. He should have condensed more and quoted verbatim in his own chapter on the Matterhorn accident, but at least he helps us to appreciate unedited Whymper. The passage, which I have just quoted, reappears in the following version :—

" To the adventurers on their ledge, it was a perfect experience. They were happy and at peace, and long after they had cooked their supper the cliffs echoed and re-echoed their songs and laughter."

Scrambles owed much of its success to the wood engravings. I have often wondered why James Mahoney, the artist responsible for the famous engraving of " A Cannonade on the Matterhorn," died in obscurity. The design and balance of this engraving are as striking as the vitality of the whole composition. The artist has interpreted with genius the duel between man and mountain. You feel the might and majesty and dominion of the cliffs, and the power of their artillery. You hear the falling stones whistling through the air, but the perfect poise of the human figure in the centre of the picture, sheltering but unafraid, is the key to the composition. It is not the mountain that wins.

For many years I assumed that Whymper had not only engraved but drawn the original sketch for this and the other pictures in *Scrambles*. This was not the case. Mr. Smythe hints more than once that Whymper, with better fortune, might have achieved outstanding greatness, but he wastes no tears on the *pictor ignotus* of the *Scrambles*. Whymper provided " slight memoranda "* in the shape of sketches, but did not draw a single one of the illustrations on the wood. James Mahoney, whose help he acknowledges in the preface, drew on wood about fifty of Whymper's slight sketches, and Whymper finished the engraving. Mahoney's work can usually be identified by his monogram. Whymper mentions in the preface another of his collaborators, Cyrus Johnson, but in the illustrations themselves, though Whymper's name usually appears, the names of the artists who drew the sketches on wood is usually suppressed, with the result that I have, as yet, only met one mountaineer who had not unconsciously absorbed the belief that Whymper was solely responsible for illustrations to which *Scrambles* owed much of its fame.

Mr. Smythe includes many of Whymper's wood engravings, but gives us no clue to the artists who drew these on wood. Their names are omitted from the list of illustrations at the beginning of Mr. Smythe's book.

Mr. Smythe's final verdict on Whymper is that he was a great man who might have been greater. " Edward Whymper passed without fulfilling or expressing himself as he might have done . . . the name of Whymper might have rung down the avenues of political, social or religious history." I disagree. No man can make a mark either in political or religious history who is as defective as Whymper in the technique of human relations, a defect which is as integral an element in Whymper's character as the qualities which ensured his success. There are people, like the *pictor ignotus* of *Scrambles*, whose gifts do not receive the recognition which they deserve ; there are others who extract every ounce of value out of their talents. Such was Whymper. There is an element of truth in Coolidge's catty suggestion, that the death of Hudson was a factor in the foundation

*" Slight memoranda," Whymper's own phrase. Mr. Smythe tells me that there are several sketches in Whymper's diaries of identical character to those in *Scrambles*. Perhaps some of these can be produced in a new edition.

of Whymper's fame. Accident played its part. Of Whymper's contemporaries, hundreds who died unknown possessed qualities of courage and pertinacity, and of these there must have been many who possessed gifts of expression equal to Whymper's, for though Whymper was a gifted and competent writer, he was by no means a genius. It was the caprice of fate which provided Whymper with the splendid theme which was the making of *Scrambles*, a glorious chance which Whymper exploited to the full. He made the best possible use of such talents as he possessed, and such opportunities as came his way. If he had been a very different man —if, that is, he had not been Whymper—he might have made a mark in " political, social or religious history," but in that case he would, in all probability, not have climbed the Matterhorn. But though I do not find any evidence in Whymper's *writings* for the existence of mystical potentialities, frustrated by environment, I concede that Mr. Geoffrey Young's interpretation of the photographs is not unconvincing. " Photographs," Mr. Smythe writes to me, " can tell a story and one reviewer devoted much space to the remarkable change in Whymper's character as disclosed by the photos."

I hope that I have not over-stressed the points on which I disagree with Mr. Smythe, for we do not disagree on essentials, and I owe much to many of his more discerning comments. We are neither of us blind to Whymper's defects, nor unmindful of the man's authentic greatness. Mr. Smythe's biography is both critical and discerning, and he has placed the whole mountaineering world in his debt by his labour of love. It is all but certain that Whymper's diaries would never have been published, had not Mr. Smythe undertaken this biography, and the diaries, as I have tried to show, provide that essential key to Whymper's character for which the reader will search in vain in his books.

CHAPTER XIX

Shadow Over Switzerland

I

I RETURNED to England from Italy just before the outbreak of war, and after six weeks in London left for the Balkans, as the occasional correspondent of a New York weekly paper. I returned from the Balkans in the middle of December and spent Christmas in Rome. I left next day for the Alps, and reached Mürren in the afternoon of December 28th.

Time, as we experience it in our waking hours, may be compared to geological strata, which have been undisturbed since they were deposited, and which are arranged in an orderly succession, the oldest strata at the bottom and the more recent at the top. Time, as we experience it in dreamland, is subject to forces analogous to those which have played such fantastic tricks with Alpine strata, thrusting the crystalline rocks of the Matterhorn pyramid above the younger sedimentary rocks upon which it rests, and sandwiching beds of primitive gneiss between the recent limestone of the Rottal face of the Jungfrau. In dreamland, experiences deposited in youth are forced to the surface, or are inextricably confused with the strata of more recent memories. Thus, in my dreams, I often play Harrow football on the rink at Mürren; shamed into some semblance of feverish activity by the abusive shouts of my old schoolmate, Cadby. And then the scene changes, and Cadby, wearing a D.H.O. badge, threatens me with "six of the best" unless I take Lone Tree Slope straight.

During the first weeks of the present war I often felt as if the realities of 1914 had intruded into a nightmare of 1939; as if I might suddenly awake to discover that Harrow football and European Wars both belonged to sediments which only the convulsions of dreamland could force to the surface. This sense of overthrust, to borrow the geological term for the inversion of strata, overwhelmed me as I entered the Palace Hotel on the afternoon of December 28th, 1939.

I had spent most of the first German War at Mürren, for an open wound condemned me to civilian activities, and I had found work in connection with the interned prisoners of war in Mürren and Montana. As I entered the Palace Hotel, I felt as if I had walked back into the Palace of 1916. I remembered digging out my ski in 1916 from a sad row of depressed boards, all stacked and labelled and ready for the winter season which most skiers were to spend in the trenches. The first label that had caught my eye bore the name of a gallant young skier who had fallen in the retreat from Mons. Would the old days, I had asked myself, ever return? Would those ski ever be unpacked? Or would the war end in universal ruin and revolution? Those were the questions which I asked myself in 1916. Those were the questions which I asked myself in 1939. Those are the questions which I still ask, and to which I still continue to return the same answer. British ski-ing will be born again.

The return in 1939 was more poignant than in 1916, for the old Mürren, which disappeared on the outbreak of the first German War, was the *Public Schools Alpine Sports Club* Mürren, which my father founded, not the Kandahar Mürren which I helped to create. Charles and Mrs. Charles gave me a great welcome.

Room 3 was as Blanche Bennett left it, neat and tidy, all ready for the 1939-1940 season. Room 4 was less tidy, for I had spent a few hours in Room 4 during the summer. . . .

The profession of letters has its compensating features. However miserable the writer may be, he can always count with confidence on the anæsthetic effect of translating his misery into words. And because I had discovered this by experience, I returned to Room 4 after wandering round the village, and covered page after page with my protracted moans. I sent the top copy to Lady Raeburn, to whom this book is dedicated, and a copy to Phyllis Holt-Needham. Here is what I wrote :—

II

De Profundis

December 28th, 1939.

I am typing this in Room 4. I have just arrived. There were three tracks at Half-Way House in soft powder snow. About one-eighth of the Rink is open. The small hotels are open, but the big ones, of course, are shut. My mind travelled back to my first visit to Mürren in the Great War ; the same sense of an epoch that is dead. I wandered through the lounge. Ghosts everywhere. The pictures had been removed. I missed Tony and Andrew

Irvine, but they would feel desolate in an empty hotel, in which one is still disturbed by echoes of the two noisiest laughs in Christendom, Tony's and Peter's.

Room 4. The Union Jack which I lowered half-mast at the Oslo Congress and raised to the salute when downhill rules were accepted —the old " K " ballot box—the Candidates' Book. I can hardly bear it. I wish I had stayed in Bulgaria. And there's a ghost of Phyllis listening in at the keyhole, and of Greta grousing away in Room 3 and refusing to serve on the K Committee and all sorts of jolly, exciting K Committee meetings, and a ghostly Deggers "UNANIMOUSLY ELECTED," or alternatively " No good, Arni," when the feminine blackballs have defeated my well-meant attempts to get a candidate elected on the decorative qualification . . . and vast " Fisses " as the FIS approached, and tremendous excitement during the final Election Committee meetings, and Doreen, a lover of tradition, saying, " No, not *there*," when a new secretary tries to put the fateful notice, "The following have been selected to represent Great Britain," not on the Kandahar Board and not on the traditional pillar near Congy's office. . . .

I have just left the typewriter for a moment and gone into the Ballroom. It was dark, and I lit a match, and it flickered feebly and revealed the black-out of war. But my mind travelled back to that glorious party—yes, a *party*, not a banquet—after the first FIS, the party which redeemed the disappointment of that snow-ruined championship. And I heard myself laughing uproariously at my own jokes in four languages, till even the sympathetic ghosts had to laugh too.

Damn it ! I was homesick for Mürren in the Balkans, but now I'm homesick for the flesh and blood which clothed the bones of Mürren. For it's only the bones that remain. Every inch of ground here has a new stab. I went into my bedroom, opened the wardrobe, and there was the Yellow Boys' tie, Wremord's club. Poor Peter. . . .

There are about thirty people in the ski school and the SAS is here, but the Schiltgrat is as powdery as in the days before the Lift was built ; and Half-Way House, I am prepared to find, much as it was in the old remote pre-Bubble days. I saw Godi. He was surprisingly cheerful, all things considered, and as amusing as ever. I asked after a mutual friend, one of the toughest of the Swiss mountaineers, who is presenting himself for the army again, having been rejected as a sickly consumptive many years ago (*arrangiarsi* applies not only in Italy but in Switzerland). "The Swiss," he said, "are warriors, not soldiers. We could fight like hell in war, but we don't like much to soldier in peace time. . . . The English are making great pressure on the neutrals now, and a damn good thing, too. There should not be any neutrals . . . we should all join in. . . . If a big man knocks a child about one cannot say, 'That says nothing to me,' and do nothing, and be neutral. . . ."

The Kleine Scheidegg is full but only until January 2nd.

Meanwhile the Nazis are staging a big meeting for February and keeping sport going hard. There was a big football match with Rumania just before I arrived, between Germany and Rumania. Object mainly financial. The gate money is worth having, and because the Nazis, being logical, and having developed sport as a branch of war in peace time, are carrying on sport during the war. The Swiss will run their championship, and a few races. About two-thirds of their men have been demobilised. They don't expect the Nazis to come through Switzerland. Rome, where I spent three weeks before coming on here, was full of rumours of peace by the Spring, as the result of a Goering *coup d'état*, but I think the wish was father to the thought.

I am going to the Kleine Scheidegg to finish a book on recent experiences in the Balkans, and then, Lord knows where I shall go. Perhaps to the front as a correspondent if there is anything doing there.

I console myself with the thought that when I came to Mürren in the last war I felt even more desolate than I do to-day. I felt that an epoch had ended, and that things would never be the same again. But they were—and better. The development of British ski-racing was one of the few things, perhaps the only good thing, which was born and grew to maturity in the twenty-year armistice between the wars. I looked at the Schiltgrat to-day and saw the Swiss sliding down it, and remembered what the local schoolmasters whom I met in the train said, "I haven't heard an English voice in Mürren," and felt really resentful. One might almost think that Mürren belongs to the Swiss by the way they go on. . . . I felt as Napoleon might have felt, had he visited Alsace during the German occupation, returning as a ghost to Colmar in 1912. . . .

What *was* the Schiltgrat till we made it? A lump of mesozoic limestone without form or beauty. But to-day it is a complex of emotions and memories. " All our dignity," says Pascal, " is born of thought," and the Schilthorn owes its dignity to a host of memories of tough, courageous chaps and chapesses hurling themselves down its icy slopes for the glory of (*a*) themselves (for I must be a realist even in moments of sentiment), (*b*) Britain, or (*c*) Kandahar or BUSC, as the case may be. Hundreds of years hence skiers will still be ski-ing down the Schiltgrat, and its snows will continue to provide youth with an arena for daring, but to none will it be the mountain that it was to the old guard, to Christopher and Deggers and Edgie and Adrian and Gee, and Tony, and Johann, and Russ and Peter, and Digby and Bill, and Greta and Doreen and Wendy. The old Mürren toughs. God bless them. A blot of a tear which will not come through on the carbon copies.

I could see against the setting sun the big wooden fence which I had built on Shambles Corner, as a protection in the heroic days of the *geschmozzel* start. I remember standing there waiting for a Kandahar with Princess Marie José, now Crown Princess of Italy. And Greta was there. Suddenly the expectant silence was broken and some thirty skiers swept over the edge in front, the low sun catching the powder thrown up by the ski. And dear old Greta exclaiming, " Now then, Digby, let the big men get through first," and Digby, aged fourteen, hurling himself in front of the big men, and shoving them aside with his sticks. (" Digby was always a tough," remarked Greta one day, as we examined a photo of another *geschmozzel* start, with Digby apparently stabbing the man in front.) Digby on that occasion finished second—or was it third ! —at any rate, high up. Peter did badly, and Peter and I walked back in gloomy silence. For those are the sort of things that mattered then. Indeed, the sanity of an age may be judged by what does seem important. In a Hitler world only guns and death matter. How I ramble on ! But I'm frightened of leaving Room 4, which is somehow becoming much more homely as the ghosts take life, and going into the black cold passages.

Digby and Peter belong to the great beetle epoch of the Kandahar, when parents still had money and could bring their children to the Alps, and the K beetles went over to the Scheidegg and took the first eight places in the Hewitt Cup. Greta and I used to accompany our beetles in search of the Hewitt Cup, which they won every time they entered for it. . . . We founded the Parents' Club. And often have we held hands waiting for the beetles and been quite well behaved when the other beetle did well and ours did badly. I remember in some A.K. slalom Godi came up and began to talk to me. " Hush, Godi," said Greta, " that's sacrilege. Even the choughs have stopped squawking, for Peter's just due to start."

In the next phase we had the Bolshy revolt against the beetles, whose speed on narrow tracks upset the elders, and the snows were marked with the mystic sign " ABC," which stood for " Anti-Beetle Club." Founder members were skiers in their prime who had been beaten by beetles and didn't like it.

I am sorry Digby could never get out for a FIS, but the Parents' Club suffer a lot during the FIS. I could never make up my mind whether it was better to know exactly when Peter was coming down, or not to know. In the latter case one had a disappointment every time a skier flashed past who wasn't Peter. In the former case there was that dreadful minute—it might be longer, it might be shorter—which separated the skier who had drawn the number before, and Peter. I remember in the '35 FIS at Mürren, rumours floating down the course, of broken legs, and then Seelos, I think, passed; and I waited and suddenly, from high up on the hill, came a faint echo of cheers, and a ghostly Peter was on the way. That was the worst FIS, because it was a race against a storm, and I watched the gathering clouds, and hoped that they would not break till Peter was past, and tried not to hope that they would break immediately after. But far, far grimmer was the " Battle of Innsbruck," and the terrible wait below the Devil's Glade and Willi Steuri staggering past with a bleeding face.

I was always accused of taking ski-ing too seriously, and no doubt with justice. But the secret of happiness in this world is to become engrossed in something which really doesn't matter, like trying to beat the Swiss in the University Race, and the secret of happiness in the next world is becoming engrossed in the one thing that does matter. And there are people who can be extremely happy seeing life *sub specie aeternitatis*. Like St. Bernard, who rode a whole day beside Geneva, and when a companion said " What a beautiful lake ! " answered " What lake ? " But I am not in the least like St. Bernard, and I am very grateful for all the gamut of emotions which those years gave to me. The intellectual pleasure of solving a problem, getting our Continental friends to realise that uphill racing is not the best criterion of downhill ski-ing ; the sporting problem, how with a handful of British to put up a good show in the FIS. We were outnumbered, but numbers aren't everything.

And the biggest thrills of my life, second only to mountaineering and watching the Nationalists storming the final ridge in the battle for the sea, have been racing or watching racing. The first Scara, which I won, and which, unimportant in itself, was important to me, but infinitely more thrilling the moments when our chaps did well. Wendy winning an A.K., Chris. and Bill Bracken and Leonard Dobbs putting it across the Swiss, Peter winning his first Kandahar and sailing past unhurt at Innsbruck. Fundamentally I am a John Bull and it pleases me to put it across the foreigners at their own game.

There was something symbolic in our come-back last winter. I was in America in the autumn of '38, and the Americans thought we had gone yellow after Munich, and Continental skiers counted us out after our Engelberg fiasco in the FIS, but last year we won the Duke of Kent and the Anglo-Swiss and Anglo-Italian, and did well in other things, too, and we're going to beat the Nazis before long. I suppose I ought to have said to compare small things with great, but I won't.

Anyhow, thank God for the good times past. They will come again. I felt that all was over when I visited Mürren in the last war. But it wasn't. And Greta will be grousing in Room 3 again and Doreen will once again be treading on the seal queen's corns, and Theo will be in this room playing chess with me and Johnny, and Dicky and Tommy and all the rest will be dropping black balls into the ballot box what time I as a toothless old man of eighty am making a last expiring effort to get Digby's daughter into the Kandahar. . . . But it's going to be very sorrowful when I take my ski out of the Bubble to-morrow. . . .

III

Never had the familiar misquotation* on the lampshade in the Scheidegg Bar seemed more apt :—

"*Tempora mutantur et nos mutamur in illis*."

Times change, and the inhabitants of the Scheidegg Bar change with them. Instead of Tom Fox, Christopher Mackintosh and

* The *et nos* which does not scan should be *nos et* which does.

Edgie Boughton-Leigh, a group of friendly Swiss officers in uniform; for the Scheidegg was the headquarters of a ski battalion throughout the winter, and notices about the *Feldpost* replaced the usual notices about ski tests. I was woken every morning by the authoritative commands of a sergeant teaching Swiss soldiers from the lowlands the elements of the stem turn.

Fritz von Allmen and Mrs. von Allmen, than whom nobody could be kinder or more charming, and I used to forgather from time to time, and sigh over the dear dead past, and exchange hopes for a happier future. I was touched by their very genuine affection for their English friends. I remember von Allmen rounding on a Swiss officer who had expressed some doubt as to our staying powers in this war. "You don't know these young English boys," said von Allmen. "I do. They don't look tough, but think what their racers have done. There's only a handful who can give the time to train seriously and we have hundreds, but when we think they are down and out for good, they come up to the top like they did last winter when they won the Anglo-Swiss Race and the Duke of Kent. They don't look as tough as our mountain boys, but they have guts. Last winter Gardner and Denis Fox and Ernst Gertsch left the Jungfraujoch to ski down to the Scheidegg. Nobody had been fool enough to come down there on ski till they did. There was a lot of step-cutting and carrying ski, and they got caught in an avalanche which broke one of the ski, but they got down somehow and then they caught a train to Thun, where Gardner had his plane, and they flew back and had a look at the Joch from above and dined in Berne, and Fox caught the train and Gardner flew home. No, believe me, England may have to go through Hell, but win they will. . ."

"Ah, it does one good to hear an English voice again," sighed a Swiss skier whom I met in the train. "The Scheidegg is terribly sad this winter. It's dead without your cheery English crowd."

The Swiss are not a demonstrative race, but they are grimly loyal to their friends. Their liking for the English has, of course, its practical side, but we were missed for reasons which have no connection with the tourist business. Ski-ing, and in particular ski-racing, has had even more effect than mountaineering on the development of understanding between the two peoples. The English mountaineer often entertained feelings of more than ordinary friendship for his guide, but they met as "Herr" and employee, and very few Englishmen ever climbed with Swiss amateurs, and therefore the English and Swiss mountaineers seldom met on terms of complete equality.

The Anglo-Swiss University Race, inaugurated in 1925, was an important event in the history of Anglo-Swiss relations, for whereas the British skiers had been unable to compete against the Swiss in langlauf and jumping, in this new development of ski-racing we could hold our own against the University skiers, and score occasional and surprising successes against the finest skiers in the country. The fact that we were usually beaten more than counterbalanced the traditional superiority complex of the British, and thus removed the only obstacle to friendly relations between ourselves and the Swiss.

British racers who distinguished themselves were automatically promoted from the proletariat of " Herren " who employed Swiss skiers as guides or teachers, to the peerage of men who met as equals in a dangerous and exacting sport, and who knew each other as Otto or Jimmy, Bill or Willy, Fritz or Peter, as the case may be. I remember the astonishment of an English lady, whose Etonian son, Bill Clyde, had just won the International University Ski Championships, when the concierge greeted her with the remark, " We were all so pleased that Bill did well at St. Moritz."

Because Bill did well, he had, *ex officio*, been promoted from the " Mr." to the " Bill " class.

The " Bills," though they tended to be classified in the *Freikarte* class, were even more missed in the Oberland than the " Misters." In spite of the fact that our racers have found it increasingly difficult in recent years to compete against the best Alpine runners, the organisers of Alpine events were as insistent as ever in their attempts to secure a British entry, for our racers helped to preserve that light-hearted atmosphere which the Nazis had done their best to destroy.

The Oberland made an effort to carry on the classic event, and I was asked by Ernst Gertsch to referee the Lauberhorn Cup. " If we can't have British competing," said Ernst, " at least we're going to have a British referee to keep alive the old Anglo-Swiss tradition of this event."

I watched the race from a point above the finish, and my mind travelled back to the dear dead days that are gone. I thought of Jackson taking the Devil's Gap straight on ice, and of our pride when Bill Bracken won the Cup from a strong Swiss and Austrian team. On that occasion (1930) the team race was won by Wengen, with Kandahar second, D.H.O. third, and the Innsbruck Ski Club fourth. Yet Innsbruck was represented by some of its best racers.

In those days the Wengen Ski Club provided about half the Swiss internationals for the FIS, and consequently the three leading Wengen events, for which they all entered, maintained a very high standard. In 1932 Peter, who was then seventeen years old, won two of these events (New Year Slalom and No Fall Race), and was second in the Lauberhorn Cup. It will not be easy for any British skier to repeat that performance after the war. We shall return to the Alps, come what may, but the golden age of British ski-*racing* has gone for ever.

Molitor, as far as I can remember, won the race, but I was living in the past, not the present, as I skied along the road of many memories from Inner Wengen to Wengen. There is a corner of that road which I never turn without hearing a ghostly shout ringing down the corridors of time, "We've won, Arni"; for it was as I passed that corner on a day in 1925, that I met a riotous group of racers who had won our first Anglo-Swiss. Wengen was full of ghosts . . . Cedric Odling in check suiting and check ski hat to match, Tom Fox, Cyril White, Ken Foster. . . . I wandered past the rink. Half-a-dozen melancholy skaters circled round, and there were a few dispirited Swiss trying to curl in Swiss-German. How I longed for the robust shouts of a well-known Wengen personality registering team spirit, and the silent subordination of self to side.

I spoke at the prize-giving. My first joke produced one laugh (from the speaker); my second fell as flat as one of Audrey Sale-Barker's spins before a FIS meeting.

IV

I stayed at the Scheidegg from Christmas to the middle of February, writing a book on recent experiences in the Balkans. For long periods I was the only Englishman in the hotel, and I was therefore grateful for the intermittent visits of Mr. Boxhall, but I did not accept his kind invitations to join him on ski, for he is a good runner, ambitious to improve, and I have only one ski-ing ambition left, to enjoy myself. Throughout those seven weeks I skied alone. Now solitary ski-ing, though it improves one's steadiness, ruins one's speed. I only fell three times in seven weeks, but I realised more than ever that one's ski-ing inevitably deteriorates unless one is consciously attempting to improve it.

I used to work in the mornings and climb the Lauberhorn in the afternoon. My first ascent of this redoubtable peak was achieved in 1895, and I can still recall the thrill with which I learned from my nurse that I was to be taken up a mountain. I knew exactly what to expect, for I had read *Scrambles in the Alps*. When the great day arrived, I looked anxiously for the guide, complete with axe and rope, who was to escort us to the summit. But there was no guide, and the great adventure began in the railway station, where the nurse took tickets for the Scheidegg. I followed her up the bridle path from the Scheidegg to the Lauberhorn with a sinking heart. When I reached the summit, I looked hopefully down the precipices on the other side. " Do we go down there ? " I asked, hopefully. " No," said my nurse.

Before I had been long at the Scheidegg I noticed that a young man of about thirty seemed to find the society of the Swiss officers in the hotel peculiarly interesting. He was always ready to join them at the bar. I first met him while he was holding ıorth on the folly of the war. " Who will gain from this war ? " he asked. " Nobody. It is *Unsinn*."

" Perhaps," I said. " But if a mad dog comes down my street, I don't say, ' Who will benefit from mad dogs ? What is the use of mad dogs ? ' Unless I, or somebody else, shoots the dog, the dog bites me."

" I suppose you regard Hitler as a mad dog," said the young man, quietly. " I fought for him in Poland."

" Oh."

" Yes, I'm not a Swiss," said the young man.

I did not apologise, but I decided that this young man wanted watching. It was clever of him not to defend Nazism in the Scheidegg bar, ingenious to concentrate on the universal ruin which the war would cause, if prolonged. He seemed to have plenty of money to spend, and it was not quite clear to me why the Nazis should release a flying officer and provide him with Swiss francs to stop in an hotel frequented by Swiss officers. Or, rather, it *was* quite clear to me why they should give him leave for this purpose. A Swiss officer to whom I hinted my suspicions seemed pained by my distrust.

I am interested in the technique of controversy, and always give a man a good mark when he makes no attempt to defend an indefensible position. The debater who refuses to concede a point, merely makes things easier for his adversary by advertising the weakness of his position, and by impressing on the memory of his audience the fact that his adversary has scored. If you drop a brick, walk smartly away in the opposite direction. Do not pick it up and play with it in the hope that it will turn into a pebble. As indeed my Nazi friend was well aware.

One evening, when a Swiss officer insisted that Hitler had broken his pledges at Munich by invading Prague, the Nazi replied : " What would you say, if I were to tell you that when the Germans entered Prague they discovered plans which the Czechs were working out with the French for a sudden joint attack on Germany ? What would you say to that ? "

" I should reply," was my answer, " by referring you to the page in Hitler's book in which he says that the propaganda value of a lie varies directly with its size."

The Nazi proved that he was well worth his pay as an agent by making no comment whatever. He changed the subject to ski-ing, and remarked that the Black Rock Run had been in perfect condition.

His conciliatory tactics were not unsuccessful, and he had many friends among the Swiss, but one evening the cloven hoof emerged, and much good work was undone. He had been unduly provoked by a rather truculent Swiss, and suddenly he lost control. " All the anti-Nazi articles," he snarled, " in your Press, which is in the hands of the Jews, are carefully filed away. It is not inconceivable that Germany may win this war, and the file is getting very thick, and it won't be too pleasant for our enemies when we do win." That was a mistake in tactics.

He often skied down to Wengen, for which he was under no necessity to offer an excuse. It was therefore silly of him to explain, more than once, that he was going to Wengen to see his tailor. Naturally this aroused my suspicions, perhaps because I find it difficult to understand why anybody should display real interest in seeing his tailor.

He was followed down to Wengen, where he visited, not the local tailor, but a fellow-German in a small hotel. After this the contre-espionage got busy, and when the ingratiating young Nazi left Wengen he was followed, and arrested after he had visited in succession Langnau, the headquarters of the Swiss G.H.Q., and Schwyz, where a new Army Corps was being constituted.

V

I left the Scheidegg towards the end of February to lecture for the British Council at Malta, Palermo, Naples and Rome. My visit to Malta coincided with the birth of a grandson. I returned to the Scheidegg from Malta and left again for another round of lectures on May 6th.

I was in Florence when the Germans invaded Holland. The sudden violence of the Italian Press, and the organised anti-British demonstrations in the streets seemed to presage an immediate Italian entry into the war. I could not cancel my remaining lecture engagements on behalf of the British Council, but I left Italy as soon as possible, for I had no desire to be interned. On my way through to Switzerland I stopped for a few hours at Pallanza to bid farewell to the dearest of friends, the Marchesa delle Valle di Casanova. Her daughter, Etta Bonacossa, had lent us her Villino, in the enchanted garden of San Remigio, and the Villino had been our summer home for two years. The Marchesa, who is Anglo-Irish by birth, had entertained in her villa the British and Italian diplomatists who had met to discuss the terms of the Anglo-Italian treaty, which brought Italy into the last war as our ally. I said good-bye to the Marchesa on the terrace, from which Mr. Runciman had so often watched the moon rise beyond Laveno.

I slept that night at Brigue. It was May 13th, a turning point of the war, for it was on May 13th that the Germans broke through the extension of the Maginot line near Sedan. On May 14th the French military attaché at Berne said to his British colleague, " We've lost the war." From dawn until sunset the Germans were massing troops and artillery along the Swiss frontier, in order to keep as many French divisions as possible on the Franco-Swiss frontier. On the night of May 13th-14th the German agents in Switzerland spread rumours to the effect that the Germans had already crossed the frontier, hoping to trap the French into an invasion which would provide the Germans with a pretext for " assisting " the Swiss to repel the French.

The Swiss were not deceived. On the contrary, they moved troops from the French to the German and Italian frontiers. I woke early to hear the rumble of army lorries on their way to the Simplon Pass. It was a glorious morning, and I left the hotel while the day was still young, and wandered up the village street to the great Benedictine Church, and joined the worshippers at an early Mass, and prayed for England, and for my son John who was having his baptism of fire on the plains of Flanders.

I lunched at the Hotel du Lac Interlaken with Walter Hofmann. Walter loves England and his faith in victory had not been eroded by Nazi victories in Poland and Norway. But, like many people in Switzerland, he had not been to bed during the long and anxious night when an invasion was hourly expected. The strain had told, and he was feeling rather despondent. " If the Nazis come," he said, " I shall stay here and hope to be shot. I have been a free man all my life and it is too late to form new habits."

I left Walter after lunch and went for a last walk through Interlaken. I found a quiet corner and sat down. The Jungfrau was veiled but not hidden by transparent mist. There were still a few streaks of snow on " Plum Pudding Hill," and I knew that there would be gentians in Wengen and soldanella in the Blumental. The green meadows were powdered by snow-white blossom, but the scented manuscript of Spring and the chorus of mountain torrents in the fullness of their triumphant release from the prison of frost had lost their magic. I looked at the beloved Jungfrau showing through a dust of silver, and felt the stab of fear. If France collapsed, could England save Europe ? And I knew that if Europe went down into the pit of Nazi slavery, and if Gauleiters were installed in Grindelwald and Mürren and Interlaken, May torrents might still make music for the Germans, but not for me.

> Three parts of Spring's delightful things
> —Aye and for me the fourth part too—

would perish, if Switzerland died.

Walter came with me to the station. I climbed into a carriage labelled, *Interlaken-Spiez-Thun-Bern-Basel*, and wondered whether I should ever find myself in a carriage labelled *Basel-Bern-Thun-Spiez-Interlaken.*

My last memory of Interlaken Ost is of Walter's disconsolate figure on the platform.

I was to spend my last night in Switzerland with Tony Torr at Berne. We were dining late at the Legation, and towards sunset I wandered along to the Terrace, from which I had so often greeted the Oberland on my arrival, and said good-bye to the mountains on leaving Switzerland. In the 'nineties there were no through trains to Interlaken, and we breakfasted at Berne on the outward and dined at Berne on the homeward journey. The ritual of the Terrace was never omitted from the Alpine *introit* or from the *De Profundis* of departure.

In those days the sorrow of parting was blunted by the knowledge that we should return, but no such consoling certitudes cheered me on May 14th, 1940. I was going back to a country which might be invaded, and to a London suburb which would almost certainly be bombed. I looked across the roofs and spires of Berne to the noble company of the Oberland, and realised that I might be seeing them for the last time.

In one's youth one thinks of death as something which happens to other people, and long after youth had faded into middle age I continued to plan my life on the tacit assumption that I should return to the Alps every winter as inevitably as the swallows go south. And as I looked at the Wetterhorn I reminded myself that even though I should, in all probability, survive the war and return to share the rejoicings of a liberated Switzerland, yet this poignant moment of parting was a salutary rehearsal of death, a foretaste of that ultimate and inescapable separation from the mountains, which I have loved this side of idolatry.

The setting sun worked its wonders on the distant snows, but there was no tranquillity in this hour of mountain peace. It was impossible to forget that the guns were thundering through the gap near ill-fated Sedan. Thousands had died that Europe might not die, but had they died in vain? Had the death rattle of France begun?

The rose of sunset withered; the snows paled and colour ebbed from the sky.

> Lo thy great Empire chaos is restored
> Light dies before thy uncreating word.
> Thy hand, dread Anarch, lets the curtain fall,
> And universal darkness buries all.

I dined with the Minister, Mr. David Kelly, Colonel Cartwright, the author of that admirable epic of escape, "Within Four Walls," and Tony Page, who, alas, died a few months later. The French were making difficulties about transit visas, and Page came to my rescue by transforming me into a King's Messenger in charge of a Legation bag. He seemed to be suffering from some misgivings as he saw me off at the station. "I hope you're not as vague as you look," he murmured, "I suppose the bag will get to the F.O."

"I have a very untidy outside," I replied, "but a very tidy inside. I classify things into those which I can lose, such as hats and overcoats, and those I can't, such as passports and Legation bags."

He did not seem to find this very reassuring, but need not have worried, for I lived up to my self-proclaimed reputation in every respect, leaving my overcoat in the train and the Legation bag at the Foreign Office. "I was told in Budapest," I added, "that a Rumanian attaché had a Legation bag stolen on the way through to Bucharest. He shot himself."

"We should, of course, expect you," said Torr, "to shoot yourself if the bag goes astray."

"Unfortunately," I demurred, "at this point the Diplomatic code seems to diverge from that of the Church to which I belong."

"Then you'd better not lose the bag," said Torr.

I arrived in Paris on May 16th, and left Havre on the night of the 17th. I had not revisited Havre since I passed through the port just before the battle of the Marne.

Would history repeat itself?

The lure of Paris was to rob the Germans once again of victory, but it was in English skies, and not on a French river, that the Germans were to suffer their first check in their attempt to enslave Europe.

CHAPTER XX

Contemporary Record

I

"THERE is a strange and disquieting parallel," I wrote as far back as 1936, " between the attitude of the untravelled Englishman to-day and the confident complacency of the men who were living in the last decade of the Roman Empire. The legend of the invincible Roman Legions lasted right up to the sack of Rome, and the legend that England will always muddle through, losing every battle but the last, will survive until England awakens to find herself a small and unimportant island in the North Sea."*

Exactly two years have passed since my prediction came true for I am writing these lines on the second anniversary of the French surrender. Only two years, and yet how difficult it is to recapture the mood of 1940—that mood of mystical faith. To-day our certitude of ultimate victory is no longer based on " the evidence of things not seen," but on the visible might of our Allies of whom one was neutral and the other unfriendly in 1940 ; and also on the ever increasing strength of our Dominions and of ourselves.

Admittedly there were moments in May and June, 1940, when faith was eroded by doubt, and perhaps one of the most remarkable phenomena of the War was the inexplicable sense of relief which we felt after France had fallen. Nobody else could let us down. We knew the worst. Until help came from the Dominions and from the U.S.A. we stood alone " a small and unimportant island in the North Sea."

And yet not alone for there are few things of which I am more certain than that we were sustained in the year of miracles by a Power other than ourselves. " This is the Lord's doing, and it is marvellous in our eyes."

The British Ski Year Book, which I had edited from its first beginning, came of age in 1941. I had to write most of it myself, and my contributions were written at odd moments and in odd places, on East coast convoys, at Hell Fire Corner overlooking Dover Harbour, and at home while bombers were droning overhead. My own memory of those eventful months is inextricably interwoven with Alpine threads, not only because I was writing about the Alps, but

* *Within that City*

also because I turned as thousands of mountain lovers turned for consolation to the memory of the mountains.

When the barrage kept me awake I read and re-read my favourite Alpine authors—Leslie Stephen, Whymper, Mummery, Geoffrey Young, and Claud Schuster.

If it were not for contemporary records I should find it difficult to believe that our faith in victory had been proof against the disasters of 1940. I have just re-read an article which I contributed to *America*, a New York weekly, in the course of which I said that whereas in May, 1940, we dreaded, in July we longed for invasion. I wrote this in all good faith, firmly convinced that an invasion would be successfully repulsed.

Because contemporary records are more convincing evidence of a passing mood than " emotion recollected in tranquillity," this chapter will consist of unedited extracts written in 1940 for the coming of age issue of the *British Ski Year Book*.

II

The British Ski Year Book Comes of Age

The twenty-first issue of the *British Ski Year Book* makes its bow in a disordered world. Twenty years ago to a day I was busy at Mürren with the first issue. Before the World War, the Ski Club of Great Britain, the Alpine Ski Club, the Scottish Ski Club and the British Ski Association had all published their own journals. Club patriotism was still strong, and many skiers resented the merging of their own periodicals in a joint publication. It was therefore important to disarm these conservative critics by a Year Book which could defy comparison with any of the publications which it replaced. No easy task, for there was little to record. British skiers had spent four winters under arms, and the fifth in occupied Germany. The first post-war season had been uneventful. In those days there was no World Championship, no Oxford and Cambridge race, no International events in downhill racing. The British Championship had not been revived, and the only references to racing in the first issue are a few remarks on the Roberts of Kandahar and the leading Wengen fixtures. Four members of the Club helped me out with articles which I was delighted to publish, but I had, in the main, to rely on myself for the remainder of the 187 pages of the first issue. " Thank you," wrote my cynical friend, C. Myles Mathews, " for sending me the first number of the new ski publication. The only result of amalgamating the ski-ing journals would seem to be that whereas, before the war, there were four journals, to all of which you contributed, there is now only one *Year Book* to which nobody seems to contribute but yourself."

I have seldom worked harder than during July and August, 1920, for I had not only to produce a *Year Book* but also a ski-ing guide to the Bernese Oberland. Hard work, but fun. My mind was engrossed with plans for the development of British ski-ing. I had already worked out some revolutionary proposals for awarding our first post-war championship, not as heretofore on langlauf and jumping, but on a downhill race and a "style competition," the embryo from which the modern slalom was to develop.

The long destructive years of war belonged to history ; the years of constructive peace belonged to us. We could plan for the future with confidence.

From the windows of the room in which the first issue of this *Year Book* was produced I could see the Gspaltenhorn ; the room in which I am writing this preface to our twenty-first issue looks out on to a field on which the Nazis dropped fifty incendiary bombs a few days ago. I am working in an officers' mess attached to an anti-aircraft battery on the North-East Coast, to which I am paying a brief visit. At the moment it is all quiet on this front, and there is a *Year Book* to be got out, war or no war.

Never has the future seemed less predictable. The great house of King & Hutchings may be struck by a bomb ; England may be invaded before these proofs have been passed for press, and the Gestapo may be busy with the back files of the Club. All things are possible, but I both hope and believe that Hannes Schneider and I will live to set another Arlberg-Kandahar slalom in a liberated St. Anton. Somebody is playing Schubert's *Unfinished Symphony* on the gramophone. I accept the omen. Hitler shall not write *Finis* to the unfinished symphony of British ski-ing.

III

The Shadow Lifts

With a portable typewriter precariously balanced on my knees, I am making the best of a quiet interlude to bring these chapters to an end. I am typing these lines within a few yards of an anti-aircraft battery overlooking Dover Harbour. The Nazis christened this stretch of the coast "Hell Fire Corner," but at the moment all is peace. White spots where butterflies settle for a moment on cornfields rippling in a summer breeze, the blue shimmer of the sea, the grey cliffs of Gris Nez, and the soft outline of the French coast, fretted with the towers and roof tops of Calais, all blend into an ordered harmony of tranquil beauty. But only a few weeks have passed since Calais was the scene of an English Thermopylæ, and only an hour has passed since the blueness of the sea was foiled with black clouds, the funeral pyres of German planes shot down in the furious battle that shattered the lazy silence of this summer afternoon.

I can just make out the tower above the Douane at Calais and the Cathedral overlooking Boulogne harbour. So near and yet so infinitely remote. Only a few miles and yet a whole world away.

I make an act of faith in the future. The day will come, I insist to myself, when once again I shall pass through the Customs at Calais or Boulogne and board a Continental Express. I recite the Litany of lovely names, Calais-Delle-Berne-Spiez-Interlaken . . . Boulogne-Berne-Brig-Domodossola-Milano-Verona-Venezia . . . but at the moment the Litany sounds sadly like a requiem for murdered happiness. Calais . . . Boulogne. Once the Gates of Paradise, to-day the portals from which hostile spirits wing their way for our destruction, only to return frustrated to St. Joan of Arc's country, which St. Joan will yet save. It is as impossible to believe that the swastika is really flying over Calais as it is tragic to realise that the Nazis have not only conquered France but driven a wedge between those whose alliance saved Western civilisation in 1914. At such times mutual recriminations are as inevitable as they are futile. Let us hope that in a happier future our skiers may help to rebuild the bridge of friendship across the English Channel.

The last Alarm has not been cancelled. The throb of distant engines breaks in upon the drowsy peace of the summer evening; the battery telephonist gives the bearing of the approaching planes and the gun swings round to meet them. A battery further down the coast reports a friendly patrol of Spitfires, and the gunners relax. "*Cancel Alarm. Cancel Alert,*" says the telephonist, as the patrol passes overhead and disappears northward towards the Estuary of the Thames.

I find myself wondering whether any of my ski-ing friends have been in action to-day in the battle which has just drawn to a close.

There is a natural kinship between ski-ing and flying, and it is no accident that skiers in general and ski-racers in particular should be well represented in the Air Force.

The peace-time casualties of the Air Force included Dick Waghorn and Tony Knebworth, who raced in the first British team to compete in a world championship (FIS, 1931). Many of our leading racers joined a famous squadron of the Auxiliary Air Force. Three of them, Max Aitken, Bill Clyde and Will Rhodes-Moorhouse, have been awarded the D.F.C.

It is a source of pride to our members that an ex-President of our Club, Sir Hugh Dowding, should be in command of our Defence Fighters. His son, who won the Army, Navy, and Air Force Ski Championship in 1938, is an officer in a Fighter Squadron.

I like to recall these links between the Air Force and our skiers, for our skiers are a representative cross-section of British youth, and I have already quoted my friend Fritz von Allmen's retort to the Swiss officer who doubted our final victory. His faith in our ultimate triumph was based on what he had seen of the spirit of our young skiers. I remember the day when it seemed impossible, save to the eye of faith, that our skiers could challenge the ski-racers of snow-rich countries, but Englishmen have won open International events, and Englishwomen have won World Championships. *Ex pede Herculem*. There is a world of difference between the risks of ski-racing and the perils of the air, yet it is not altogether unreasonable to draw reassuring conclusions from a sport in which we were hopelessly outnumbered.

It was a German who popularised the phrase "Justification by Faith," but it is the British who have proved in war the practical value of Luther's slogan. Those men at the battery, whom I have watched in action, cherish a genial and good-humoured conviction of tranquil superiority to the enemy. There is a morale which no dive-bombing can destroy.

Still more majestic shalt thou rise,
More dreadful from each foreign stroke
As the loud blast which tears the skies
Serves but to root thy native oak.

Their serene confidence in ultimate victory is inspired partly by experience, for they realise that when we have achieved parity we shall command the skies, as we now command the sea. And they are emboldened by the intuitive conviction that free men fighting for their own independence are, as Herodotus insisted many centuries ago, more than a match for slaves. There is, indeed, a recurring pattern running through human history, for the battle between tyrannies and free men has to be fought out anew in every age. And though cowards will always counsel surrender, free men will continue to reply as the Athenians replied to the Envoy of the Persian Führer : " You need not remind us that the Persian is many times mightier than we. We know that, yet we shall fight him with confidence, for we are inflamed by the love of freedom. Waste no more words in seeking to persuade us to make a Pact with the Barbarian, but carry back this answer to Mardonius. Tell him that Athens would have him know that so long as the sun keeps to his ordained course, we will not seek to appease Xerxes, but will oppose him with all our strength, putting our trust in the gods, and in the heroic dead."

War is not only the squalid business which it was represented to be in the mud-blood school of Pacifist authors, for War has its redeeming moments of beauty. My Dover week is ended, but the pageantry of these air battles lingers in my memory. As I write I can see the diving planes and the tracer shells flashing up to meet them, the diamond sparkle of Messerschmitts glinting in the rays of the declining sun. I remember the pools of light on the low cloud ceiling as the searchlights hunted for the dark invader. I remember a pillar of cloud, the signature of a diving airman who had suddenly swooped from a height of five and twenty thousand feet ; the imprint of white shell-bursts against the blue sky, and the dynamic pattern of planes in this furious mêlée of the sky.

But even more beautiful than the visible pageantry of battle is the invisible splendour of the spirit which informs the Chivalry of the Air. As I watched the contemptuous courage with which they met and repelled superior forces, I remembered the tribute paid more than two thousand years ago to the Athenians :—

" They face dangers with a high heart, unresting in victory and stubborn in defeat. In the service of their country they use their bodies as though they were the bodies of quite other men, but their minds as though they were wholly their own." (The subtlety of this distinction is characteristically Greek.) " They are born neither to enjoy peace themselves nor to suffer men to enjoy it."

The British Ski Year Book terminates with a " Review of the Year," from which the following paragraphs are quoted :—

IV

" Review of the Year " (1940)

" I wandered into the Alpine Club the other day. The gallery of Presidents, and the framed menu cards of Winter Dinners, seemed to belong to another world, the world of that complacent security in which our fathers and grandfathers lived their serene lives. But I am glad to have lived on into these difficult but heroic days, for the Englishman of to-day has far more reason for pride of race than those who were never called upon to face the ordeal through which we are living, the ordeal which we shall triumphantly survive.

" When I think of Wren's bombed and gutted churches in the City I remember the reply of the Athenians when the Spartans voiced their fears lest Athens might make peace with the Persian Tyrant, a Dictator even more formidable in his day than Hitler in ours.

" Knowing the mood of Athens you dishonour us by your fears, for there is not gold enough or land in the world which could bribe us to join the Mede for the enslaving of Hellas. And even if we would there be many things which would prevent us. First and above all else, our burnt shrines and images of our gods, which we must revenge rather than come to terms with the doer of these things, and in the second place there is our Greek blood and speech, and the link of common temples and like ways of life—if Athens betrayed these things it would not be well."

" And if England betrayed these things it would not be well for England ,Europe, and mankind."

" There are few better forms of escapism than that provided by the classics. Our Victorian grandfathers believed that savagery and war would soon vanish from the world. We know better. The myth of inevitable progress has been killed by the two World Wars. We know that there can be only an uneasy truce in the unending struggle between the spirit of freedom and the tyrants. In every age there will be men who counsel surrender, and there will always be periods when the lamps of freedom go out one by one. It is therefore heartening to read the story of earlier struggles between free men and slaves.

' Athens,' said Demosthenes, in words which may serve to-day for England,* ' has never in her history surrendered to an oppressor,

*This was written before the modern Greeks revealed to the world the glory that *is* Greece.

however formidable, or bartered freedom for servile security. . . . Men of Athens, be very sure that you did well when you imperilled yourselves for the safety and for the freedom of all. . . .'

'*Of all*, for the freedom of Austria, Bohemia, Poland, Holland, Belgium, and France, no less than of Britain, depends to-day on the British Commonwealth of free nations, and on the Austrians, Czechs, Poles, Dutchmen, Belgians, and French who are still fighting in our ranks."

"A few nights ago I was listening to the *Unfinished Symphony* on the wireless, when the London Regional went off the air, to avoid assisting the navigation of approaching bombers. And suddenly a Swiss station, normally drowned by the London Regional, came through. And I heard how a Bundesrat had died, and how Soleure had won the Gymnastic tournament, and learned that conditions were excellent for climbing. The old familiar accent of the Swiss broadcaster seemed like a voice from the dead, a voice which recalled

The Sleep that is among the lonely hills.

And then the anti-aircraft went into action.

"King Leopold of the Belgians is an honorary member of the Club. I have heard the whole story of the campaign from a distinguished British officer, not unknown to members of this Club, who was with King Leopold to the last. My informant, who can document his statement by copies of telegrams, states that King Leopold proved himself in every way a worthy son of a gallant father. He will be vindicated by history."

"In sanguine moments I have sometimes toyed with the thought that an occasional skier might find it amusing to browse among back numbers of the *Year Book*, but I never foresaw the modest, if useful, role which this publication would play in time of war.

"When I returned from town last night, I found my wife and daughter struggling downstairs, their arms clasped round the complete set of the *British Ski Year Book*. I was touched by their choice of wartime reading, but I was soon undeceived.

"Our home has been promoted from the class of *Noises off* to the more honourable category of *Noises on*. A station, a few hundred yards away, and various batteries of anti-aircraft guns have been the objective of sustained attack. Our home has rocked like a pine in a Foehn hurricane to the melody of high-explosive bombs.

" We have recently provided a home for a large family whose house has been destroyed, and the dining-room has been turned into a dormitory for six children. We have no cellar or shelter. To protect them from the effects of blast or flying shrapnel, we have barricaded the windows with selections from my library. Hence my wife's sudden and unprecedented interest in the *British Ski Year Book*.

> Imperious Cæsar dead and turned to clay
> May stop a hole to keep the wind away ;
> And Arnold's prosy record of the winters
> Now plugs a gap to keep away the splinters.

" I have just had a look at the barricade. The *Encyclopædia Britannica* should certainly be worth its weight in lead. The Library Edition of Ruskin will stand up to anything but a direct hit. *The Story of the Heavens*, which fills a convenient gap, will need a new edition after the war. Goering might contribute a chapter. *Our Island Home* looks a little dated and Lea's *History of Sacerdotal Celibacy* reminds me of a remark made by a woman in Dockland, whom I met on her way back to a ruined home : ' The trouble with Hitler is that he's fifty and has never looked at a woman. It's not human. If he had a wife and kiddies of his own he wouldn't be so savage to other people's kiddies.'

" War has its little ironies. At the entrance of a road punctured by a mine crater I read the following notice :—

Private Road. Heavy Traffic prohibited.

And on the only wall that was left standing of a demolished house in Dockland I saw the following disregarded warning :—

Anybody who commits a nuisance will be prosecuted."

" The greatest of all philosophic distinctions, more important than the differences between rival creeds, is the distinction between those who believe in universals and those who believe only in particulars. If England is nothing more than a collection of particulars, Tom, Dick and Harry, it is unreasonable that Tom should die for Dick and Harry, but if England exists as a universal, apart from the particulars, England is worth dying for. Where the belief in universals disappears, the spirit of endurance is eroded. If man is nothing more than a group of atoms, there is no reason why he should not move hurriedly to the rear when giant tanks and dive-bombing fray his nerves. Why sacrifice oneself for other atom groups?

"The English genius is empirical rather than intellectual. We seldom push any belief to its logical conclusion. Even those who describe themselves as materialists still act as if they believed in the supremacy of the spiritual. Patriotism, which is derived from a mystical and quasi-religious conception of the *Patria*, persists even among people who repudiate mysticism in all its forms.

"And it is, perhaps, because we distrust intellectualism and despise logic that we are still fighting. We are not intellectual enough to recognise the logical proof of our inevitable defeat. We are indeed so silly that we shall continue to fight until we have won."

"In these difficult but glorious days, many of us turn for consolation to the hope and memory of the hills. My body is confined within the four walls of a house which may not be standing to-morrow, but my spirit is free to wander where it will. Beyond the skies, patterned with bursting shells, I can see, if only with the eyes of faith, the great escarpment of the Oberland, softened and subdued in the twilight, the spirit of the dawn moving across the quiet waters of Maggiore, and the sudden shock of green fields from the discovery of a glacier pass in May. There are many who dare not allow their mind to dwell on lost happiness, many who hold with the poet that

> Sorrow's crown of sorrow is remembering happier things.

I am not of their number, perhaps because I believe in universals. To me the Wetterhorn is something more than a collection of particulars, so much limestone and so much snow and ice. I know that the beauty of the Wetterhorn is the manifestation in time and space of a beauty that is timeless and eternal. I accept the Platonic distinction between αὐτὸ τὸ καλὸν (beauty itself) and τὰ πολλὰ καλά (many beautiful things); that is, between beauty as a universal and beauty in its particular manifestations. I believe that there is an imperishable element in the happiness of the hills, that things trivial vanish, but that the best remains, an eternal possession beyond the dominion of time. I may never see the Wetterhorn again, but I know that the beauty which I have loved is only a foretaste of Plato's 'full and perfect vision.'"

CHAPTER XXI

Yosemite and Sun Valley

WASHINGTON has a place of its own in my American memories, for 1315 Nineteenth Street is the American home of Mrs. Wade Martin, who never failed to arrive at Mürren with the spring flowers, and seldom left before the first autumn snows. She loves and is loved by the Mürrenites, and her Washington home was an asylum to which I returned again and again during the second winter of the war. The Alpine classics on her shelves, the Alpine pictures on her walls and the jolly yodelling gramophone records helped me " to beget the golden time again."

I was in Washington when the Japs attacked Pearl Harbour, and I reminded Mrs. Wade Martin of an argument in the lounge of the Palace, Mürren, just before the outbreak of the war. She had maintained that America would not intervene, and I replied by quoting a remark alleged to have been made by the American Ambassador during the Czech crisis. " We shan't let you drown but we shall wait until you are coming up again for the third time before coming to your help."

On the evening of the Japanese attack, I walked from my hotel to the White House. Floodlit against the stars, it was a symbol of the beacon of hope towards which millions had turned for comfort in the dark night of the European tragedy. I remembered a gloomy dinner in the Athenæum in the middle of October, 1940, shortly before I left for the States. " You are wasting your time," said a very distinguished fellow member, " I know the facts. Within a year from to-day we shall have exhausted our foreign exchange, and shall have to surrender at discretion. We had far better make terms now while the Germans are still in some doubt as to the chances of America financing the war."

I did not agree, for I was convinced that America would intervene. None the less his pessimism depressed me. On our way upstairs I glanced at the portrait of Huxley which hangs in the hall ; Huxley fingering a skull with a smug look of self-conscious indifference as if determined to convince us of his calm acceptance of death as a biological fact. But Huxley did not live in a world in which members of the Athenæum might be disintegrated into skulls over a glass of port, or foresee a day when England herself would be facing the prospect of annihilation.

We drank our coffee in the long drawing-room, lined with books, which has changed so little since Dickens dozed in his favourite chair and Carlyle played bad billiards in the Athenæum. The secure climate of Victorian complacency still survives in this most Victorian of clubs. The thunder of the guns in St. James's Park seemed wholly unreal, the crazy intrusion of a Wellsian nightmare. On the other hand, the Bishop dozing by the fire was the symbol of that unchanging England which still survived within the walls of the Athenæum. A bomb fell in Whitehall, and the Bishop awoke with a start, rang the bell and ordered a glass of port.

England was coming up for the third time when American intervention began. The fifty destroyers which were handed over to us in 1940 turned the tide in the Battle of the Atlantic. Never before in the history of the world has so much depended on one man, for I doubt if anybody but Mr. Roosevelt could have coaxed America into that undeclared war which America was waging long before the attack on Pearl Harbour. The Isolationist case was the more difficult to refute, since it was based not on reason but on emotion, on the emotional premise " It can't happen here." If America was as impregnable as the Isolationists affected to believe, it was irrational to spend billions on re-armament. Yet the overwhelming majority of Isolationists supported re-armament, while opposing help to the one country whose continued resistance gave America time to re-arm.

National motives are as complex as individual motives, and American foreign policy, like our own, is a complex of many factors, of which the idealistic crusading factor is neither the most nor the least important.

The realistic conviction that America would be in grievous peril, if England fell, would not have sufficed to bring America into the war had it not been reinforced by an idealistic hatred of tyranny and by sympathy with the free peoples who were resisting Hitler.

The Government policy of Government aid was reinforced by thousands of Americans who were prodigal both of money and of time in their works of charity on behalf of the victims of war. The Americans are the most generous people in the world, and I hope that a real effort will be made, when peace returns, to prove our gratitude. I suggest that some of our artistic masterpieces should be presented to America.

I arrived in the States on November 5th, as a private lecturer, receiving no subsidy direct or indirect from the Government. I had therefore to finance my lecture tour by fees, most of which were paid by Catholics. Now the American Catholics are mainly of Irish, German or Italian background and are therefore not predisposed in our favour. None the less the courage of our civilians in the bombed cities of Britain had made a profound impression and Isolationists were almost as ready as Interventionists to welcome an Englishman who could tell them something about "The Battle of Britain."

During the six months which I spent in America I travelled 25,000 miles, crossing the continent twice from coast to coast. My furthest north was Halifax, my furthest south Miami. I lectured on the Battle of Britain to Catholics and to Protestants; to various groups of Jews who were consistently pro-British; to clubs such as The Century which corresponds to the Athenæum; to Rotarians; to British War Relief Societies; to dons and to undergraduates.

I have described the political aspects of my American journey which began on November 5th, 1940, and ended May 3rd, 1941, in my book *And the Floods Came.* I therefore propose to devote this chapter to my ski-ing and mountaineering experiences, for I was lucky enough to enjoy an aggregate of some ten days ski-ing in the course of the winter.

I spent a few days in New York before starting on my travels. I am always tempted to linger in New York, for I have many ski friends there—Roland Palmedo and Alice Kiaer, formerly Alice Wolfe, and Beverley Robinson, the uncle of Peter Robinson the Canadian skier whose famous line down the Kandahar course on the Schilthorn is still remembered.

On my way to the West Coast I spent nearly a week as the guest of the Loretto Heights College where I lectured. Loretto Heights looked out on to the long line of the Rockies, crested by the first snows of November. It was good to be among the mountains again, and the windy red dawns which I saw from Loretto have a place of their own in my mountain memories, but it would be silly to pretend that this section of the immense Rocky range is distinguished by grandeur or variety of mountain form. A range of which some of the highest summits are accessible in a car cannot be compared with the Alps. The Teton region of the American Rockies and the Canadian Rockies are magnificent, but the Colorado Rockies are sub-Alpine rather than Alpine in appearance. The Lauberhorn towers two thousand feet above the topmost pines of Wengernalp, and the highest crests of the Colorado Rockies, which attain a height of 14,000 feet, are two thousand feet above the Colorado tree-line with the result that though they are as high as the Finsteraarhorn, they are scarcely more impressive than the Lauberhorn. There are no glaciers, no sharp ridges or towering cliffs to disturb the equable charm of a range which recalls the Jura. It is all but impossible to believe that these charming wooded hills are as high above Denver as the Matterhorn above Zermatt.

Jerry Hart, former secretary of the Oxford University Mountaineering and the Oxford University Ski Clubs, invited me as his guest to the dinner of the Colorado Mountain Club, and Dudley Smith motored me up to Berthoud Pass and gave me lunch in the Colorado Alpine Club, the walls of which were gay with Swiss posters.

After leaving Denver I continued my journey westwards, and spent three weeks at San Francisco as the guest of Mr. and Mrs. Maurice Harrison. Oliver Kehrlein drove me out to Mount Lassen and asked me to set the slalom for the opening meet of the season. The last slalom at which I had officiated was at Zakopane. Before I left San Francisco, Joel Hildebrand, one of the pioneers of ski-ing on the West Coast, invited me to dinner to meet a group of his colleagues, ardent interventionists to a man. On my return to the East Coast I stayed at Boston, and lectured to the Appalachian Mountain Club. Henry Hall, one of America's leading mountaineers, gave a dinner party for me at which I met an old friend, Miriam Underhill, the pioneer of "manless" climbing. Miriam and a French lady climbed the Grépon together.

I spent Christmas with Hannes Schneider at North Conway. Hannes spoke with sincere gratitude of Mr. Harvey Gibson, who built the principal hotel at North Conway, and who was instrumental in bringing him to America. Hannes lives in a comfortable house with his son Herbert, aged 20, and his daughter Hertha, aged 19. His wife died shortly after they arrived at North Conway.

On the afternoon of the 24th Hannes took me along to the Eastern Slope Inn, where he had prepared a wonderful surprise.

As I came into the bar the band struck up the famous Mürren Waltz.

Warum trifft sich denn alle Welt
In Mürren, in Mürren im Schnee?
Weil's jedem hieroben so gut gefällt
In Mürren, in Mürren im Schnee.

And who should I see but the quartet who had played at Mürren in the last of the pre-war winters; the old Palace Band, Charley Zumstein, a superb comedian, Futran, author of the Mürren Ski Waltz, Niedermann and Perratone. They had come over to the U.S.A. for the World Fair and stayed on ever since.

And then a girl from Spiez sang *Stille Nacht, Heilige Nacht*, which I had last heard during Midnight Mass at Mürren. And as she sang, I remembered the sudden contrast between the hilarious festivities within, and the quiet of the Alpine night as one left the Palace and oo k the road to the little Church. I remembered the moonlight leeping on the ice boss of the Mönch, and the shadowy shape of the Gspaltenhorn blotting out the western stars. *Stille Nacht, Heilige Nacht*. I looked at my watch. It was almost midnight in the Alps. A few faithful souls would be crunching along the path to the Chapel. And the Eiger, Mönch and Jungfrau would loom up across the valley remote, shadowy, and serenely detached from these our mortal ills. Mürren was still there. The Eiger had not been dive-bombed. The Jungfrau was unblitzed. But it was as difficult to believe that Mürren still existed as to realise that powder snow lay deep in the Blumental when Christ was born. Mürren seemed to belong to a world as remote as the Bethlehem of the Nativity.

And then somebody sang a song of old Vienna. And Hannes bowed his head. And I thought of the moonlight reversed in the swift cold waters of the Inn, and the harsh voice of a Nazi explaining to the Innsbruckers how fortunate they were to be Austrians no longer, but citizens of the Greater Germany, and of that earlier Innsbruck which I had learned to love in the days of the Habsburgs, the Innsbruck still gay with the deciduous colours of the autumn of that great culture of the West, colours which have now been killed by the Nazi frosts.

Old Vienna will never be reborn, but it still lives for us in the magic of Mozart. And I was glad that this Christmas spent with Austrian friends will always be linked in memory with Austria's supreme musician. The parish priest, Father Belford, has seen some reference of mine to Mozart, and he sent me a message to the effect that his gramophone and his records of *Figaro* and *Don Giovanni* were at my disposal, and I spent a happy hour listening to my favourite *arias* before sitting down to a supper party with Mozart's countrymen.

Toni Matt, probably the finest downhill racer on the American Continent, Otto Tscholl, Koessler and Oestermann turned up for supper and we talked of the old days. Hannes showed me a handsome volume of pictures of the World Championship in Zakopane, a present from my old friend Bobkowski, who is now in Switzerland. "Gute alte Zeiten," he wrote on the dedication page, "müssen wiederkommen," and then followed the date, January 10th, 1940.

I had been awakened that morning by an earthquake. The bed shook violently and the house, none too firmly built, swayed to and fro. The top of the chimney collapsed and scattered bricks in the road. Hannes was already in the road before I reached the front door. The earthquake was violent enough to start a fire next door. I watched this fire for a few minutes with serene detachment, a complete isolationist. Inspired by the example of our neighbours who were helping to remove furniture from the burning house, I decided on a policy of all aid short of war on the flames, and joined the convoy parties. I rushed into the house and seized a large picture, but before removing it I had one look at this work of art and resolved to abandon it to the kindly flames. So I compromised on an armchair.

On Christmas Day Hannes motored me to the local "Allmendhubel," a hill about the height of the famous Mürren "Bubble," or perhaps a little higher since it provides about a thousand vertical feet of ski-ing. A moving staircase and an endless series of small cars on to which one hops as they pass, carries skiers to the top of this hill. Hannes, with infinite patience, had cleared two broad continuous runs of trees and brushwood so that this hill provides real "open ski-ing," which is something of a rarity in New Hampshire. Hannes' boys with assistance from the natives have cleared about five trails through the woods, and this took some doing, for it was not only trees which had to be removed but rocks.

There is a little Inn at the top, and a wooden bench outside, and Hannes and I sat in the sun and thought of the days that are gone. It was one of those mild windless days haunted by the ghosts of an Indian summer masquerading as the first deceptive hints of the far distant spring. I was glad to be with Hannes, glad to be among mountains, but *how* I longed for the Mountains of Youth, those beloved hills every wrinkle on whose friendly old faces I know and love. And we talked of the old days, of the " Stimmung " of Kandahar prize-givings, of " laughter and the love of friends " . . . And Hannes said, " All depends on England. If England holds out my country will rise again from the dead."

" We shall hold out," I answered, " and you will be there on the platform to greet me, when I return to St. Anton for the Victory Arlberg-Kandahar."

Love of mountains is a complex of many factors. We are influenced not only by colour and form, but also by historical and literary associations. " The snows of Mont Blanc," writes Leslie Stephen, " and the cliffs of the Matterhorn would have their charm in the midst of a wilderness ; but their beauty is amazingly increased when a weather-stained chalet rises in the foreground ; when the sound of cowbells comes down through the thin air ; or the little troops of goats return at sunset to the quiet village. . . . If the mountains could be swept clear of all life which has been growing up amongst them for centuries and which harmonises them as the lichens mellow the scarred masses of fallen rock they would be deprived of half their charm. The snow ranges of California, or the more than Alpine heights of the Caucasus may doubtless be beautiful, but to my imagination, at least, they seem to be unpleasantly bare and chill, because they are deprived of all those intricate associations which somehow warm the bleak ranges of Switzerland."

A century-old aquatint of the Bernese Oberland range, as seen from the Faulhorn, faces me as I write, and some assorted photographs of American mountains are protruding from the usual chaos on my desk. I am prepared to maintain that the Oberland mountains, tested by an exclusively æsthetic standard, are without rival both for grandeur and for variety of mountain form. But their appeal is not purely æsthetic. I grew up among these mountains and they are linked in my mind not only with the very beginnings of our sport, but also with my own first adventures among the hills. But one need not be a mountaineer to feel that the Alps are unique. Even Ruskin, who hated climbers as men who profane the mountains, would have been the first to insist on the essential difference between the Alps and the mountains of Colorado or Alaska. Peaks which have only watched the nomadic wanderings of Indian tribes could never have inspired the Ruskinian rhetoric of passages such as this : " Iseran who shed her burial sheets about the march of Hannibal ; Cenis who shone with her glacier light about the descent of Charlemagne ; Paradiso who watched with her opposite crest the stoop of the French Eagle to Marengo."

A visit to the Grand Canyon enabled me to isolate the purely æsthetic factor in love of mountains, for I knew nothing of the history of the Canyon before I saw it, and what little I have learned since has failed to capture my imagination.

I arrived in a snowstorm, which cleared during the night, and the drift of retreating clouds next day conjured up effects of light and shadow unknown on cloudless days.

In the course of the morning I heard Mr. Kolb's famous lecture. Mr. Kolb travelled for several hundred miles down a series of canyons in which he risked death, not only by drowning but also by starvation, for there are many points in the Canyon where a swimmer escaping from a capsized boat, would find himself on a narrow bluff below vertical and inaccessible cliffs.

Facing us across the Canyon, there was an hotel on the opposite rim, twelve miles away. Only twelve miles, yet a letter to that hotel would take longer on the journey than a peacetime mail between London and Constantinople, and would cross some half-a-dozen States in transit.

Millions and millions of years ago, the river meandered down through the plains, and in those days there was no Canyon. The calm of the earth's surface, at this particular point, was disturbed by a crustal movement, a wave which has been gathering force for millions and millions of years. The level of the river has changed very little, but it has cut through the upland as it rose, and carved out a canyon, five thousand feet in depth.

The archaic igneous rocks near the river bed are crowned by sedimentary strata, sculptured by wind and weather into an infinite variety of fantastic forms, minaret and pylon, sphinx and Doric temple. And from the sepulchral depths of the Canyon rises the faint hiss of the snake-like Colorado river, as it coils and winds its way to the distant sea. The scenery has the fantastic inconsequence of one of Coleridge's opium dreams :

In Xanadu did Kubla Khan
A stately pleasure-dome decree,
Where Alph, the sacred river, ran
Through caverns measureless to man
Down to a sunless sea.

Long, crazy sloping knife-edge ridges, interrupted by the staccato of crazy pinnacles, sloped down from mountains whose tops had been sawn off and planed down to the same mass-produced standardised height.

The walls of the Canyon revealed an incredible range of fantastic colour, deep crimson, steely greens, brick dust, ochre, and light blue. The young grass on the shelving plateaus caught and reflected the sun. In the afternoon we drove to a point from which we had a wonderful view of the Painted Desert, aptly so called, for its surface was like the surface of painted clay on which the colour has congealed, or like some polychromatic pattern on enamel. Far, far away on the frontier of the Painted Desert, sun-rays slanting through rain clouds picked out the gullies of the sentinel cliffs which keep guard over this land of ancient mystery.

The human associations of the Canyon, as I have already conceded, meant nothing to me when I arrived, and mean nothing to me still, in spite of, or perhaps because of, the specimens of Indian art which I studied in the local museum. The Canyon, therefore, provided what I was in search of, mountain colour and form isolated from all personal, literary and historical associations. And yet it would be foolish to assert that the appeal of the Grand Canyon is purely æsthetic. Its historical associations may be uninteresting, but there are few places in which I have been more conscious of the remoter background of pre-history, of the mysterious influence of this ancient earth, of a majesty which owes nothing to man or to associations with man. The Canyon inspires no affection. The Alps are my friends, but even if I had spent my childhood near the Canyon, I doubt if I should ever have got on to terms of intimacy with the crazy pinnacles and polychrome walls of this uncanny chasm. The Canyon has enchantment but no charm ; is compelling but not appealing.

But oh ! that deep romantic chasm which slanted
Down the green hill athwart a cedarn cover !
A savage place ! as holy and enchanted
As e'er beneath a waning moon was haunted
By woman wailing for her demon lover . . .
And 'mid these dancing rocks at once and ever
It flung up momently the sacred river.

My lecture programme took me away before I had time to follow the winding track down to the river five thousand feet below. Had I done so, I should have found one river and lost another, the river torrent which flowed through Coleridge's opium dreams :

> Then reached the caverns measureless to man,
> And sank in tumult to a lifeless ocean.

I left the Grand Canyon at night, and awoke next morning to discover the South. There were orange groves, and palms and soft hills, whose tone and texture recalled the mountains which stoop to Maggiore. And the grass was as young and as green as the March fields on the southern slopes where Mottarone meets the lake. The train swung round a corner, and something in the look of the hills recalled a curve below Domodossola and the feel of Maggiore, unseen yet sensed beyond the dividing ridge. I looked at my watch. It would be late afternoon at Pallanza, and the Simplon range would be a confusion of misty pencilled valleys, and sharp crests etched against the western sky, and the campanile of St. Remigio would reflect the late sun, and the cypress avenue would be in deep shadow. And a friend, English by birth and Italian by marriage, would perhaps be on the terrace, where we had said good-bye a few weeks before Italy entered the war, the terrace from which Mr. Runciman had so often watched the moon rise beyond Laveno after a busy day working out the treaty which brought Italy into the last war—as our ally.

The train drew up at a side station at the end of a street with the inevitable petrol pump, coca-cola advertisements and texaco signs ; and Pallanza seemed very far away. But it was wonderful to be approaching once more the Pacific coast with its flavour of the latin south, and its heritage of lovely names which Spain has bequeathed. The grace of a bygone day still lingers in the names of many of the great Alpine peaks. How much better "Jungfrau" or "Finsteraarhorn" than "Mount Cook" or "Mount Mackenzie!" I am glad that Sierra Madre and the Mount St. Antonio which greeted me beyond the plains as the train drew in to Los Angeles were not called Mount Hofman or Mount Baldy. California has been baptized into the Faith, and the place-names read like a litany of saints, San Francisco, Santa Barbara, Santa Monica, San Bernardino. There was once a movement to re-christen them and to turn these latin saints into hundred per cent. Americans, but the vandals are losing ground, and America is becoming increasingly tenacious of past traditions. Many years ago they changed the name of St. Joseph, Indiana, to South Bend (St. Joseph, it was objected, had a Popish flavour, perhaps because St. Joseph worshipped the Virgin Mary) but the California Babbits were defeated and the Sierra Madre has not yet been re-christened Mount Mother's Day.

Many American place-names are beautiful, such as Savannah, Providence and New Haven, and some are amusing. "There's a man in Washington," said an American friend of mine, "who is known as 'Slim Killer of Hot Coffee, Mississippi.'" With a name like that he couldn't help being good. Many years have passed since a German-American born in Hamburg called the sandwiches which he served Hamburgers. And somebody seems to have thought that a Hamburger was a ham sandwich, for I have been offered a cheeseburger, and there was a snack bar at Los Angeles, called "Air Raid Shelter" where they served snack sandwiches called Blitzburgers.

At Los Angeles I stayed with the Paulist Fathers in a lovely house, with a patio like those in Spanish homes, and a shady colonnade running round it, called Strada San José de Buenos Ayres. And there were palms and spring grass in the middle distance, and snow-dusted peaks rising beyond the plain, like Monte Rosa beyond the soft distances of Piedmont.

> How faintly flushed, how phantom fair
> Was Monte Rosa hanging there,
> A thousand shadowy pencilled valleys
> And snowy dells in a golden air.

Is half a loaf better than no bread? Are mountains which remind one of Italy a consolation or a torment? My answer varies with my mood. I awoke one morning to find the soft southern sunshine flooding my room, and for one fleeting moment I was back in the Villino at St. Remigio. How the past stabs one in these fleeting moments when one is neither asleep nor awake, moments which divide the dreams which are the flower of the past from waking consciousness pregnant with the seeds of future anxieties! Old scents and sounds and sights are reborn with a vivid exactness. Inconsequential memories vainly attempt to follow the dreams across frontiers into a country which even Hitler has yet to claim as his Lebensraum.

The smell of the limes near the Adler at Grindelwald, the ding-dong of station bells as the train crosses the Swiss frontier, lizards sunning themselves on the wall of the Villino, Venice by moonlight, April dawns from the Lauberhorn, the Alpine horn awakening echoes in the Mettenberg, and the sound of cow-bells coming up through the thin air. And then the vision fades, and one tries to remember those who are infinitely worse off, Poles under the Nazi heel, for instance, or Roger and Cedric prisoners of war in Germany, but it is difficult to cure toothache by thinking of the martyrs on the rack.

It was Aldous Huxley, with whom I spent a memorable afternoon at Los Angeles, who encouraged me to explore the surrounding hills. And so, one day, after lecturing at Marymount College, a most attractive building in the old Spanish colonial style of architecture, I wandered up the path to Brentwood heights, and climbed up a tributary ridge, until it petered out in a hummock of fresh young turf, splashed with the vanguard of spring flowers. Los Angeles was out of sight, and out of mind. And though there were no campanili or hill shrines to recall the gracious past, there were no coca-cola signs to remind one of the vulgar present. The town of Santa Monica was only a faint mist of greyness against the Pacific. Far away to the south a pumice isle floated on the shimmering blueness. The music of an invisible torrent drifted up through the warm and drowsy air. Man may defile the land, but the sea, as Euripides says, cures the evils of man. Even the Pacific beaches, crowded with sunbathing filmstars, are cleansed by

> The moving waters at their priestlike task
> Of pure ablution round earth's human shores.

The Sierra Madre, rising at points to some ten thousand feet above the sea, were still deep in snow. A girdle of iridescent cloud separated the phantom fairness of St. Antonio, " hanging there " from the Piedmont plain of California. Of course it was not *the* Piedmont, but suddenly I remembered that Monte Rosa and St. Antonio are only mediums through which we discern the broken reflections of a beauty which is beyond and above the accidents of time and space, eternal and unchanging, present for those who have eyes to see in California no less than in the Alps. And I opened my pocket book and took out a letter from a friend in a far-off country.

" To-day I went for a few hours to St. Remigio, grey and frosty, not as you know it and love it. I know just what you meant about Plato. Time and change are the only true enemies, eternity and fixity the only comforters. One can see the fixed stars through the mortal storm, but it takes so much will power to look beyond the rushing waves of pain and horror. And yet, one moment's effort, a prayer, or the word of a friend warning us from far away to look up and there stand the types in their unshrinking truth and splendour. . . ."

In the middle of March Oliver Kehrlein motored me to the Yosemite for the Far West Kandahar Challenge Cup, which had been presented by the Kandahar Club, and which is held alternately in the Yosemite and on Mount Hood. This was not my first visit to the Yosemite. I saw it first in all the glory of its autumn colouring, and it left an ineffaceable impression upon my mind. It reminds one of the Lauterbrunnen Valley, but the great granite cliff of El Capitan is far more impressive than the limestone crags over which the Staubbach falls. This tremendous wall of smooth polished granite, over three thousand feet in height, is definitely Boik, a word which I present to the English language. It is Best-Of-Its-Kind. It has no rival among the granite cliffs. El Capitan, New York Skyscrapers, the Grand Canyon, the Charleston Gardens, the Silver Springs and Okala, are all Boik, and things which are Boik are worth going a long way to see. But the Yosemite Valley has not only grandeur but charm. The vast escarpments of granite cliffs are decorated by waterfalls.

> A land of streams ! some, like a downward smoke,
> Slow-dropping veils of thinnest lawn, did go ;
> And some thro' wavering lights and shadows broke,
> Rolling a slumbrous sheet of foam below

Spring without running water is like dinner without wine, as I was to realise among the arid Rockies in which Sun Valley lies.

Chris Schwarzenbach won the Slalom, and was the first amateur and the second competitor on the Combined, which was won by Martin Fopp. The Ladies' Straight Race and Combined was won by Yvonne Blossom, a charming and accomplished racer from Pasadena.

I was impressed by the high average standard of the ski-ing, and by the excellent organisation for which Charlie Proctor, an honorary member of the Kandahar and an old Olympic and Dartmouth skier, was mainly responsible. My happiest memory of Yosemite is of a pleasant idle hour on spring snow with Don Tressider, the King of the Yosemite. We pottered about in the spring sunshine, and discussed the possibilities of the Yosemite. The runs, which are served by automobile and rope tows are, as yet, a little on the short side, 2,000 feet drop, but there is an inexhaustible range of long tours for those who still love real ski-ing, as opposed to mere robot sliding.

I had met Tressider many times in Europe, at the historic Innsbruck FIS and at more than one Kandahar. " What struck me about the Kandahar," said Tressider, " was its atmosphere. I remember being impressed by the contrast between the warlike atmosphere of the Innsbruck FIS and the friendliness of the Arlberg-Kandahar. That atmosphere was, of course, a creation of you and Schneider. St. Anton during the Kandahar was like a big family party : that is the atmosphere we hope to create here."

I think they will succeed. William Janss, who finished high up, said to me, " I enjoyed the Kandahar. A real party. I competed recently in a big event where all the competitors sat round without drawn faces as if they were going over the top in a big offensive, but here everybody enjoyed themselves both before and after the race."

It would be hopeless for the organisers of the Kandahar to compete against races such as the Harriman Cup, for the Union Pacific, with its immense resources, is behind Sun Valley, and the Harriman Cup inevitably bears the same relation to the American Championship as the Arlberg-Kandahar to the World Championship, but Tressider, George Henderson, Kehrlein, Hildebrand and Proctor have managed to re-create on the West Coast the genuine Kandahar atmosphere, which is all and perhaps more than all that the club dared to hope for when they presented the Cup.

And then there was the banquet, and I thought of the old Mürren ballroom filling up, and Hannes obstinately refusing to utter, and Deggers clowning superbly and the silly jokes (mine) which met with such a generous response. " Ah," said Fopp, " those were days. We raced hard but we did not mind if we did badly. How I miss David Zogg, and ' Matterhorn ' Furrer and Hannes. Of course you are here, and *Das ist immer noch etwas* (That is always something)" a compliment which was all the more welcome because it was so characteristically Swiss.

On my way through from San Francisco to Sun Valley I paid a short visit to Mount Angel, which was founded by Benedictine monks from Engelberg. A dear old prior with a long beard spoke to me in a language which he fondly believed to be high German, the medium of communication which Swiss employ in their intercourse with foreigners, nicer by far than the High German of Germany, but nothing like so attractive as the beloved Swiss dialect in which—to his surprise—I replied to him. From the windows of the monastery I could see the distant snows of Mount Hood and plains as green as the fields round Lucerne, where spring was waiting us when Phyllis Holt-Needham and I travelled back from the World Championship in Engelberg, 1938. 1938–1941. Engelberg, Switzerland, Mount Angel, Oregon. *φευ, γαιής ὅσσον ἀφ' ἡμετέρης·* " Alas ! How long the road between ! " George Henderson, who is interested in the Timberline Lodge, Mount Hood, drove me into Portland, where I was entertained by a group of skiers. I visited Mount Hood in November, 1937, and offered a small prize for an informal race which has since developed into a big event, the first race of the Mount Hood season. We discussed plans for the Far West Kandahar which was held on Mount Hood in March, 1942. Henderson sent his greetings to Helen Palmer-Tomkinson, who had competed on Mount Hood just before the war. It is easy to make a mistake of one minute in timing racers, and many of her friends thought that she had been credited with one minute too much in the downhill race. " I think," said Henderson, " that the timing was correct, and we were all impressed by the sportmanship of Miss Tomkinson. She made no comment and it was not she, but her friends, who raised the point." An American skier, who was present, had spoken to me of this incident and contrasted Helen's attitude with the noisy protests of a famous European skier who believed himself to have been credited with one minute too much at another very important meeting. During all the years in which I have been connected with ski-racing I have never known a British racer launch a protest to the Race Committee against a timekeeper or against the decision of a referee, flag-keeper, etc., but I myself am responsible for defrauding one small competitor out of a cup which he appeared to have won. I had watched the race for the Arnold Lunn Cup, the senior Kandahar Ski Club event, and was convinced that the timekeepers had made a mistake in crediting Peter, who was then twelve years old, with first place, so I added a minute to his time, but I did not dare to confess my arbitrary action until he won the Cup some years later.

I caught the night train from Portland and arrived in Sun Valley in time for tea. I was the guest of Mr. Averell Harriman, the Chairman of the Board of Directors of the Union Pacific. The popular manager of the Sun Valley Hotels, Mr. Rogers, welcomed me on my arrival, fitted me out with ski, ski boots, and a fine choice of ski garments, and did everything in his power to make my visit a success. The free pass on the local funiculars, with which he provided me, was a welcome reminder of the fact that I still belong to the most famous of all British ski-ing clubs, the great freemasonry of the Freikarte.

Mr. Harriman is the creator of Sun Valley as a ski-ing centre. He sent his messengers before him to spy out the land, and they brought back glowing reports of a nameless valley, destined to become the St. Moritz of America.

In the Alps the development of tourist travel has been gradual. The early travellers found accommodation with the local curé; then came a modest inn, and in the fullness of time, that ultimate symbol of our hygienic but unlovely age, a palatial hotel with hot and cold water in every room. The great Alpine centres have each their own particular tradition, a tradition which has matured slowly during the long passage of years, but the hotels, ice rinks, and theatre of Sun Valley were planted down, ready made. The nearest equivalent to Sun Valley in the Alps is Sestrières which, like Sun Valley, was invented and, so to say, manufactured overnight. But traditions do not take long to develop and before long those who visited Sun Valley in its first seasons will be speaking as nostalgically of the old days as the original members of the Kandahar of the Hotel des Alpes before the fire. The organisation is superb, I had hardly been in the hotel five minutes before I was asked which ski-ing class I should like to join, beginners, moderate runners or experts. I demurred politely. "Maybe you're an expert and don't need lessons." "On the contrary, I've been a bad runner for forty years and I'm past praying for and past teaching."

Otto Lang is in general charge of the winter sports. Lang graduated from Innsbruck University, and like many other university men in the poverty-stricken Austria of the post-war period drifted into ski-teaching, *faute de mieux*. We talked of many things, other than

Opposite: *YOSEMITE VALLEY. EL CAPITAN* (on the left).
By kind permission of Ansel Adams

ski-ing, of the old Austria which may yet be reborn, of Spengler, and of America and its future.

The ski school is run by Friedl Pfeiffer, who has married the daughter of a banker of Salt Lake City. Pfeiffer won the Arlberg-Kandahar in 1936, racing for the Arlberg Club. Whereas the Kandahar Ladies won the Ladies' Cup on four occasions, the Arlberg racers missed victory again and again by a narrow margin, until at last Pfeiffer and Gerda Paumgarten, who was also at Sun Valley, won the double event in 1936. There was something symbolic in this Götterdämmerung victory, for this was the last occasion on which the race was held in St. Anton, and it would have been very sad had Hannes never had the joy of seeing the Arlberg colours carried to victory.

Sun Valley was full of old friends, such as Mrs. Kiare, Betty Woolsey Fraser, Clarita Heath, a teacher in the school, Rettles de Cosson, and many others. Rettles, whose mother was American, was in the States when the war broke out and is hoping to sail for Egypt on the first available boat.

Sun Valley compares favourably with the more popular Alpine centres, so far as snow conditions and terrain are concerned. There are four mountains, the summits of which can be reached by chair-lifts, Mount Baldy, Mount Proctor, Mount Ruud and Dollar Mountain. The first of these provides a descent of about 3,200 vertical feet, the remaining three descents from 1,000 to just under 2,000 feet. There are no less than six superb runs on Mount Baldy, of every degree of difficulty. These are trail runs, cut through the trees, and the snow is usually, but by no means always, hard and tracked, but the other mountains, which face north, are open and provide the powder-snow enthusiast with ample scope for deep-snow practice.

The scenery and the ski-ing at Sun Valley are rather reminiscent of Gstaad.

The National Four-Event Championship was being held at Sun Valley when I arrived, and the Harriman Cup was being competed for concurrently, and was decided on the combined result of the Straight and Slalom Races in the Four-Event Championship.

Friedl Pfeiffer won the Slalom and the Combined, but the hero of the Harriman Cup was Chris Schwarzenbach, who had flown over from the West Coast, arriving on the eve of the race, and had

Opposite: *JUSTISSIMA TELLUS* (Near Soglio, Bergell).
By kind permission of A. Steiner.

finished third in the Straight Race and second in the Slalom, and second in the Combined. He was the first amateur in both races and in the Combined. The Combined Ladies' Event was won by Gretchen Fraser, whose husband skied for America in the 1936 Olympics. It was a great pleasure to meet him again at Sun Valley. Nancy Reynolds, winner of the 1940 Far West Kandahar, was second.

The Four-Event National Championship was won by the Norwegian-born Alf Engen.

Mrs. Fraser has, I believe, never skied in Europe. She is a very dashing and finished skier with superb technique, who should do well in a World Championship. Her success is encouraging as evidence of the fact that American snows can produce skiers fit to compete with the finest products of Alpine centres. So far as the men are concerned the principal events are still the monopoly of European competitors or of Americans, like Dick Durrance, who learned to ski in Europe. Dick Durrance has won the Harriman Cup and various American Championships on several occasions. He is still the outstanding American-born ski-racer. I was shown the scene of his fantastic straight run in last year's Harriman Cup, almost as sensational as Sigmund Ruud's legendary line in the A-K of 1935.

The standard of the leading American-born and American-trained skiers is about the same as that of our best runners—a high standard. In the last pre-War season, British University Ski Teams defeated the Swiss and Italian University skiers, and Readhead won the Duke of Kent's Cup.

Walter Prager finished sixth in the Harriman. Prager is not yet an American citizen but he has been called up for military service, for the U.S.A. insist that those who are domiciled in and earning their living in the States shall help to defend the country in time of war, a very reasonable point of view.

American ski-ing is even more infected by the downhill-only disease than our own. In the remote past, ski were welcomed as the key to the winter Alps, as the passport to untracked snow and unexplored slopes. The pioneers were explorers, and not racers. Sun Valley has never passed through that phase. There is a large notice on the summit of Mount Baldy warning skiers that it is forbidden to leave the trails ! Those who have a taste for solitude and distaste for trails had better avoid Mount Baldy. I am not as unsocial as Walter Raleigh and do not endorse his indictment of the human race in the moving lines which begin

> I wish I loved the human race,
> I wish I loved its silly face,
> I wish I liked the way it talks,
> I wish I liked the way it walks,
> And when I'm introduced to one
> I wish I thought—what jolly fun.

I am only misanthropic on ski, and this is mainly due to vanity. If I paid any attention to the best medical advice, I should be ski-ing in an iron contraption or, perhaps, not ski-ing at all. As it is, when people complain that the snow is slow, I reply by quoting a famous remark of King Albert's at Mürren, " I do not find that my particular style of ski-ing *demands* any great speed." All would be well if I had not written books about ski-ing urging other people to proceed with the maximum of velocity downhill. People who have read those books are disappointed when they see me on ski. I hope that I shall never meet in the snows a nice Italian officer, my chance companion on a journey to Milan, who asked me if I skied, and if I had met Arnold Lunn. He had read the French translation of a book by Arnold Lunn in which Signor Lunn said that you should never fall, you should wait till the ground got up and hit you in the face. Magnificent ! The true spirit of Fascist Italy ! " He must be a fine man, this Signor Lunn." " He is indeed," I replied, " those words you have quoted are characteristic of the man. They express his superb contempt for danger. You should just see him pointing his ski downhill." But I shall take very good care that he never does. Chess is the only sport in which I give public performances. I played the Chess Champion of Nevada State at Sun Valley and scored a win and a draw out of four games. A year before I had tied a match with the Chess Champion of Malta. So nobody can say I didn't do my bit in the Great War.

My determination to ski alone at Sun Valley was reinforced by the fact that I was ski-ing in Mr. Rogers' boots which were built for a man with normal legs, and not for a skier whose right foot is two inches shorter than his left. But solitary ski-ing is not easy on Mount Baldy. Having taken the last chair-lift to the summit of Mount Baldy, after admiring the afternoon lights, I prepared to slide cautiously downhill. I was soon overtaken by four guardians of the mountain who were sweeping up for stragglers. I begged them not to bother about me. They pointed out that they were under orders to see that no injured skier was left out on the mountain all night. Now I have skied alone on Alpine glaciers, and made more than one solitary ascent of the great Oberland peaks, and I resented the suggestion that I could not find my way down Mount Baldy. But my protests were unavailing and they dry-nursed me to the bottom. Very right and proper, no doubt, for the management has to dry-nurse incompetents, but after that experience I specialised on Mount Proctor and Mount Ruud.

Surely the time has come for those in authority to revive *real* ski-ing. Downhill-only racing is a magnificent sport, but it is a by-product of real ski-ing, and racing is not what it was. A race like the Mürren Inferno from the top of a peak to a valley over seven thousand feet below over untracked snow, wind-blown, powdery and sun-crusted as the case may be, still bears a recognisable relation to cross-country ski-ing, and still tests snowcraft and mountain sense, but racing down a prepared track, with every bump of which the skier is familiar, has no relationship to ski-ing, as understood by the pioneers, magnificent though it be as a test of stamina, courage and quick thinking.

As a veteran ski-mountaineer, I envy the young skiers of America. To-day every ski-able Alpine peak has been climbed, every snow pass crossed, but the vast ranges of the American Continent are still virgin ground. These opportunities are far greater than those which I enjoyed when, as a boy, I made one of the early ski traverses of the Oberland glaciers.

Every effort should be made by the authorities to encourage ski exploration. The Sierra Club of California has set a good example by instituting a really tough ski-mountaineering test.

But who am I to complain? I had just finished this moving exhortation to the Americans to return to the happy pre-Lunn epoch in European ski-ing when I received the following blast from Mr. C. J. Lambert.

"Before the *Year Book* goes through its period of travail I would like you to give the following viewpoint on ski-ing your earnest consideration.

"There used to be a happy time when ski-ing was not considered the perfect background for emulating the feats of the Gadarene swine.

"Enthusiasts could sally forth to Wengern Alp or elsewhere and reach their hotel without that filthy sound of ski rattling over ice still ringing in their ears.

"You along with countless other misguided people have hammered home to everyone that the enjoyment of this wonderful sport consists in passing between two given points in the shortest possible distance in the shortest possible period of time.

"To this end you have organised tests and races, which have changed delightful runs into nightmarish bobsleigh tracks.

"You have deliberately organised schools to teach skiers to increase speed and displace cartilages—and Dr. Goebbels has nothing of propaganda to teach you in achieving these ends.

"I submit (and not humbly either) that you are largely responsible for the present Gadarenish attitude of skiers, and your sins should weigh heavy upon you.

"The true art of enjoying the sport entails passage over the greatest possible distance between two given points, at the greatest possible speed.

"Anyone seen indulging in a stem or any form of turn incorporating the stem turn should be ruthlessly expelled with ignominy from the ski-ing resort.

"Equipped with a good eye for country, a graceful kick turn and a cast-iron derrière as a standby for use in dire emergency, a skier is perfectly equipped for the complete enjoyment of the sport.

"No longer would Alpine trains disgorge hordes of pin-toed and exhausted lads and lassies, heavily sunburned both ends as a result of five daily trips above the chauffage.

"People could fall in comfort on soft snow with little fear of being torpedoed.

"Huge sums of money would be freed for liquid refreshment, which would rejoice the hearts of those both sides of the bar.

"Uncle Arni, right this great wrong which you have done, for young skiers are clay to fashion as you wish.

"Let the slopes abound once more with gracefully waving legs and that heaven-sent spectacle of the skier who has fallen downhill in the midst of a kick turn.

"It is not too late to mend your ways and make ski-ing fields fit to fall in.

"Remove the knife edges from the ski and let us revert once more to delightful round edges, which hurt one so little.

"I have spoken."

The ski-ing at Sun Valley more than fulfilled expectations, but the spring was disappointing. The Rockies are unbelievably arid.

There was one dispirited stream meandering through the valley, and sage brush and bunch grass and dirty brown earth were beginning to merge on the slopes facing the sun. I thought of Grindelwald in April, and the chorus of song with which a hundred torrents greet the triumph of the sun. I remembered the green grass on southern slopes and marsh marigolds clustering beside the stream beds.

Mr. Jeffers, Chairman of the Union Pacific, paid a surprise visit to Sun Valley just before I left. He very kindly invited me to a dinner party. Fraser proposed my health, which gave me a chance to express our gratitude to America and Mr. Jeffers drank a toast to England.

I was sitting between Countess Potocka, the wife of the Polish Ambassador, and an exceptionally pretty girl, who worked as an assistant in the ski shop run by Monsieur Picard, of Lausanne and St. Moritz. I am always tongue-tied in the presence of youth and beauty, but my companion made a heroic effort to steer the conversation into channels suitable for the aged. It seemed that she and her father always argued about the respective merits of Plato and Aristotle. She was an ardent Aristotle fan. I put in a good word for Plato. " But Plato," she objected, " was anti-democratic. He was the spiritual father of Communism." I admitted that his political views were open to criticism. What appealed to me was the Platonic doctrine of Beauty. " And it seems to me," I added, " less important that a man's views about politics should be sound than his views about beauty, or even, for that matter, about beauties." I thought this rather a promising opening, but at this point an irritating man on the other side of the Aristotle fan insisted on talking to her, so I shall never know whether I converted her to Platonism.

Countess Potocka is a Peruvian by birth. We met again a year later in Lima. It was with real delight that I saw her husband in the lounge of the Bolivar, for I had always hoped that I should have the chance of renewing our friendship, the foundations of which were laid at Sun Valley.

I was very sorry not to meet Mr. Harriman at Sun Valley. He had already left for London where he has been appointed Minister to the Court of St. James with the special mission of arranging for the expeditious arrival of American supplies. His daughter, Kathleen Harriman, is a fine skier and has had the enterprise to secure an appointment as a Press correspondent in London. I watched her race at Sun Valley and hope that she will survive such blitzes as London may still be called on to endure, and return to win her father's Cup at Sun Valley when victory has been achieved.

The Council of the Ski Club of Great Britain recently invited Mr. Harriman to become an honorary member. We are glad to welcome into the Club this distinguished American, who has rendered outstanding service to the sport, and who holds to-day a position of great responsibility in the organisation of that American aid to Britain which will ensure the final victory.

Two days after leaving Sun Valley my professional lecture tour came to an end, and for the next three weeks I travelled at my own expense through the South and deep South in order to give " Thank You " lectures to various societies who were working for British War Relief.

I left America May 4th in one of the small Cutters which the American Government had handed over to us, Cutters about the size of Corvettes. I was the only civilian on board. Our Cutter was helping to escort over 50 ships, some of whom were very slow, with the result that we were nearly three weeks crossing the Atlantic. Apart from a little trouble with a submarine, which was depth charged but not sunk, we had a tranquil crossing. The Captain could not have been kinder. He gave me the freedom of the bridge, and I was able to study the chart on which the hypothetical positions of submarines were pencilled according to the messages which were received from time to time.

Few things are more moving than the curt messages flashed by sinking ships to convoys in the neighbourhood. The spirit of the Greek mariner, whose epitaph is the noblest in the Greek anthology, is reborn in our Merchant Service :

> A shipwrecked sailor buried on the coast
> Bids you set sail
> Full many a gallant barque when we were lost
> Weathered the gale.

On our last lap we were warned that a raider was on the sea and we changed our course accordingly. Just before we landed we met a battleship escorted by a tribal destroyer on their way to do battle with the *Bismarck*.

Two days later I learnt that a ski-ing friend, Vice-Admiral L. L. Holland, had gone down with the *Hood*.

CHAPTER XXII

ALPS AND ANDES

ON Good Friday, 1942, I flew from Montreal to Newfoundland. My neighbour in the bomber was General Sikorski. I am writing this chapter on Easter Sunday, but there is, as yet, no resurrection for crucified Poland. "*Is it nothing to you all you who pass by? Behold and see if there be any sorrow like unto my sorrow that is done unto me.*"

"Two hundred thousand Poles," said the General, "including most of our intellectual leaders have been shot certainly since the Germans occupied Poland. I told Mr. Roosevelt that time is not an ally of Poland in this war for these mass murders are still continuing."

The weather forecasts are encouraging, and there is every hope that we shall take off from this airport to-night. I have crossed the Atlantic, since the beginning of the war, in a passenger ship, in a man-of-war, and in the Clipper and I am looking forward with great interest to a bomber passage. It is difficult to believe that this time to-morrow I shall be in England.

Through the windows of the room in which I am writing I look out on to windswept snows, bleak forests and the grey skies of this northern clime. The gales, which sweep across the frozen lakes, are unsoftened by the rumour of Spring, but it is less than a fortnight since I said good-bye to the Indian summer of the Chilean autumn. I left Santiago on Passion Sunday, and reached New York on Wednesday, took the night train for Chicago and, after flying to Washington, reached Montreal in time for breakfast on Palm Sunday, having travelled over eight thousand miles in a week. I had passed from the Autumn of Chile through the eternal Summer of the tropics to the Winter of Canada. But in England April is neither Autumn nor Winter but Spring. I can pay no greater tribute to Chile than to admit that even the joy of returning home and the prospect of April in England cannot wholly banish my nostalgic regrets for the city which Valdivia founded in the valley he named the Vale of Paradise.

There is, at least, one crime of which I am guiltless—taking happiness for granted. Not for me the Virgilian reproach, *O fortunatos nimium sua si bona norint*—"Ah, if we'd only known how lucky we were in those pre-war days!" I have never echoed this familiar complaint, for I did know—only too well. Indeed I have sometimes felt as if a wholly delightful present was being experienced in the past tense, as if I were looking back at the passing moment from a wholly unpredictable future. I remember an afternoon at the Santiago Country Club, in the course of which I seem to have communicated this sense of prophetic retrospectiveness to my friend, Norma Murray. "I have an odd time-machine feeling," said Norma, " as if I were seeing you and this swimming-pool through a mist of memory, as if I were already looking back to this lazy hour, as something very nice which happened a long time ago, as if Mary and my namesake Norma and Lionel and you were people whom I had met long ago, and lost touch with."

Norma Murray was working in the States when the war began, and she wrote at once to offer her parents a refuge from bombs and blitz. "It was very kind of you," her mother replied, " to invite your father and me to stay with you in America, but we were born in England, and can see no reason for dying anywhere else." Norma was earning a big salary in the States, but that letter decided her. She returned to Europe, joined a French ambulance unit, drove an ambulance through the invasion, and escaped after the fall of France with fragments of a bullet in her leg, and—after many adventures—ended up in the Chancery at Santiago.

On that Sunday afternoon at Santiago the war seemed very remote. It was difficult to believe that the boy who had just performed a double somersault off the top diving-board was leaving next week to join an R.A.F. training squadron, or that Joan and her sister, who were sunbathing on the bank were sailing in a few days to join the Wrens.

Norma Spinney, who had spent most of her life in Morocco, where she had not only climbed but also skied, and Mary Dignam, a charming Canadian, dived into the swimming-pool. They were working at the Chancery, and I began to understand a remark attributed to Dick Allen, the First Secretary: "The Chancery reminds me of the title of Proust's novel, *A l'ombre des jeunes filles en fleur*."

Even a brief visit to South America checks any tendency to generalise about South Americans. The difference, for instance, between Peru and Chile is as marked as between Portugal and Spain, or even between Spain and Italy.

Lima is still a capital of the Spanish culture, but Santiago is a cross-section of Europe. There are homes in Lima which might have been transported brick for brick from Spain—patios which reminded me of Seville—and a gracious way of life which is part of the Spanish heritage. The upper classes are great travellers in times of peace. Their culture is cosmopolitan, but Spain is the spiritual home even of those who have lived for years in Italy, in France or in England. Their forefathers threw off the political yoke of Spain, but the cultural ties remain.

Modern Chile, on the other hand, owes less to the Spaniards than to the British, German and Italian settlers. A few names selected at random from the leading members of the Ski Club Chile is characteristic of the Chilean mosaic. Agustin Edwards is the descendant of an English naval surgeon, Arturo Podesta of an Italian, Mitrovich is the son of a Croatian, Miss Ganaan's mother was a Belgian, and Mrs. Pfenniger, the lady national champion of Chile, is of mixed German and Swiss ancestry. Edwards, the owner of the oldest newspaper in the Spanish language, the *Mercurio*, is the son of a popular and influential ambassador at the Court of St. James. He was educated at Eton, where he won the rackets championship, and at Oxford where he rowed for his college. I met him at Mürren in 1937 where he was elected to the Kandahar. No man has done more for ski-ing in Chile, and we are proud to number him among the honorary members of the Ski Club of Great Britain.

As a city Santiago is less attractive than Lima. It has been even more grievously damaged by earthquakes and vandalism, and the old buildings which remain are not of great interest, but few cities have a nobler setting. It is far enough from the sea to escape the aridity caused by the Humbolt current, with the result that the valley of the Mapocho in which Santiago lies is relatively fertile, and the Andean giants, some twenty thousand feet in height, are a complete contrast to the coastal ranges which overlook Lima. The view from San Cristobal is Italian in character. The immediate foreground has a softness of colouring which one has learned to associate with Lombardy, but it is a Lombardy without the lakes. And the snowy peaks faintly flushed at sunset have a touch of Monte Rosa as seen from the north Italian plains. The foothills, some eight thousand feet in height, are less fertile than the Jura, but infinitely less arid than the hills which overlook Lima. Their sunburnt slopes speckled with sparse green shrubs are similar in tone and texture to the foothills which keep one company on the journey between Milan and Verona.

In 1647, two hundred years before fashion was prepared to concede that mountains were not repulsive objects, a Chilean-born Jesuit, Alonso Ovalle, described the view from Santiago in a passage which is interesting as an early tribute to mountain beauty. " Then when the sun is shining on that immensity of snow and on the steep slopes and white sides and ridges of those far spread mountains, it is a sight that even to us who were born there and are accustomed to it, is wonderful, and gives cause to render praise to the Maker who could create so much beauty."

Many a time have I climbed San Cristobal to watch the sun setting on Paloma and Altar, " the Dove " and " the Altar." What beautiful names ! How much better than Mount Cook or Mount Evans !

Paloma is the only mountain on the American continent which inspires in me that quasi-personal affection which I feel for the Alps. The Andes command respect, but do not encourage intimacy, perhaps because their scale is too vast, and their majesty too overpowering. From their roots in Venezuela to the Straits of Magellan the Andes wind through more than five thousand miles. To grasp this scale, you must imagine a mountain range which begins at Snowdon, which straggles across Europe and Asia, attaining its greatest height somewhere near Ararat and which fades out in the Himalaya.

But comparisons such as this only dimly convey the immensity of the Andes ; and it was not until I flew along the range, for rather more than half its length, that my imagination began to register its dimensions. We took off from Santiago shortly after the dawn and landed just after sunset. As the plane rose from Santiago, Paloma and Altar sank, and the immensities of Aconcagua climbed into the sky, dwarfing the lower ranges in spite of the fact that some of their minor peaks were four thousand feet higher than Mont Blanc. The green valley of the Mapucho disappeared all too soon, and for hour after hour we flew over the unforgiving desert, chequered spaces of dull ochre, smooth and lifeless like painted enamel, feathered with a fringe of spidery green lines, the irrigation canals which coax the furtive trickles of grudging water from the mountains to the burning plains. We slept at Lima, which is rather less than two thousand miles from Santiago, about as far as from London to Istanbul, and took off at dawn next day. As we approached Ecuador we escaped from the dominion of the Humbolt current, and the arid deserts gave way to tropical jungles. But the unending Andes continued to unfold their inexhaustible panorama of glacier-capped volcanoes, Aconcagua, Misti, Coropuna, Huancaran, Cotopaxi, Caramba, few of them under, most of them well above the twenty thousand feet mark. It was not until the third day of our flight that our plane dipped down over "a peak in Darien" to the foothills of Panama.

The Andean rivers are as majestic as the mountains, and have the same note of immensity. Shortly before I left Peru, I followed the Rimac from the grey and arid coastal ranges to its source in the many-coloured splendour of the central chain. Thanks to the kindness of my friends, the Mesneys, who motored me to Oroya, and of the Colleys who entertained me at Oroya, I crossed the continental divide by the highest motoring road and returned by the highest railway in the world. The former crosses the pass of La Cima at a height of 4,835m., 15,863 ft. above the sea, and the railway tunnels through just below the pass at much the same height as the summit of Mont Blanc. From La Cima I could see glaciers and gleaming snows, and rocks which ranged through a gamut of colours from rust red to steel blue, and green valleys and a mountain tarn as blue as the Oeschinensee. An unassuming little stream, a source of the mighty Amazon, issues from this lake, a frolic of rippling blue of which we caught recurring glimpses as the car swung down the curves below the pass. Enriched by snow-fed tributaries from the mountain constellations which empty their waters into the valley we were descending, this stream attains the dignity of a river before it reaches Oroya. Below Oroya it falls rapidly to the tropic plains, merges into other sources of the Amazon, and flows on and on and on through many a sweltering league of jungle towards the still far distant Atlantic. The Amazon delta is no less than two thousand miles in the direct line from the little tarn just below the pass of La Cima.

Size and scale, not variety, are the key to the incomparable grandeur of the Andes. The Alps within small compass display a far greater range of mountain form than the Andes in all their pride of territory. The individuality of the Oberland peaks is due to the intricate interplay and overfolding of limestone and granite. The rhythm of the granite ridge which soars from the Jungfraujoch to the Jungfrau summit, fluted by ice, indented by frost and softened by snow, is the more striking by contrast with the smooth monotony of the polished limestone cliffs which fall in vertical sweeps to the Lauterbrunnen Valley far below. And the foil of gothic aiguilles provides the perfect balance to the baroque dome of Mont Blanc.

There is some magnificent ice work in the Andes, but a lamentable dearth of enjoyable rock work, for the Andean rock is, in the main, so brittle that many ridges are absolutely unclimbable. The softness of the material does not lend itself to the finer effects of mountain sculpture. One wearies of the unending volcanoes, for one volcano is very like another, and even Puntiagurdo, which strikes out a new line of volcanic architecture, does not deserve its name, "the Matterhorn of the Andes."

"The Matterhorn," said a patriotic Swiss, "is like a sound tooth; Puntiagurdo like a decaying tooth."

Those who love Nature in proportion as Nature is uncontaminated by man, and who maintain that Switzerland has been irretrievably ruined by trippers will, of course, prefer the Andes to the Alps, and the Chilean to the Alpine lakes. The Lago Todos los Santos in the Chilean lakeland is often compared with Lake Lucerne, but I can well believe that this comparison might be repudiated with equal indignation by Andean and by Alpine enthusiasts.

Lake Lucerne and the Emerald Lake, as the Lago Todos los Santos is sometimes called, have much in common, a cruciform ground plan, narrow inlets and winding bays with sudden and everchanging disclosures of snow peaks and wooded hills, but the resemblances between the two lakes must have been infinitely more striking in the prehistoric ages before man had tamed and domesticated the surroundings of Lucerne. Man is a comparatively late comer to the Emerald Lake, but in the Alps man has been co-operating for thousands of years with other geological agents in changing the face of Nature. He has carved from primeval forests a *Lebensraum* for the cow, and incidentally provided not only the cow with pasture but also the skier with open slopes. In the Chilean lakeland man has won only his first skirmishes against Nature. The mountain slopes, mirrored in the Emerald Lake, are choked and strangled by forests. Only a few scanty plots have been liberated from the tyranny of trees.

Fire is the man's chief weapon in his war against the Chilean forests, and fire does not confine itself strictly to the ground which it is proposed to clear. Thousands of leafless blackened trunks strike a macabre note which spoils the idyllic beauty of the lake.

To compare Lucerne and the Emerald Lake is to do justice to neither lake. The loveliest effects on the Emerald Lake are oriental rather than Alpine. I remember, for instance, a fascinating vignette, the glacier-capped and Fuji-esque volcano Orsono showing through a frame-work of coije trees, very similar to the trees which are so familiar a feature in Japanese prints.

The Swiss and Italian lakes owe their appeal to the marriage between the art of God and the art of man. How I missed the signature of Man in the savage forests of Todos los Santos ! How I longed for little villages nestling near the lake shore, for Gothic spires or Romanesque campanili, for friendly little paths climbing past weather-stained chalets to the green grazing alps, dotted with slow-moving cattle. I am happiest where neither Man nor Nature is completely supreme. Chicago and the Sahara are impressive, but I do not want to live in Chicago or to cross the Sahara.

If Todos los Santos may be compared to Lucerne, Lake Llanquiheue has something of the spacious grandeur of Lake Leman. I liked it all the better because here man has won his first battles against the forest. The faint gold of distant wheat fields on the lower slopes of Osorno melted into the dark greens of the forest and provided that contrast for which one looked in vain on Todos los Santos. Teutonic farmhouses, set among fields of flax and barley and hemp, bear witness to the industry of the German settlers and recall the shores of Tirolese and Bavarian lakes.

Chile, which extends from the tropics to the subantarctic, has three zones, the southern in which it is extremely rainy, the central in which the climate is not unlike that of Switzerland, and the northern desert where it hardly rains at all. The Humbolt current is responsible not only for the aridity of the coast but also for the low average temperature. The summer snowline at latitudes which correspond to Naples, sinks to about 5,000 feet, the height of Mürren, and glaciers flow into the sea at points no further from the equator than Birmingham. If the Humbolt current swept round the shores of Britain, the icebergs from the great Snowdon Glacier would break off on the shores of the Irish Sea.

The Humbolt current not only lowers the temperature, but also deflects rain from the western coast of South America between Central Chile and Ecuador. I shall never forget the first impact of the Peruvian coastal range near Trujillo. I had slept on deck, and awoke to see mountains in reverse, snow-covered lower slopes leading up to snow-free crests above. In that moment of drowsy awakening, I wondered whether crossing the equator not only reversed the seasons but also transposed the kingdoms of rain and frost. I rubbed my eyes and the snow mirage vanished, to be replaced by white sand deposited during long æons of unending drought.

We sailed at sunset. Sullen clouds, which never relent into healing rain, brooded over the desiccated rocks, rocks which ranged in colour from rust red to ochre. The great sweep of white sand on the lower slopes, in the dull light of a shadowed sun, looked like the old and tired snow of an Alpine summer. Suddenly the sun burst through the clouds. The white sand gleamed, and the middle slopes flared up into a vivid, imperial purple.

Of all ranges on the American continent, north and south, none is richer in historical and prehistorical associations than the Andes. The Chichlin museum near Trujillo contains fascinating work by the Chimus, who preceded the Incas, and who created an advanced civilisation long before the Homeric age in Greece. The nomad Indians of the Rocky Mountains enriched neither art nor architecture but the Chimu artists could stand comparison with all save the greatest of the Greeks. Greek sculpture is, for the most part, impersonal, but the Chimu artists had as keen a flair for personality as a Hollywood agent, and their work is probably, for that reason, of far greater value in reconstructing their civilisation than the idealised and impersonal stock types which are reproduced again and again in Greek sculpture.

Chimu, Inca and Spaniard. The gulf of time, which divides the ruins of Chan from the lovable absurdities of the Rococo Carmelite church at Trujillo, exceeds by many centuries that which separates Argos from the miniature cathedral at Athens. It is not wholly fanciful to suggest that the Andes, though far less rich in historical and human associations than the Alps, derive some spiritual enrichment from the successive layers of culture which have been deposited on the plains which they overshadow.

No student of modern architecture can rest content until he has seen the New York sky line, but he will find few new buildings of outstanding merit south of the equator. On the other hand South America has some charming examples of the older styles, which are unrepresented in the United States.

The puritan settlers in New England had broken with their own past ; the founders of the new Spain like the founders of Virginia and Georgia were conservatives who carried with them to the new world the traditional loyalties which they had inherited in the old. The puritans left England because they were in revolt against the established religion and the political structure of their country. The Conquistadors were fanatic Catholics and devoted servants of his most Catholic Majesty the King of Spain. New England soon evolved her own colonial aristocracy, and consequently her own architectural style, but the puritans were concerned to create a *bourgeoisie* democracy in which counting-houses would take the place of castles, and chapels of cathedrals. The Conquistadors, on the other hand, were anxious to emulate in the new world the architectural glories of the court of Spain and they proved their loyalty to the European culture of which they were the trustees by building stately palaces and baroque cathedrals.

The savage and pitiless splendour of the Andean range provided a perfect setting for the ruthless epic of the Spanish conquest. Pizarro started out with 188 men for the conquest of Peru. Swallowed up in the immensities of an unexplored continent he emerged again in the Inca capital and an ancient empire and advanced civilisation disintegrated under the impact of his extravagant self-confidence. His was no systematic invasion but the most reckless of commando raids—a raid from which there was no possibility of return.

I flew from Lima to the city which Valdivia founded. He started from Cuzco in Peru, which is nearer to Santiago than Lima. My journey was completed between sunrise and sunset ; his lasted for twelve months. Only a small remnant of those who had crossed the desert under his command, creeping round the roots of the

Opposite : *SUMMIT RIDGE (Piz Bernina).* *By kind permission of A. Pedrett.*

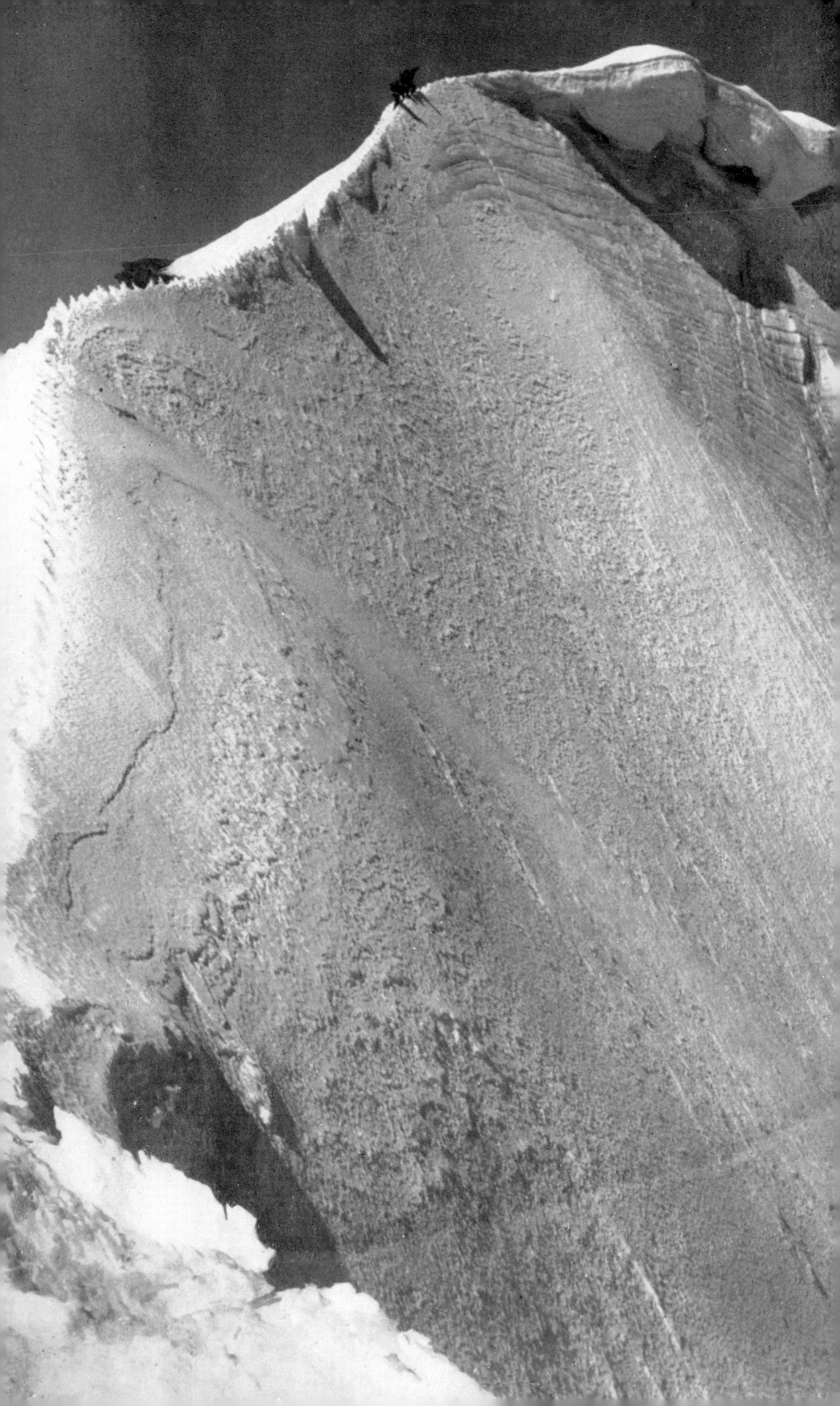

mountains, hurrying from one scanty trickling stream to the next, lived to set foot in that " Valparaiso " in which Valdivia founded his city, but the destitute and starved adventurers who completed the march had lost nothing of their superb confidence, and yet another empire collapsed at the approach of these extraordinary men.

The Conquistadors were impelled forward in the unknown by a complex of many motives, ambition, greed of gold, and patriotism. Their unshaken certitude of success was derived from their fanatic faith in their mission, the conquest of a new world for Christ for the Church and for Spain. They were undisturbed by the inconsistency between the methods which they adopted and the teaching of Him whose kingdom they believed themselves to be advancing. Indeed they were unaware of any conflict between the creed they professed and the code which they practised. They were as pitiless as they were brave, as ruthless as they were devout, and it is perhaps not surprising that they should provoke little but distaste in the minds of those who lack not only their defects but also their heroic qualities. The more anæmic type of historian, who is equally disedified by their ferocity and by their faith, often seeks to explain away and belittle their extravagance of superhuman courage. In all recorded history of war there is no record of an invasion more impudent than Pizarro's conquest of a great empire with a handful of 188 adventurers. Mr. E. J. Payne, after a few sneers at these " vile and sordid adventurers," airily dismisses the problem of their success by one of the silliest sentences ever written by a learned man : " The facilities of marching which a century of well-organised aboriginal rule had established from one end of the dominion to the other and in several places between the coast and the mountain made Pizarro's progress easy."*

As if " facilities of marching " were only accessible to the invader, helped on his forward movement by roads reserved for one-way traffic.

The Conquistadors did not confine themselves to the coastal roads : some of their mountain marches were at least as striking as Suvoroff's Alpine campaign, but by common consent the most impressive mountain campaigns in history were those achieved under the generalship of Bolivar during the war of liberation against Spain.

It is not easy, within the limits of a chapter, to compare the

* *Cambridge Modern History*, Vol. I, p. 46.

Opposite : *THE URNS OF THE SILENT SNOW.* *By kind permission of H. Gorny.*

physical characteristics of the Alps and Andes, and also to discuss, if only in outline, the cultural and historical background of this tremendous range. And the result may not justify the attempt. There are mountaineers for whom a mountain is only a problem in technique, and there are skiers for whom mountains are nothing more than things down which to slide. But there are others, and it is for them that I write.

An Airport in Newfoundland.
Good Friday to Easter Sunday, 1942.

CHAPTER XXIII

Better than a Thousand

Καὶ τόδε Φωκυλίδεω πόλις ἐν σκοπέλῳ κατὰ κόσμον οἰκεσα σμικρὴ κρέσσων Νίνου ἀραινούσης.

Thus saith Phocylides. A little well-ordered city, set on a rock, is better than all your frenzied Ninevehs.

NOBODY could have been more helpful than the officers of the Ferry Command who fitted us out with warm clothing and boots, and coached us in the intricacies of the oxygen mask. Indeed, at times the solicitude of Squadron Leader G. McDougal, who accompanied us, was a little embarrassing. As an old mountaineer I was technically interested in the effects of altitude, but my removal of the oxygen mask at the height of Everest's North Col, 24,000 feet, did not long escape his eagle eye or stern remonstrance.

" We shall have head winds again," said the Captain, before we took off, " and there'll be a low cloud ceiling over Scotland, but there'll be holes in the ceiling through which we can get down and we'll be there in ten hours." We landed ten hours after taking off to the second, and we dived through a hole in the cloud ceiling, exactly as the Captain had forecasted. I was deeply impressed by the accuracy of modern weather prediction.

We flew at night. It is desirable to keep awake, as the oxygen requires attention, and I was glad to discover in my travelling companion, Mr. Blair, a chess player. I had no mittens, and as one cannot handle chess men with ski gloves there were times when my fingers looked a little blue, for the temperature in our cabin sank to some sixty degrees below zero, fahrenheit.

I have visited twenty-five countries, and travelled eighty thousand miles since Hitler invaded Poland, and I should not be sorry if I were kept at home for the rest of the war. Be that as it may, it is certainly good to be in England " now that April's here."

I am spending an April week-end with my old ski-ing friends the Aitchesons, and the room in which I am writing looks out on to an enchanting stream, bordered with primroses and violets, the next best thing to the Alpine gentians and soldanella of which Hitler has robbed me. Still, I will be just even to Hitler and admit that but for him I should probably never have seen Santiago. Few people can resist the spell of Chile and the charm of the Chileans. Even John

Gunther, whose book *Inside Latin-America* is the fine flower of a disintegrating puritanism, softened in Santiago.

Santiago has a very special niche in my memory. And this for many reasons. I liked the town and the surroundings. I met an astonishingly large number of most attractive people, Chileans, Americans, British and Swiss. And finally there are buildings, a house in the suburbs and a ski hut in the surrounding ranges, which are extra-territorial, fragments of Switzerland in a Chilean setting.

On my first Sunday at Santiago, Otto Pfenniger and his wife, Elsa, motored me out to Alphalar, a meadow below a cliff not unlike the cliff over which the Staubbach falls, but covered with cacti instead of spray. Still, there was a touch of Lauterbrunnen about the valley and a look of the Grimsel peaks in the rocky range at its head, and the Swiss atmosphere was reinforced by the beloved dialect in which Otto and Elsa talked, when they weren't talking English to me.

Otto comes from Lucerne. He has a long list of brilliant first ascents to his credit in this region of the Andes, and is accounted, so I was told in Santiago, one of the most distinguished mountaineers in Chile.

In 1938, he was asked to represent the leading German-Chilean mountaineering club at the General Assembly of German Alpine Clubs. The first item on the agenda was to substitute good Nazis for the Austrian officers of the Austrian clubs, who owed their position to such irrevelant considerations as their status in the mountaineering world. Seyss-Inquart, for instance, was recommended as the Sport-leader for German mountaineering on three grounds. First, he was a good party man and had rendered distinguished services to the Party. Secondly, he had been wounded in the war. Thirdly, he was a mountaineer. The Nazis have spent enormous sums on propaganda in Chile, and were ready to welcome with effusive politeness the representative of a German-Chilean Club, but Otto did not respond to the glowing compliments and sat glumly silent. He was tempted to point out that he had been misled, for he had accepted their invitation under the impression that he was representing a mountain club at a meeting of mountaineers, only to discover that he had let himself in for a Nazi Party meeting.

Otto soon tired of being told that, in pre-Hitler Germany, the Jews had obtained a strangle-hold on finance, on the professions, on the Press and on medicine. " I told one of these Nazis that if we

Swiss could not hold our own against Jewish competition, I should be much too ashamed to advertise this fact to a foreigner." Characteristic of that Swiss realism which is a perfect foil to Swiss idealism. In Otto's case the stubborn Swiss realism was reinforced by all that he had seen and heard in Germany. He presented a report to his committee which did not please them, and when Germany invaded Holland, he resigned from the club, for he could no longer endure to climb with, or meet, men who were ready, as most German Chileans were ready, to condone evil and cruel things.

Elsa, his wife, is Chilean born, of mixed German and Swiss ancestry, but Swiss without reservation in her allegiance. Her delightful children, a boy and a girl, not only looked but spoke Swiss-German.

Otto took me one evening to the Swiss Club, where the President and members were entertaining (in their shirt sleeves) a distinguished guest, a Swiss officer who had just arrived from Switzerland. In 1940, after the collapse of France, there were timid voices who hinted that it would be futile for Switzerland to resist an invasion, that Germany had won the war, that England would soon surrender, and that Switzerland must come to terms with Hitler. " But the great mass of the people thought differently. Even if Germany was irresistible we were determined to resist. It was a character test. Are we men or are we dirty dogs ? "

The Swiss informed the Nazis that, in the event of an invasion, they would begin by blowing up the Simplon and Gotthard tunnels, essential for the German communications, not only with Italy, but also with Libya. They would abandon the plains, and concentrate their stores of food and munitions in the Rhône valley. Defeat would be only a matter of months, perhaps weeks, but the Swiss believed that they could kill 200,000 Nazis before surrendering and thus contribute a noble service to the cause of all free men. And even in 1940, when it seemed as if resistance was futile and Hitler invincible, the Swiss took the long view and knew that they would not die in vain, if they preferred death to surrender. Their children and their children's children would still be proud to be Swiss and from the seed of their pride would flower the spirit of resistance which would one day liberate enslaved Europe from the Nazi tyranny.

Otto told me that there were only two members of the Swiss colony in Santiago who were not whole-heartedly pro-ally. One of them had served on the committee of one of the Swiss institutions, but when he recently came up for re-election he did not receive a single vote. Two members of the Club, however, inscribed on their secret ballots the words, " Our Swiss Quisling."

I dined several times in Otto's home. Most of my favourite Alpine views were represented on the walls : Hertenbühl, Lungern with the triple-crested Wetterhorn, and Lucerne. There was a delightful Swiss " Stube," with Swiss chairs and table, and the arms of the cantons round the wall, and a cuckoo clock, and the dear unlovely Bernese pewter pots, replicas of which are often given in Oberland ski races.

Elsa had only once visited Europe, but her English was both fluent and correct, which was sad, because I should have far preferred her to talk Swiss-German. She is widely read, and also the best Chilean lady skier, and has twice missed the international championship by the narrowest of margins. The Greeks saw nothing odd in the scholar-athlete combination, but in our age of specialisation the fact that a champion in any sport should also be keenly interested in the things of the mind often excites surprise. It is perhaps even more surprising that somebody as widely read as Elsa should also be a wonderful cook. Cooking has to be either very good or very bad to attract my attention. On one occasion I sent for a head-waiter to complain that an hour had passed since I ordered my dinner, and that I did not propose to wait much longer. To which he replied that I had not only ordered, but eaten and paid for the dinner in question. It is therefore no small tribute to Elsa's cooking to record the fact that my mouth still waters at the thought of her masterpiece, a cream pudding of Parthenesque perfection. It is not surprising that Otto should have begun to propose to Elsa when she was sixteen and married her at seventeen. The realistic Swiss do not believe in giving their rivals, either in love or business, an unnecessary start.

On March 15th, my last Sunday in Chile, I left Santiago after lunch to spend a night in the Ski Rifugio of San Lorenzo, of which Otto is the architect and owner.

We motored up a winding valley to the Fundo of a friendly Bavarian, who had fought in the first World War but who hated Hitler and his regime. His Fundo was about 1,000 metres, the Rifugio 2,700 metres above the sea ; over 5,000 feet to be climbed, approximately the height of the Faulhorn above the Grindelwald Valley. We left at 5.30 p.m. on horseback.

The summer and winter holidays of my youth were spent in the Alps, and I have only ridden a horse three or four times in my life. It would seem, from what Elsa said, that there is a subtle distinction between the European and South American riding technique. It was certainly consoling to reflect that my difficulties would not be aggravated by a riding style acquired on the other side of the Atlantic.

I mounted a large white horse by a method which owed more to Alpine Club than to Cavalry Club technique. Elsa's horse sneered, and my horse did not conceal its chagrin. Snobbery is as rampant in the animal kingdom as in human society.

Once astride my horse, I resolved to apply a technique recommended in a song which made a great impression on me when I first heard it in the summer of 1938. I had been invited to attend the opening meeting of one of Dr. Buchman's House-parties, which was to be held at Interlaken. A young man, accompanying himself with a guitar, sang a song called " Wise Old Horsey," the theme of which was the unnecessary difficulties encountered by a rider who relied on his own judgment as to the direction in which to proceed. " Why not drop the reins," said wise old horsey, " and accept God-guidance ? "

I therefore resolved to adopt a policy of non-intervention, which was very successful, not perhaps for the reason advocated in the song, but because my horse had no option but to follow Elsa's horse. It was only when we reached a level field, between two steep climbs, that there was choice of movement, and my rider-snobbish horse chose this moment to revolve slowly in a complete circle, after which he resumed his journey with a contemptuous snort, as if to say, " My friends and I happen to be going in this direction, but pray do not flatter yourself that your wishes have anything to do with my movements."

Slowly the shadows crept up from the valley, and the details of the lower slopes, tree and shrub and cactus, disappeared. The twilight ebbed from the mountains overlooking the valley, picking out in strong relief the narrow strata of white calcite which gleamed between massive bands of red and purple rock. The angry flush of an Andean sunset lingered on the remoter glaciers.

The Alps have been humanised rather than vulgarised by human contacts. Their austere majesty has, perhaps, been diminished, but there has been gain as well as loss, for even trippers and picture postcards contribute something to the personality which the Alps have acquired by long association with Man. Man is at home in the Alps, an intruder in the Andes.

" The Alps " is a little more than a geographical expression, for one does not think of the range as a range. One thinks of individual peaks, each with its own name, personality and tradition. But the Andes has a group soul. The individual personalities of the mountains are subordinated, as in a Communist film, to the mass personality of the range as a whole. And though most of the great peaks in the Andes have been named, charted and climbed, a suggestion of remote anonymity is still the keynote of the Andean theme. Even those, so I am told, who have lived among these mountains and climbed them never feel that they have established those same relations of intimate friendship which the Alps have the faculty of inspiring.

The steep, primitive bridle track eased out as we approached the gentle flaring slopes above the precipitous ramparts which overhang the valley. It was clever of Otto to discover the ski-ing paradise in which his hut is built, for these slopes are invisible from below, and nothing could look less inviting than the range as seen from the valley.

Night fell just before we reached the first Rifugio, the property of Otto's Bavarian friend. After a short halt we rode on, and two hours later reached Otto's Hut.

The Rifugio del San Lorenzo is very small, little more than twelve square metres in area, but Otto has exploited to the full the available space. He has found room for six comfortable bunks, the stove, and cupboard, and has tucked some Alpine pictures into the remaining niches of empty wall space. San Lorenzo is a symbol of that well-ordered land where every available hectare of cultivable land is lovingly exploited. The pundits assure us that there is no future for little countries. It may be so, for centralisation is one of the symptoms of a dying culture, and the great culture of the West, which was born within the economy of the small town, village and farm is, perhaps, destined to perish, as other cultures have perished in the sterile climate of a centralised megalopolitan civilisation. Art flourished in Periclean Athens and died in Alexandria, precursor of the world cities of to-day. And as I looked at San Lorenzo, a symbol of little things, and of little Switzerland, an old Greek saying came back to me : " A little well-ordered city, set on a rock, is better than all your frenzied Ninevehs."

After supper I went outside. Night among the mountains blots out the visible evidence of man's presence in the hills, the campanile and timber-stained chalet no less than the ugly scar of funicular and mammoth hotel, and throws into strong relief the basic mountain form which has changed so little since Man first followed the retreating glaciers into the Alpine valleys. Night breaks down the bridge of associations which Man builds between himself and the mountains ; the Matterhorn is no longer Whymper's mountain but that same nameless obelisk which towered above the uncharted glaciers when mammoths were still lumbering across the Piedmont plain. Night re-establishes the autonomy of the hills and restores their memories of a life which is infinitely older than Man.

The darkness eliminates surface differences between the humanised Alps and the austere Andes with the paradoxical result that the Andes seem far friendlier and more approachable by night than by day. Through the open doorways I heard Otto and Elsa talking in Swiss-German, and these snatches of the familiar Alpine speech reinforced the extra-territorial illusion. It was easy to believe that the shadowy presences in communion with the star-pointed night were the mountains of my youth. The snow-fed torrent which filled the night with music sang the same song as streams conceived in Alpine glaciers, and the years fell away and I was a boy again, outside the Orny Hut, on my way to my first big climb.

I slept well and awoke to hear Elsa and Otto busy with the preparations for breakfast. I made a co-operative gesture which was firmly repulsed. *Grossvaters* have great prestige among the Teutons, but even so I am not wholly reconciled to allowing the young and beautiful to wait upon me. I concede, however, there is something to be said for the Teutonic and Latin view of woman's role on this planet.

After breakfast, we set forth on my Golden Jubilee expedition. We loaded our ski on the equine snob, the nearest local equivalent to the Mürren " Bubble."

We wandered along a gentle valley, carpeted with flowers, and climbed for an hour up to a little pass which was about a thousand feet above the Rifugio, and more than six thousand feet above the Fundo, from which the patient horses had transported our ski. And in return for all this we hoped for just under a thousand feet of running, a Mürren " South Slopes." But *qualitas* cannot be measured in terms of *quantitas*, and though this Golden Jubilee expedition was a miniature of mountain experience, it was a very perfect miniature. There was the cool beauty of the early morning lights on the snow, the cheerful hosannas of a mountain stream, the flower patterns in the valley, the never-fading wonder of the apocalypse of the pass with its sudden discovery of distant ranges, and a short but happy frolic down sun-softened crust, firm and true and easy.

The muleteer, who had never seen ski-ing, was astounded when Otto and Elsa led off with rapid *schusses*, and was even impressed by the sedate stemmbogens with which I followed them. Otto overheard him describing these strange sights to a herdsman on the alp. " The Englishman was no good on a horse, but you should see him on those long bits of wood." To the uninitiate straight running is impressive, but continuous turning on these long, clumsy planks nothing short of a miracle. I remember—in 1903—how we gaped our astonishment when Rickmers linked six stem turns down a slope at Adelboden.

The sun-softened snows petered out into a grassy slope, flecked with flowers. It was autumn in Chile, but the winter had been unusually severe and long, and the spring flowers were in full bloom near San Lorenzo. Fate which had cut me off from the Alpine spring, was making amends by decking out the Chilean autumn in the trappings of an Alpine May, for the *Stimmung was the Stimmung* of a May glacier tour, the same regret as one linked the last of one's christies down the vanishing snows, the same tranquil happiness as one crossed the frontier where the vanguard of flowers presses hard on the rearguard of winter, and the same liquid melody of snow-fed waterfalls.

The level valley, between San Peladoros and the rocky ridge on which the Rifugio stands, was a sheet of glorious colour, yellow buttercups, Chilean edelweiss (perezia), the yellow Soldado, the pink pilgrim flower, and the Violeta de la Cordillera, most fascinating of all violets.

A letter from Otto lies before me as I write. The little alp down which we skied is to be called the Arnialp. " This is quite neutral, for there is an Arnialp above Engelberg." Otto has his alibi in case he is taxed with naming places after a belligerent.

I am glad that the place-name of this enchanted valley will henceforward link it with Switzerland. I am grateful to the Arnialp and to the mountains which guard it. Between them they conspired to make perfect my Golden Jubilee expedition. San Peladoros did his best to look like the Schilthorn, and the rocky ridge to the East tried hard to disguise itself as the Belalp Fusshorner.

We lunched at the Rifugio, and rode slowly down to the valley. At the point of abrupt transition between the gentle slopes of the ski-ing paradise and the steep fall of the wall which overhangs the valley, we paused for a few minutes. A faint murmur drifted up through the evening air from the river far below. Only a faint shimmer on the grey streak showed where the tumult of its waves broke on the boulders of its bed.

The twilight played havoc with the succession of ridges which stretched away westward to the golden haze above the plain in which Valdivia founded his city. The last rays of the sun illuminated the vivid green on the gentle sloping shelves above the narrow V-shaped valley which had been cut by the Colorado river. And then the night fell, and the stars came out, the southern stars.

My heart sank when first I saw the Southern Cross, the symbol of a new world, separated by the Equator from old familiar and beloved things, but thanks to San Lorenzo the Southern Cross has to-day an unmistakable Helvetian flavour.

" One day in Thy courts are better than a thousand." One feels that the Psalmist might have expressed this more tactfully and removed a painful ambiguity by adding " better than a thousand elsewhere," but one knows what he meant.

This chapter, begun in April, ends on May 27th, the thousandth day of the war. Hence the title of this chapter, *Better than a Thousand*, for that day at San Lorenzo " in thy courts " had built a bridge across a thousand days of war to the golden years of peace. Just as a restorer removes the grime of years from a painting, so those hours at San Lorenzo have " restored " my mountain memories, cleansing them from the layers of oblivion, and restoring the pristine colours of mountain joy in all their radiant glory.

LONDON.
May 27th, 1942.

CHAPTER XXIV

"IN HEAVEN IS EARTH"

IT is not easy to typewrite in a chair which shoots across the floor every time the little freighter in which I am crossing the Atlantic disputes the right of way with an Atlantic roller. The taciturn Norwegian steward has just looked into our diminutive lounge to announce that of our two lifeboats one has just been swept away by the gale. But only a few more days remain of 1942, and I am determined to complete this book within the year in which I had hoped to celebrate my mountain jubilee in Grindelwald. My last faint hope of revisiting the Alps in 1942 vanished some weeks before the Nazis reached Toulon. To-day Switzerland is entirely surrounded, an island of freedom in an ocean of tyranny, an ocean

> . . . whose waters of deep woe
> Are brackish with the salt of human tears.

Meanwhile in this war, as in the last, the Swiss are proving themselves to be the good Samaritans of Europe, and their country is still the clearing house for such corporal works of mercy as are still possible. A friend of mine who works in the War Office department concerned with the interests of our prisoners of war tells me that it is impossible to praise too highly the unassuming courage and quiet persistence with which the Swiss have stood up to the Nazis and the Japanese in defence of our prisoners of war.

The reserve of mountain people is not conducive to quick and easy friendships, but those who have made their home in Switzerland will endorse a recent tribute from the author of one of the best books which this war has produced, *For the Heathen are Wrong*. "In those fifteen months," writes Mr. Bagger, "I came to regard Switzerland as the finest democracy in the world, a democracy based on the effort of hard thinking, on the dignity of hard work, on the beauty of self-imposed discipline. It was the one democracy in Europe that was, on the one hand, truly democratic, and that, on the other hand, *worked*; and this was because of all European democracies, it had remained most faithful to the Christian origins of our civilisation. It was the most advanced of European nations because it was the most conservative."

The Mountains of Youth was written at Grindelwald in secure possession of all that makes life worth living. This book has been written in exile, but I try to draw consolation from the thought that exile has some compensating advantages for a writer. Ovid's greatest poems, perhaps his only great poems, were those written beside the bleak Euxine. On my fifty-third birthday, which I celebrated in exile, thousands of miles from my native land and from my mountain home, I remembered Ovid's reproaches to his natal God for adding to, instead of cutting short, the years of the miserable exile.

> Dure quid ad miseros veniebas exulis annos
> Debueras illis inposuisse modum
> Si tibi cura mihi, vel si pudor ullus inesset
> Non ultra patriam me sequerere meam

These lines stuck in my memory because as a boy I tried to translate them into English verse. They meant very little to me then, probably because the word " exile " merely suggested living abroad, and as the happiest moments of my young life were those when I watched the cliffs of Dover disappearing I had no imaginative conception of what exile could mean to a man who loved Rome as I loved Grindelwald. But when I remembered Ovid's birthday lamentations on April 18th, 1941, it was not only Grindelwald, but battered and heroic London which tugged at my heart strings, and across the bridge of centuries I saluted the exile of Tomis. " Passages which to a boy," writes Newman, " are but rhetorical commonplaces which he imitates as best he can in his own flowing versification and thinks neither better nor worse than a hundred others, at length come home to him when he has had experience of life and pierce him with their sad earnestness and vivid exactness. Then he comes to understand how it is that lines, the birth of some chance morning or evening at an Ionian festival or among the Sabine hills have lasted for generation after generation for thousands of years with a power over the mind and a charm which the current literature of his own day with all its obvious advantages is utterly unable to rival." I hope that memory has not played me any tricks, but it is no use asking the steward whether the ship's library contains *The Grammar of Assent.*

Ovid only discovered what Rome meant to him when he was exiled to Tomis, and it was not until I said good-bye to the Oberland, on the day that the Maginot Line was turned, that I fully realised how little there was of value in my life which was not directly or indirectly linked with the mountains. It was in the home of a great ski-ing pioneer, Canon Savage, that I first met my wife, and it was among the mountains that I met most of my intimate friends. The love of mountains is the key to a great brotherhood, and there are few places in which one cannot find a group of mountaineers or skiers. In my wanderings in Europe and in the Americas, north and south, I have never failed to find friends among the mountaineers or skiers, friends who could be counted on in sickness and in health, as indeed I discovered in Montreal, where two of the kindest people who ever lived, Sydney Dawes, a great skier, and his wife, Elspeth, were prodigal of kindness during the long weeks in St. Mary's Hospital, a hospital which I shall always think of with gratitude and affection.

Again it was among the mountains that my religious and political beliefs took shape, and not only the creeds which I am prepared to defend at the bar of reason but also those "Overbeliefs," which as Goethe says, "are the poetry of life." One can, at least, hope that there will be gentians in heaven, and mountain torrents, and the "linked sweetness long drawn out" of Telemarks in deep crystal powder snow, and the divine originals of Wetterhorn, Eiger and Jungfrau. And the angelic choir will, perhaps, include at least one finished performer on the Alpine horn to reawaken in the celestial sphere those melodious echoes which I have so often heard surging back from the cliffs of the Mettenberg to the road which leads to the Upper Glacier. "Do our eyes indeed," wrote Francis Thompson, "close for ever on the beauty of earth when they open on the beauty of heaven? I think not; I would fain beguile even death himself with a sweet fantasy . . . I believe in heaven is earth."

At least we may believe that there will be a beauty in heaven which bears the same relation to the beauty on earth as the procession in Plato's parable to the shadows cast by that procession on the cavern wall. And even on earth there are moments when the clouds pass and the thinning mists disclose a fugitive glimpse of the "hid battlements of eternity." We cannot tell whether "in heaven is earth" but we know that earth will be very near to heaven on the day that we return to the sunlit mountains of peace. How often have we rehearsed that journey in our dreams! The shadowy plains of France faintly showing beneath the stars, dim figures moving about station platforms at night, the hiss of escaping steam while the train is at rest, the first ripplement of hills in which the eye of faith can see the hope and promise of the mountains, the familiar clang of station bells beyond the Swiss frontier, the confident self-assurance of Swiss villages with their orderly houses, the limestone gorges of the Jura, which are the entry and introduction to the Alps, and then . . . and then . . .

Beyond the blue dominion of the lake, and beyond the green surge of sentinel hills, uncrested with snow, the power and the glory of the immutable and undiminished heights.

North Atlantic,
December 21*st*, 1942.

PRINTED AT
THE CHAPEL RIVER PRESS,
ANDOVER, HANTS